Microsoft® Office 4.2
For Windows™
Simplified

D1370602

IDG's **3-D Visual**™ Series

IDG BOOKS
From **maranGraphics**™

IDG Books Worldwide, Inc.
An International Data Group Company
Foster City, CA • Indianapolis • Braintree, MA • Chicago • Dallas

Microsoft® Office 4.2 for Windows™ Simplified

Published by
IDG Books Worldwide, Inc.
An International Data Group Company
919 E. Hillsdale Blvd., Suite 400
Foster City, CA 94404
(415) 655-3000

Library of Congress Catalog Card No.: 95-079677
ISBN: 1-56884-673-8
Printed in the United States of America
10 9 8 7 6 5 4
Distributed in the United States by IDG Books Worldwide, Inc.

Distributed by Computer and Technical Books in Miami, Florida, for South America and the Caribbean; by Longman Singapore in Singapore, Malaysia, Thailand, and Korea; by Toppan Co. Ltd. in Japan; by IDG Communications HK in Hong Kong; by WoodsLane Pty. Ltd. in Australia and New Zealand; and by Transworld Publishers Ltd. in the U.K. and Europe.

For general information on IDG Books in the U.S., including information on discounts and premiums, contact IDG Books at 800-762-2974 or 317-895-5200.

For U.S. Corporate Sales and quantity discounts, contact maranGraphics at 800-469-6616, ext. 206.

For information on international sales of IDG Books, contact Helen Saraceni at 415-655-3021, Fax number 415-655-3295.

For information on translations, contact Marc Jeffrey Mikulich, Director of Rights and Licensing, at IDG Books Worldwide. Fax Number 415-655-3295.

For sales inquiries and special prices for bulk quantities, write to the address above or call IDG Books Worldwide at 415-655-3000.

For information on using IDG Books in the classroom, or ordering examination copies, contact Jim Kelly at 800-434-2086.

Trademark Acknowledgments

©1994, 1995
maranGraphics, Inc.

The animated characters are the
copyright of maranGraphics, Inc.

U.S. Corporate Sales	U.S. Trade Sales
Contact maranGraphics at (800) 469-6616, ext. 206 or Fax (905) 890-9434.	Contact IDG Books at (800) 434-3422 or (415) 655-3000.

About IDG Books Worldwide

Welcome to the world of IDG Books Worldwide.

IDG Books Worldwide, Inc., is a subsidiary of International Data Group, the world's largest publisher of business and computer-related information and the leading global provider of information services on information technology. IDG was founded more than 25 years ago and now employs more than 5,700 people worldwide. IDG publishes more than 200 computer publications in 63 countries (see listing below). Forty million people read one or more IDG publications each month.

Launched in 1990, IDG Books is today the fastest-growing publisher of computer and business books in the United States. We are proud to have received 3 awards from the Computer Press Association in recognition of editorial excellence, and our best-selling ...For Dummies series has more than 10 million copies in print with translations in more than 20 languages. IDG Books, through a recent joint venture with IDG's Hi-Tech Beijing, became the first U.S. publisher to publish a computer book in the People's Republic of China. In record time, IDG Books has become the first choice for millions of readers around the world who want to learn how to better manage their businesses.

Our mission is simple: Every IDG book is designed to bring extra value and skill-building instructions to the reader. Our books are written by experts who understand and care about our readers. The knowledge base of our editorial staff comes from years of experience in publishing, education, and journalism — experience which we use to produce books for the '90s. In short, we care about books, so we attract the best people. We devote special attention to details such as audience, interior design, use of icons, and illustrations. And because we use an efficient process of authoring, editing, and desktop publishing our books electronically, we can spend more time ensuring superior content and spend less time on the technicalities of making books.

You can count on our commitment to deliver high-quality books at competitive prices on topics customers want to read about. At IDG, we value quality, and we have been delivering quality for more than 25 years. You'll find no better book on a subject than an IDG book.

John Kilcullen
President and CEO
IDG Books Worldwide, Inc.

IDG Books Worldwide, Inc., is a subsidiary of International Data Group. The officers are Patrick J. McGovern, Founder and Board Chairman; Walter Boyd, President. International Data Group's publications include: ARGENTINA'S Computerworld Argentina, Infoworld Argentina; AUSTRALIA'S Computerworld Australia, Australian PC World, Australian Macworld, Network World, Mobile Business Australia, Reseller, IDG Sources; AUSTRIA'S Computerwelt Oesterreich, PC Test; BRAZIL'S Computerworld, Gamepro, Game Power, Mundo IBM, Mundo Unix, PC World, Super Game; BELGIUM'S Data News (CW) BULGARIA'S Computerworld Bulgaria, Ediworld, PC & Mac World Bulgaria, Network World Bulgaria; CANADA'S CIO Canada, Computerworld Canada, Graduate Computerworld, InfoCanada, Network World Canada; CHILE'S Computerworld Chile, Informatica; COLOMBIA'S Computerworld Colombia, PC World; CZECH REPUBLIC'S Computerworld, Elektronika, PC World; DENMARK'S Communications World, Computerworld Danmark, Macintosh Produktkatalog, Macworld Danmark, PC World Danmark, PC World Produktguide, Tech World, Windows World; ECUADOR'S PC World Ecuador; EGYPT'S Computerworld (CW) Middle East, PC World Middle East; FINLAND'S MikroPC, Tietoviikko, Tietoverkko; FRANCE'S Distributique, GOLDEN MAC, InfoPC, Languages & Systems, Le Guide du Monde Informatique, Le Monde Informatique, Telecoms & Reseaux; GERMANY'S Computerwoche, Computerwoche Focus, Computerwoche Extra, Computerwoche Karriere, Information Management, Macwelt, Netzwelt, PC Welt, PC Woche, Publish, Unit; GREECE'S Infoworld, PC Games; HUNGARY'S Computerworld SZT, PC World; HONG KONG'S Computerworld Hong Kong, PC World Hong Kong; INDIA'S Computers & Communications; IRELAND'S ComputerScope; ISRAEL'S Computerworld Israel, PC World Israel; ITALY'S Computerworld Italia, Lotus Magazine, Macworld Italia, Networking Italia, PC Shopping, PC World Italia; JAPAN'S Computerworld Today, Information Systems World, Macworld Japan, Nikkei Personal Computing, SunWorld Japan, Windows World; KENYA'S East African Computer News; KOREA'S Computerworld Korea, Macworld Korea, PC World Korea; MEXICO'S Compu Edicion, Compu Manufactura, Computacion/Punto de Venta, Computerworld Mexico, MacWorld, Mundo Unix, PC World, Windows; THE NETHERLANDS' Computer! Totaal, Computable (CW), LAN Magazine, MacWorld, Totaal "Windows"; NEW ZEALAND'S Computer Listings, Computerworld New Zealand, New Zealand PC World, Network World; NIGERIA'S PC World Africa; NORWAY'S Computerworld Norge, C/World, Lotusworld Norge, Macworld Norge, Networld, PC World Ekspress, PC World Norge, PC World's Produktguide, Publish& Multimedia World, Student Data, Unix World, Windowsworld; IDG Direct Response; PAKISTAN'S PC World Pakistan; PANAMA'S PC World Panama; PERU'S Computerworld Peru, PC World; PEOPLE'S REPUBLIC OF CHINA'S China Computerworld, China Infoworld, Electronics Today/Multimedia World, Electronics International, Electronic Product World, China Network World, PC and Communications Magazine, PC World China, Software World Magazine, Telecom Product World; IDG HIGH TECH BEIJING'S New Product World; IDG SHENZHEN'S Computer News Digest; PHILIPPINES' Computerworld Philippines, PC Digest (PCW); POLAND'S Computerworld Poland, PC World/Komputer; PORTUGAL'S Cerebro/PC World, Correio Informatico/Computerworld, Informatica & Comunicacoes Catalogo, MacIn, Nacional de Produtos; ROMANIA'S Computerworld, PC World; RUSSIA'S Computerworld-Moscow, Mir - PC, Sety; SINGAPORE'S Computerworld Southeast Asia, PC World Singapore; SLOVENIA'S Monitor Magazine; SOUTH AFRICA'S Computer Mail (CIO),Computing S.A.,Network World S.A., Software World; SPAIN'S Advanced Systems, Amiga World, Computerworld Espana, Communicaciones World, Macworld Espana, NeXTWORLD, Super Juegos Magazine (GamePro), PC World Espana, Publish; SWEDEN'S Attack, ComputerSweden, Corporate Computing, Natverk & Kommunikation, Macworld, Mikrodatorn, PC World, Publishing & Design (CAP), Datalngenjoren, Maxi Data,Windows World; SWITZERLAND'S Computerworld Schweiz, Macworld Schweiz, PC Tip; TAIWAN'S Computerworld Taiwan, PC World Taiwan; THAILAND'S Thai Computerworld; TURKEY'S Computerworld Monitor, Macworld Turkiye, PC World Turkiye; UKRAINE'S Computerworld; UNITED KINGDOM'S Computing /Computerworld, Connexion/Network World, Lotus Magazine, Macworld, Open Computing/Sunworld; UNITED STATES' Advanced Systems, AmigaWorld, Cable in the Classroom, CD Review, CIO, Computerworld, Digital Video, DOS Resource Guide, Electronic Entertainment Magazine, Federal Computer Week, Federal Integrator, GamePro, IDG Books, Infoworld, Infoworld Direct, Laser Event, Macworld, Multimedia World, Network World, PC Letter, PC World, PlayRight, Power PC World, Publish, SWATPro, Video Event; VENEZUELA'S Computerworld Venezuela, PC World; VIETNAM'S PC World Vietnam

Credits

Author & Architect:

Ruth Maran

Technical Consultant:

Wendi Blouin Ewbank

Illustrations:

Dave Ross
David de Haas
Suzanna Pereira

Layout:

Christie Van Duin
Carol Walthers

Screens:

Tamara Poliquin

Editors:

Judy Maran
Kelleigh Wing

Proofreaders:

Paul Lofthouse
Brad Hilderley

Indexer:

Mark Kmetzko

Post Production:

David McKenna
Kris Gurn
Robert Maran

Acknowledgments

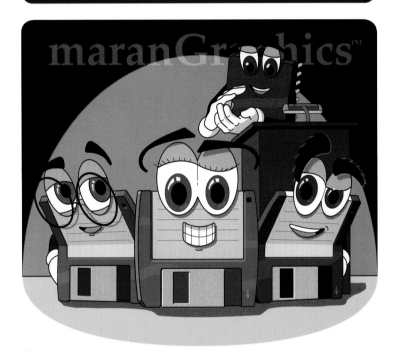

Special thanks to Wendi B. Ewbank for her insight and dedication in ensuring the technical accuracy of this book.

Thanks to Saverio C. Tropiano for his assistance and expert advice.

Thanks to the dedicated staff of maranGraphics, including Robin Clark, David de Haas, Brad Hilderley, Paul Lofthouse, Judy Maran, Maxine Maran, Robert Maran, Sherry Maran, Suzanna Pereira, Tamara Poliquin, Dave Ross, Christie Van Duin, Carol Walthers and Kelleigh Wing.

Finally, to Richard Maran who originated the easy-to-use graphic format of this guide. Thank you for your inspiration and guidance.

TABLE OF CONTENTS

INTRODUCTION TO MICROSOFT OFFICE

WORD

Getting Started

Edit Your Documents

Smart Editing

Save And Open Your Documents

INTRODUCTION TO MICROSOFT OFFICE

WORD

EXCEL

POWERPOINT

MAIL

EXCHANGE OBJECTS BETWEEN PROGRAMS

INDEX

Format Pages

Working With Tables

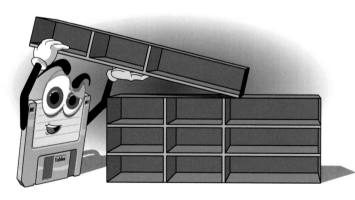

EXCEL

Getting Started

Save And Open Your Workbooks

Edit Your Worksheets

INTRODUCTION TO MICROSOFT OFFICE

WORD

EXCEL

POWERPOINT

MAIL

EXCHANGE OBJECTS BETWEEN PROGRAMS

INDEX

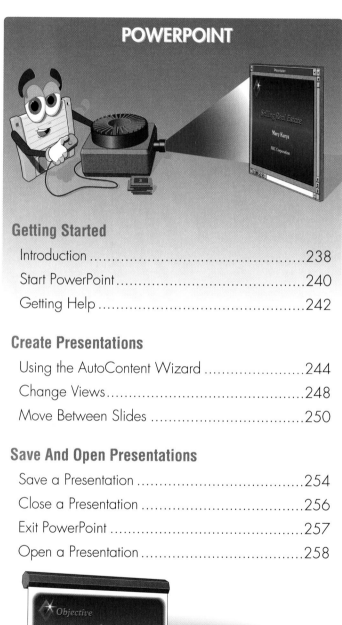

POWERPOINT

Edit Presentations

Add Objects

INTRODUCTION
TO MICROSOFT
OFFICE

WORD

EXCEL

POWERPOINT

MAIL

EXCHANGE
OBJECTS
BETWEEN
PROGRAMS

INDEX

Enhance Presentations

Fine-Tune Presentations

EXCHANGE OBJECTS BETWEEN PROGRAMS

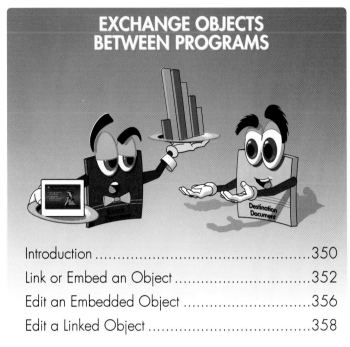

INDEX

INTRODUCTION TO MICROSOFT OFFICE

WORD

EXCEL

POWERPOINT

MAIL

EXCHANGE OBJECTS BETWEEN PROGRAMS

INDEX

In this section you will learn the basic skills needed to use the Word, Excel, PowerPoint and Mail programs.

INTRODUCTION TO MICROSOFT OFFICE

Microsoft® Office includes Word, Excel, PowerPoint and a license to use Mail. These programs will help you accomplish everyday tasks.

The Professional version of Microsoft Office also includes the Microsoft Access program. This program is useful for managing a large collection of information called a database.

This book does not cover the Microsoft Access program.

WORD

Word is a word processing program that lets you create letters, reports, memos and newsletters quickly and efficiently.

- **Microsoft Office**
- Using the Mouse
- Start a Program
- Switch Between Programs
- Exit a Program
- Select Commands

EXCEL

Excel is a spreadsheet program that helps you manage, present and analyze financial information.

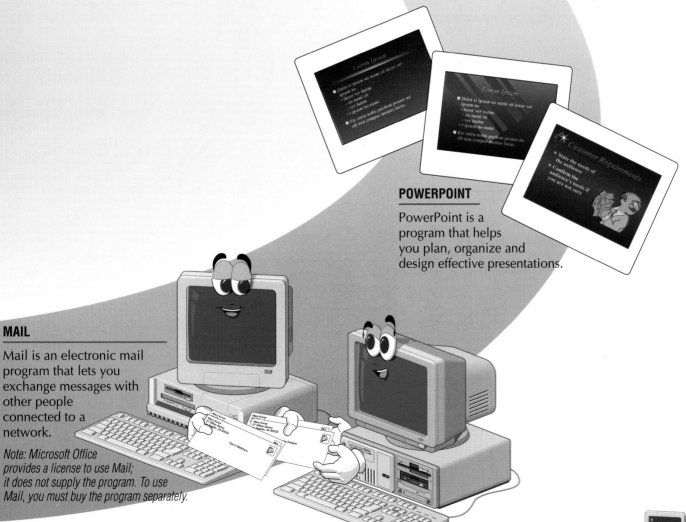

POWERPOINT

PowerPoint is a program that helps you plan, organize and design effective presentations.

MAIL

Mail is an electronic mail program that lets you exchange messages with other people connected to a network.

Note: Microsoft Office provides a license to use Mail; it does not supply the program. To use Mail, you must buy the program separately.

USING THE MOUSE

The mouse is a hand-held device that lets you quickly select commands and perform tasks.

USING THE MOUSE

◆ Hold the mouse as shown in the diagram. Use your thumb and two rightmost fingers to guide the mouse while your two remaining fingers press the mouse buttons.

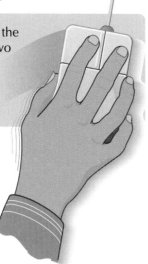

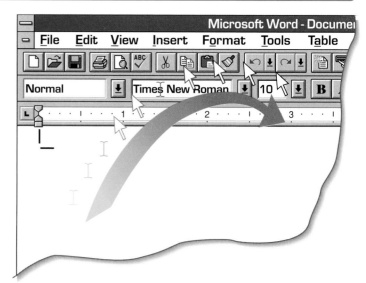

◆ When you move the mouse on your desk, the mouse pointer (I or ↖) on your screen moves in the same direction. The mouse pointer changes shape, depending on its location on your screen and the action you are performing.

- Microsoft Office
- **Using the Mouse**
- Start a Program
- Switch Between Programs
- Exit a Program
- Select Commands

PARTS OF THE MOUSE

◆ The mouse has a left and right button. You can use these buttons to select commands and choose options.

Note: You will use the left button most of the time.

◆ Under the mouse is a ball that senses movement. To ensure smooth motion of the mouse, you should occasionally remove and clean this ball.

MOUSE TERMS

CLICK

Press and release the left mouse button once.

DOUBLE-CLICK

Quickly press and release the left mouse button twice.

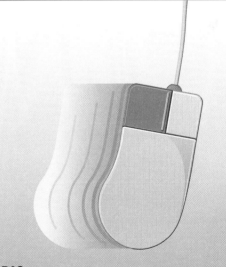

DRAG

When the mouse pointer (I or ⬚) is over an object on your screen, press and hold down the left mouse button and then move the mouse.

You can use the Microsoft Office Manager to quickly start a program.

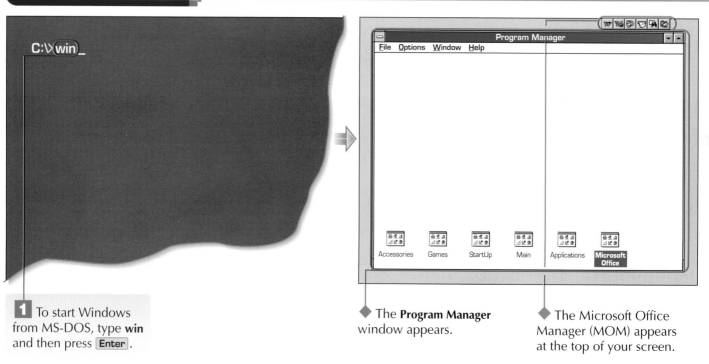

C:\>win_

1 To start Windows from MS-DOS, type **win** and then press **Enter**.

◆ The **Program Manager** window appears.

◆ The Microsoft Office Manager (MOM) appears at the top of your screen.

- Microsoft Office
- Using the Mouse
- **Start a Program**
- Switch Between Programs
- Exit a Program
- Select Commands

The Microsoft Office Manager provides a button for each of the four Office programs.

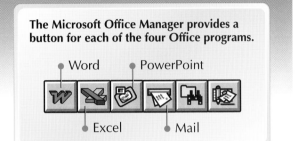

Word   PowerPoint

Excel   Mail

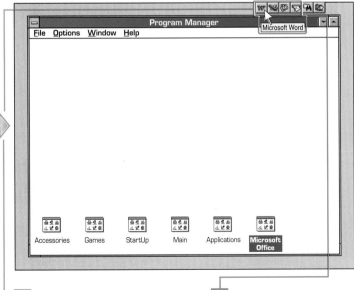

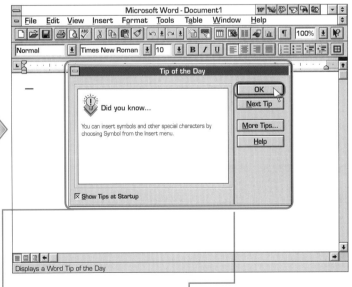

2 To display the name of a button, move the mouse over the button (example: w).

◆ After a few seconds, the name of the button appears.

3 To start a program, move the mouse over the button (example: w for Word) and then press the left button.

◆ The program appears on your screen.

◆ When you start the Word program, the **Tip of the Day** dialog box appears.

4 To close the dialog box, move the mouse over **OK** and then press the left button.

You can work with several programs at the same time. For example, you can create a presentation while preparing an income statement.

SWITCH BETWEEN PROGRAMS

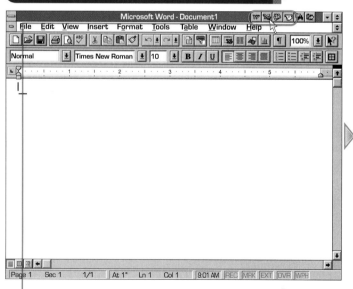

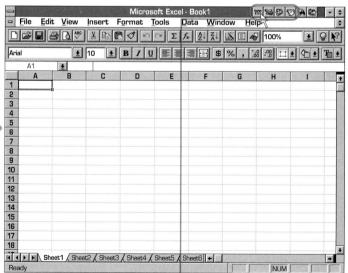

1 To open a second program, move the mouse ⟨ over the button (example: ▨ for Excel) and then press the left button.

◆ The program appears on your screen.

Note: In this example, the Excel program covers the Word program.

2 To return to the original program, move the mouse ⟨ over the button (example: ▨ for Word) and then press the left button.

10

- Microsoft Office
- Using the Mouse
- Start a Program
- **Switch Between Programs**
- **Exit a Program**
- Select Commands

When you finish using a program, you can exit the program.

EXIT A PROGRAM

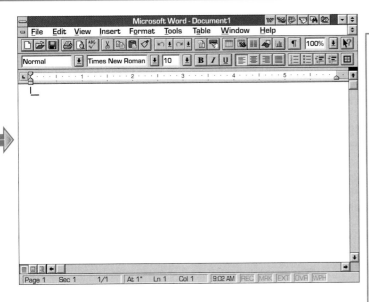

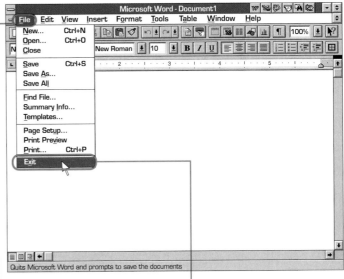

◆ The original program reappears.

Note: In this example, the Word program covers the Excel program.

1 Move the mouse ⌖ over **File** and then press the left button.

2 Move the mouse ⌖ over **Exit** and then press the left button.

SELECT COMMANDS

You can open a menu to display a list of related commands. You can then select the command you want to use.

USING THE MENUS WITH THE MOUSE

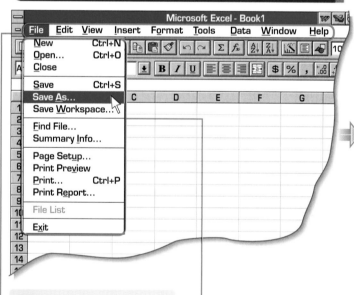

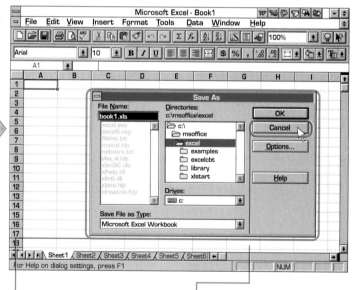

1 To open a menu, move the mouse ⅍ over the menu name (example: **File**) and then press the left button.

Note: To close a menu, move the mouse ⅍ outside the menu area and then press the left button.

2 To select a command, move the mouse ⅍ over the command name (example: **Save As**) and then press the left button.

◆ A dialog box appears if the program requires more information to carry out the command.

3 To close a dialog box, move the mouse ⅍ over **Cancel** or **Close** and then press the left button.

- Microsoft Office
- Using the Mouse
- Start a Program
- Switch Between Programs
- Exit a Program
- **Select Commands**

INTRODUCTION TO
MICROSOFT OFFICE

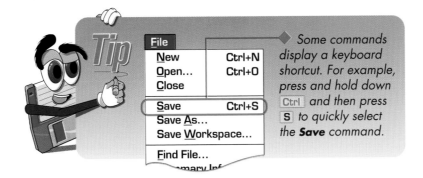

Some commands display a keyboard shortcut. For example, press and hold down `Ctrl` and then press `S` to quickly select the **Save** command.

USING THE MENUS WITH THE KEYBOARD

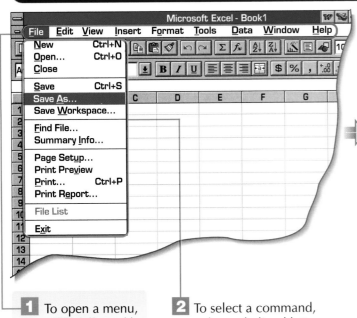

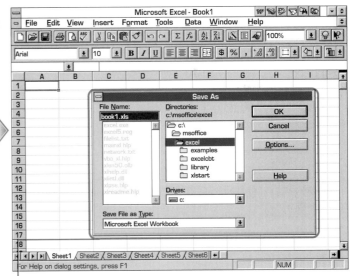

1 To open a menu, press `Alt` followed by the underlined letter in the menu name (example: `F` for **File**).

Note: To close a menu, press `Alt`.

2 To select a command, press the underlined letter in the command name (example: `A` for **Save As**).

◆ A dialog box appears if the program requires more information to carry out the command.

3 To close a dialog box, press `Esc`.

SELECT COMMANDS

You can use the buttons on your screen to quickly select the most commonly used commands.

USING THE BUTTONS

Each button displayed on your screen provides a fast method of selecting a menu command.

For example, you can use 💾 to quickly select the **Save** command.

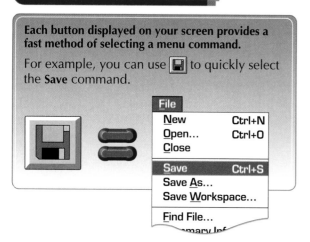

File	
New	Ctrl+N
Open...	Ctrl+O
Close	
Save	**Ctrl+S**
Save **As**...	
Save **Workspace**...	
Find File...	

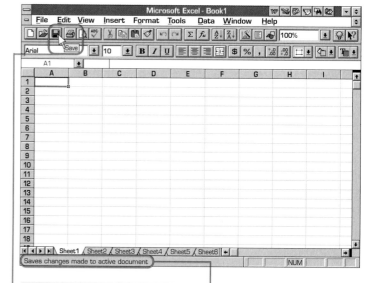

1 Move the mouse ⌖ over a button of interest (example: 💾).

◆ After a few seconds, the name of the button appears.

◆ A short description of the button also appears at the bottom of your screen.

2 To select the button, press the left mouse button.

- Microsoft Office
- Using the Mouse
- Start a Program
- Switch Between Programs
- Exit a Program
- **Select Commands**

A shortcut menu displays a list of commonly used commands for an area on your screen.

USING THE SHORTCUT MENUS

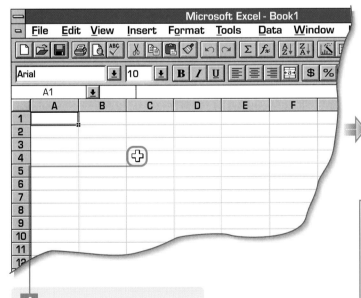

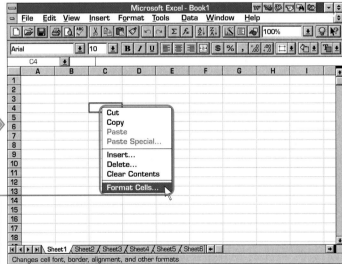

1 To display a shortcut menu, move the mouse ⊕ over an area on your screen and then press the **right** button.

◆ A shortcut menu appears.

2 Move the mouse ⇖ over the command you want to use and then press the left button.

Note: To close a shortcut menu, move the mouse ⇖ outside the menu area and then press the left button.

15

WORD

tion

ne

Reasons
to
e The Earth

ernet Newsgroup

ave Ross
M.B.A.
University of Washington

January 12, 1995

ABC Computer Corporation
P.O. Box 2501
Krikkit, VA 22106

Re: Position Opening-Receptionist

To whom it may concern:

Regarding your advertisement of January 9, 1995, I am pleased
to submit my résumé for review and wish to be considered as
an applicant for the above-named position.

My professional experience does include using Word.
I am well versed in the program capabilities and able to apply
the features accurately. Should you find my background and
qualifications acceptable, I would be delighted to interview
for this position at your convenience.

Thank you for your assistance in this matter. I look forward to
discussing this career opportunity with you.

cerely yours,

Susan Johnston

Johnston
re

Word lets you produce impressive-looking documents quickly and efficiently.

WHAT YOU CAN CREATE WITH WORD

PERSONAL AND BUSINESS LETTERS

Word helps you efficiently produce personal and business letters.

REPORTS AND MANUALS

Word provides editing and formatting features that make it ideal for producing longer documents, such as reports and manuals.

NEWSLETTERS AND BROCHURES

You can use the formatting features and graphics that Word provides to produce attractive newsletters and brochures.

- **Introduction**
- **Start Word**
- Enter Text
- Move Through a Document
- Select Text
- Getting Help

When you start Word, a blank document appears. You can type text into this document.

START WORD

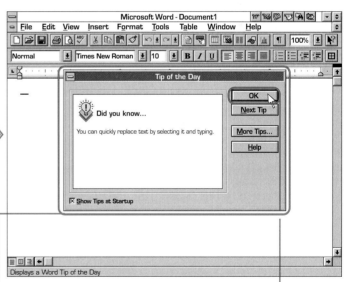

1 To start Word, move the mouse ⍾ over 🅆 and then press the left button.

◆ The **Microsoft Word** window appears, displaying a blank document.

◆ Each time you start Word, a tip about using the program appears.

2 To close the **Tip of the Day** dialog box, move the mouse ⍾ over **OK** and then press the left button.

ENTER TEXT

When typing text in your document, you do not need to press **Enter** at the end of a line. Word automatically moves the text to the next line. This is called word wrapping.

When you use a word processor to type a letter, the text au...

When you use a word processor to type a letter, the text automatically wraps to the next line as you type.

ENTER TEXT

◆ In this book, the design and size of text were changed to make the document easier to read.

Initial or default font	→	New font
Times New Roman 10 point		Arial 12 point

Note: To change the design and size of text, refer to page 88.

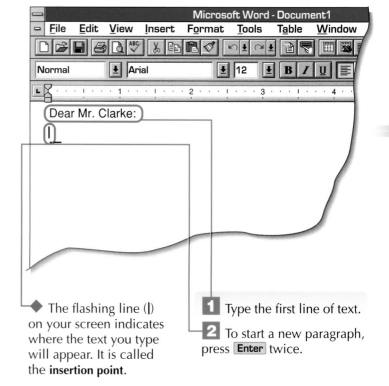

Dear Mr. Clarke:

◆ The flashing line (I) on your screen indicates where the text you type will appear. It is called the **insertion point**.

1 Type the first line of text.

2 To start a new paragraph, press **Enter** twice.

WORD

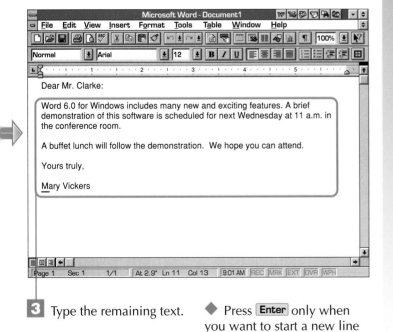

3 Type the remaining text.

◆ Press **Enter** only when you want to start a new line or paragraph.

STATUS BAR

The status bar provides information about the position of the insertion point and the text displayed on your screen.

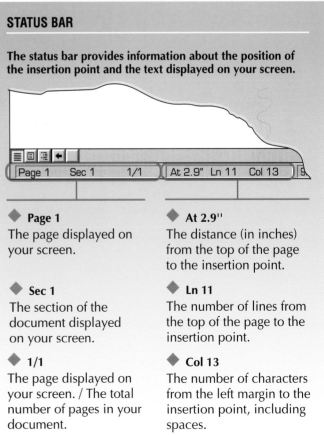

◆ **Page 1**
The page displayed on your screen.

◆ **Sec 1**
The section of the document displayed on your screen.

◆ **1/1**
The page displayed on your screen. / The total number of pages in your document.

◆ **At 2.9"**
The distance (in inches) from the top of the page to the insertion point.

◆ **Ln 11**
The number of lines from the top of the page to the insertion point.

◆ **Col 13**
The number of characters from the left margin to the insertion point, including spaces.

If you create a long document, your computer screen cannot display all the text at the same time. You must move through the document to view other areas of text.

IMPORTANT!

You cannot move the insertion point below the horizontal line (▬) displayed on your screen. To move this line, position the insertion point after the last character in your document and then press **Enter**.

MOVE TO ANY POSITION

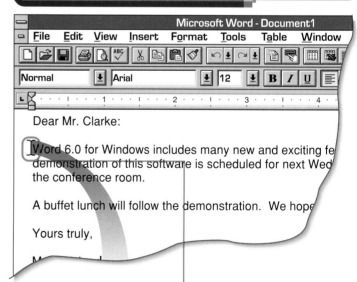

The insertion point indicates where the text you type will appear in your document.

1 To position the insertion point at another location on your screen, move the mouse I over the new location and then press the left button.

GETTING STARTED

- Introduction
- Start Word
- Enter Text

- Move Through a Document
- Select Text
- Getting Help

WORD

SCROLL UP OR DOWN

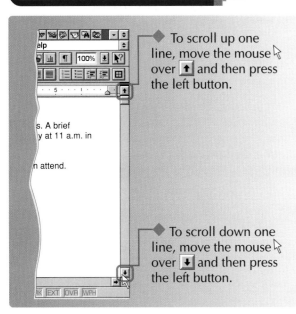

◆ To scroll up one line, move the mouse over ⬆ and then press the left button.

◆ To scroll down one line, move the mouse over ⬇ and then press the left button.

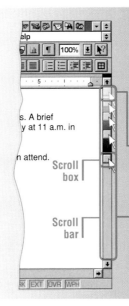

Scroll box

Scroll bar

The location of the scroll box on the scroll bar indicates which part of your document is displayed on the screen.

For example, when the scroll box is in the middle of the scroll bar, you are viewing the middle part of your document.

1 To quickly scroll through your document, move the mouse ⬚ over ⬚ and then press and hold down the left button.

2 Still holding down the button, drag the mouse ⬚ along the scroll bar. Then release the button.

KEYBOARD SHORTCUTS

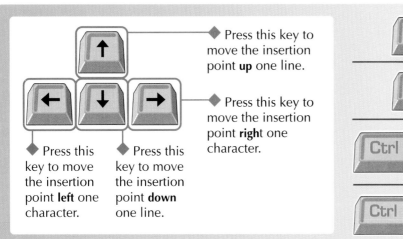

◆ Press this key to move the insertion point **up** one line.

◆ Press this key to move the insertion point **righ**t one character.

◆ Press this key to move the insertion point **left** one character.

◆ Press this key to move the insertion point **down** one line.

Page Up

Press this key to move **up** one screen.

Page Down

Press this key to move **down** one screen.

Ctrl + Home

Press these keys to move to the **beginning** of your document.

Ctrl + End

Press these keys to move to the **end** of your document.

23

SELECT TEXT

Before you can use many Word features, you must first select the text you want to change. Selected text appears highlighted on your screen.

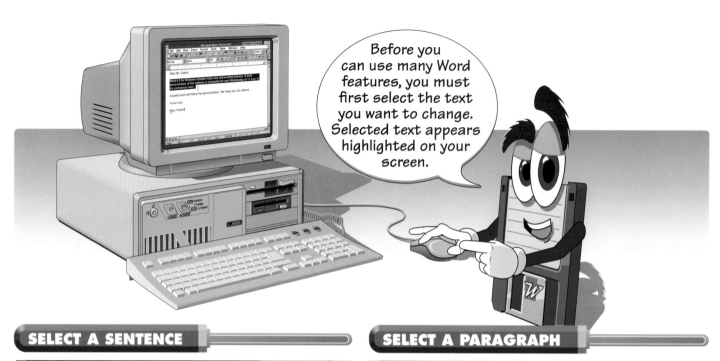

SELECT A SENTENCE

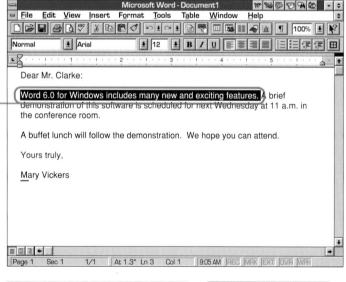

1 Press and hold down `Ctrl`.

2 Still holding down `Ctrl`, move the mouse I anywhere over the sentence you want to select and then press the left button. Then release `Ctrl`.

TO CANCEL A TEXT SELECTION

Move the mouse I outside the selected area and then press the left button.

SELECT A PARAGRAPH

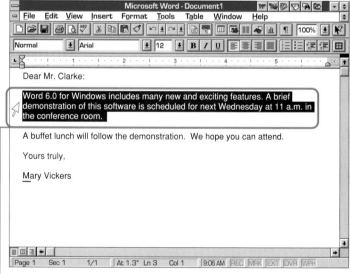

1 Move the mouse I to the left of the paragraph you want to select (I changes to ⁀) and then quickly press the left button twice.

GETTING STARTED

- Introduction
- Start Word
- Enter Text
- Move Through a Document
- Select Text
- Getting Help

WORD

SELECT A WORD

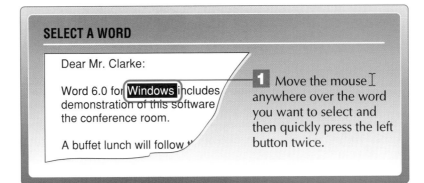

Dear Mr. Clarke:

Word 6.0 for Windows includes demonstration of this software the conference room.

A buffet lunch will follow

1 Move the mouse I anywhere over the word you want to select and then quickly press the left button twice.

SELECT YOUR ENTIRE DOCUMENT

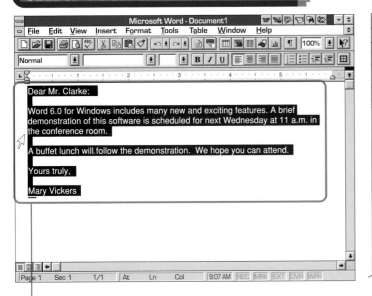

1 Move the mouse I anywhere to the left of the text in your document (I changes to ⇗) and then quickly press the left button three times.

SELECT ANY AMOUNT OF TEXT

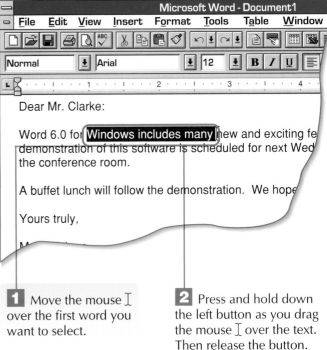

1 Move the mouse I over the first word you want to select.

2 Press and hold down the left button as you drag the mouse I over the text. Then release the button.

If you forget how to perform a task, you can use the Word Help feature to obtain information. This can save you time by eliminating the need to refer to other sources.

GETTING HELP

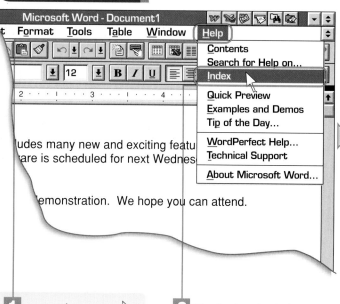

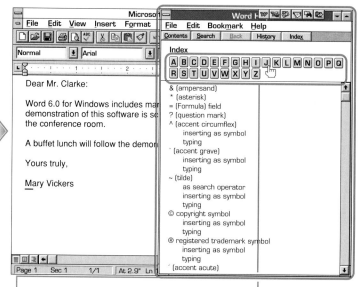

1 Move the mouse over **Help** and then press the left button.

2 To display the help index, move the mouse over **Index** and then press the left button.

◆ The **Word Help** window appears.

3 Move the mouse over the first letter of the topic you want information on (example: **J** for **Justification**) and then press the left button.

GETTING STARTED

• Introduction
• Start Word
• Enter Text
• Move Through a Document
• Select Text
• Getting Help

WORD

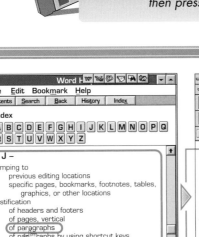

You can easily print the help topic displayed on your screen.

◆ Move the mouse over Print in the **How To** window and then press the left button.

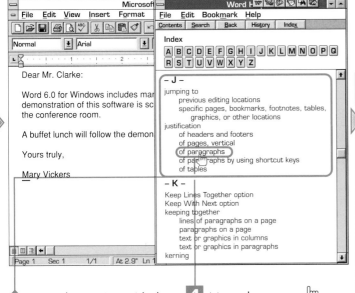

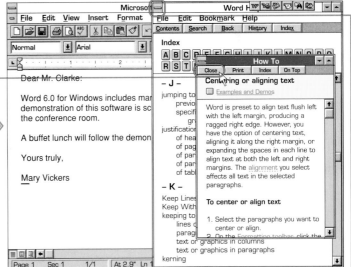

◆ Topics beginning with the letter you selected appear.

Note: You can use the scroll bar to view other topics in the index. For more information, refer to page 23.

4 Move the mouse over the topic of interest (example: **justification of paragraphs**) and then press the left button.

◆ Information on the topic you selected appears.

5 To close the **How To** window, move the mouse over **Close** and then press the left button.

6 To close the **Word Help** window, move the mouse over ▬ and then quickly press the left button twice.

INSERT TEXT

Word makes it easy to edit your document. To make changes, you no longer have to use correction fluid or retype a page.

INSERT A BLANK LINE

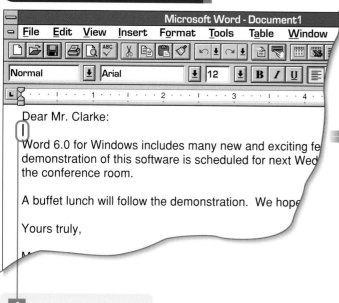

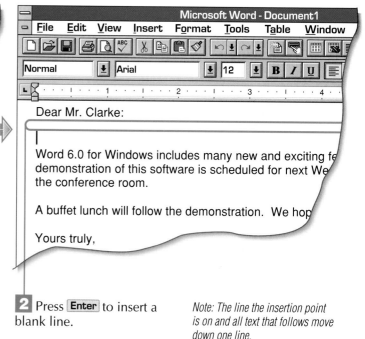

1 Position the insertion point where you want to insert a blank line.

2 Press **Enter** to insert a blank line.

Note: The line the insertion point is on and all text that follows move down one line.

- **Insert Text**
- Delete Text
- Replace Selected Text

- Undo Changes
- Redo Changes
- Change the Case of Text

- Move Text
- Copy Text
- Change Views

IMPORTANT!

Make sure you save your document to store it for future use. If you do not save your document, it will disappear when you turn off your computer.

Note: To save a document, refer to page 64.

SPLIT AND JOIN PARAGRAPHS

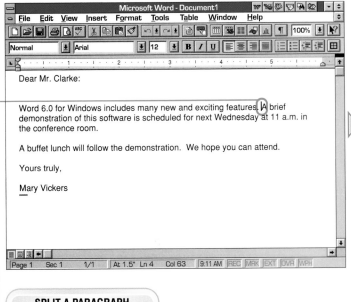

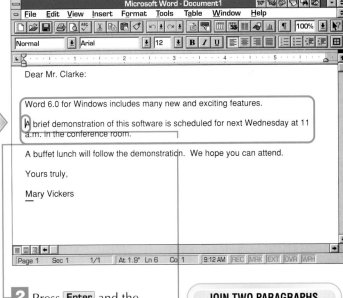

SPLIT A PARAGRAPH

1 Position the insertion point where you want to split a paragraph in two.

2 Press **Enter** and the paragraph splits in two.

3 To insert a blank line between the two paragraphs, press **Enter** again.

JOIN TWO PARAGRAPHS

1 Position the insertion point to the left of the first character in the second paragraph.

2 Press **+Backspace** until the paragraphs are joined.

29

INSERT TEXT

In the Insert mode, the text you type appears at the insertion point location. Any existing text moves forward to make room for the new text.

This sentence moves forward as you type.

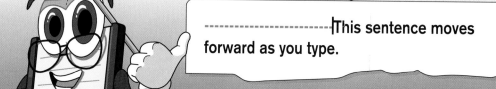

-------------------------This sentence moves forward as you type.

INSERT TEXT

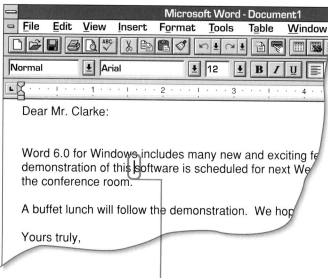

Microsoft Word - Document1

File   Edit   View   Insert   Format   Tools   Table   Window

Normal   Arial   12   **B** *I* U

Dear Mr. Clarke:

Word 6.0 for Windows includes many new and exciting fe
demonstration of this software is scheduled for next We
the conference room.

A buffet lunch will follow the demonstration. We hop

Yours truly,

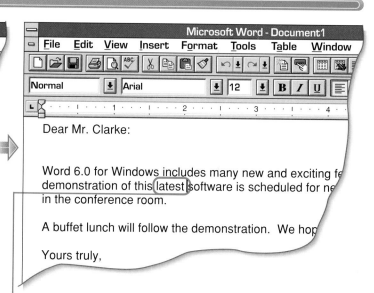

Microsoft Word - Document1

File   Edit   View   Insert   Format   Tools   Table   Window

Normal   Arial   12   **B** *I* U

Dear Mr. Clarke:

Word 6.0 for Windows includes many new and exciting fe
demonstration of this latest software is scheduled for ne
in the conference room.

A buffet lunch will follow the demonstration. We hop

Yours truly,

When you start Word, the program is in the Insert mode.

1 Position the insertion point where you want to insert the new text.

Note: If the letters OVR appear in black (OVR) at the bottom of your screen, press Insert on your keyboard to switch to the Insert mode.

2 Type the text you want to insert (example: **latest**).

3 To insert a blank space, press the **Spacebar**.

Note: The words to the right of the inserted text move forward.

- **Insert Text**
- Delete Text
- Replace Selected Text

- Undo Changes
- Redo Changes
- Change the Case of Text

- Move Text
- Copy Text
- Change Views

WORD

This sentence disappears as you type.

xxxxxxxxxxxxxxxxxxxxpears as you type.

In the Overtype mode, the text you type appears at the insertion point location. The new text replaces (types over) any existing text.

OVERTYPE TEXT

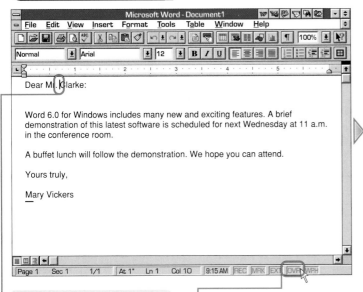

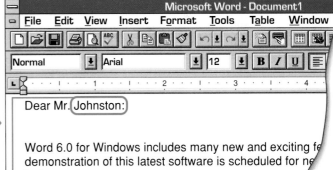

1 Position the insertion point to the left of the first character you want to replace.

2 To turn on the **Overtype** mode, move the mouse over OVR and then quickly press the left button twice (OVR changes to OVR).

3 Type the text you want to replace the existing text (example: **Johnston:**).

Note: The new text types over the existing text.

4 To turn off the **Overtype** mode, repeat step **2** (OVR changes to OVR).

Note: You can also press Insert *on your keyboard to turn on or off the* **Overtype** *mode.*

DELETE TEXT

You can use Delete to remove the blank line the insertion point is on. The remaining text moves up one line.

DELETE A BLANK LINE

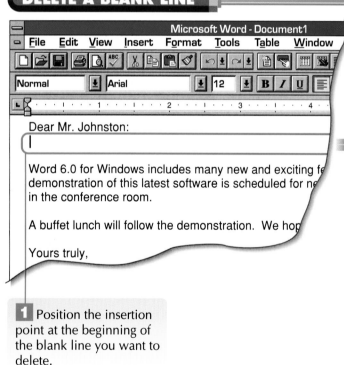

1 Position the insertion point at the beginning of the blank line you want to delete.

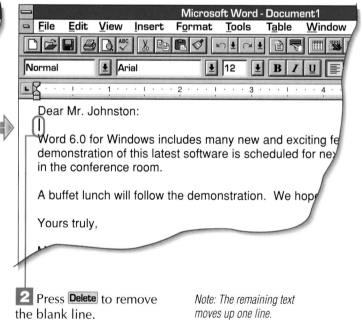

2 Press Delete to remove the blank line.

Note: The remaining text moves up one line.

- Insert Text
- **Delete Text**
- Replace Selected Text

- Undo Changes
- Redo Changes
- Change the Case of Text

- Move Text
- Copy Text
- Change Views

> You can use **Delete** to remove the character to the right of the insertion point. The remaining text moves to the left.

DELETE A CHARACTER

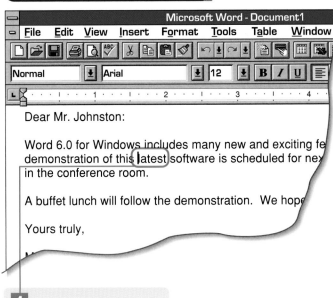

1 Position the insertion point to the left of the first character you want to delete (example: l in latest).

2 Press **Delete** once for each character or space you want to delete (example: press **Delete** seven times).

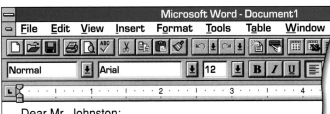

You can also use this key to delete characters. Position the insertion point to the right of the character(s) you want to delete and then press **←Backspace**.

You can use Delete to remove text you have selected. The remaining text moves up or to the left.

DELETE SELECTED TEXT

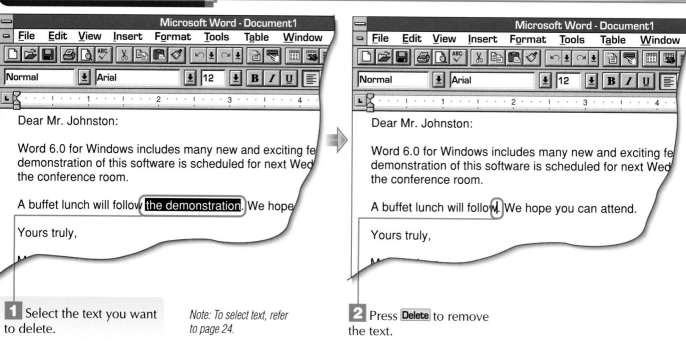

1 Select the text you want to delete.

Note: To select text, refer to page 24.

2 Press Delete to remove the text.

- Insert Text
- **Delete Text**
- **Replace Selected Text**

- Undo Changes
- Redo Changes
- Change the Case of Text

- Move Text
- Copy Text
- Change Views

Word allows you to replace text you have selected with new text.

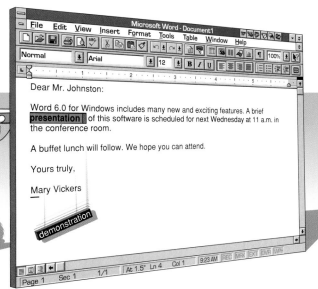

REPLACE SELECTED TEXT

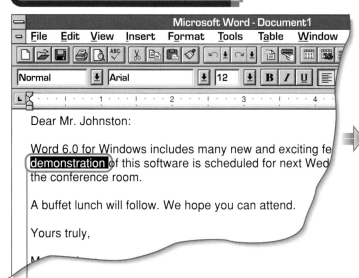

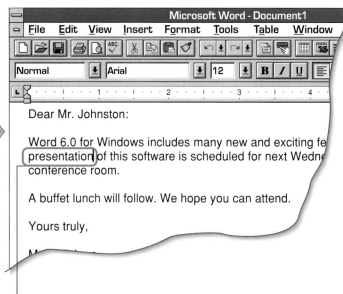

1 Select the text you want to replace with new text.

Note: To select text, refer to page 24.

2 Type the new text (example: **presentation**). This text replaces the text you selected.

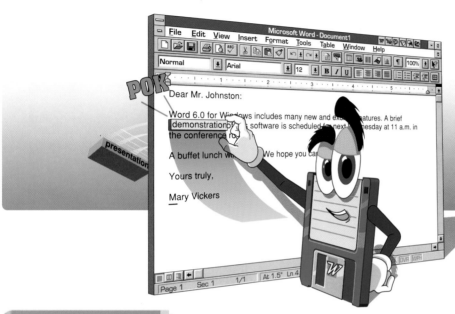

Word remembers the last 100 changes you made to your document. If you regret these changes, you can cancel them by using the Undo feature.

UNDO CHANGES

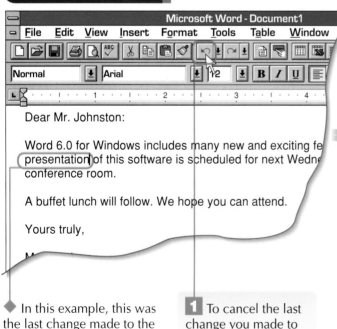

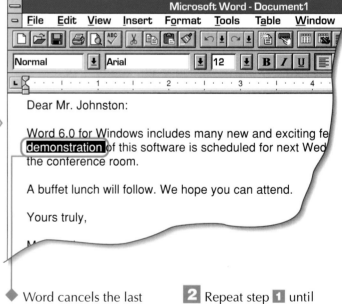

◆ In this example, this was the last change made to the document. The word **demonstration** was changed to **presentation**.

1 To cancel the last change you made to your document, move the mouse ⌖ over 🔄 and then press the left button.

◆ Word cancels the last change you made to your document.

2 Repeat step **1** until you restore all the changes you regret.

- Insert Text
- Delete Text
- Replace Selected Text

- **Undo Changes**
- **Redo Changes**
- Change the Case of Text

- Move Text
- Copy Text
- Change Views

The Undo and Redo features are very helpful, but there are some commands that Word cannot undo.

For example, you cannot use the Undo feature to cancel the save and print commands.

REDO CHANGES

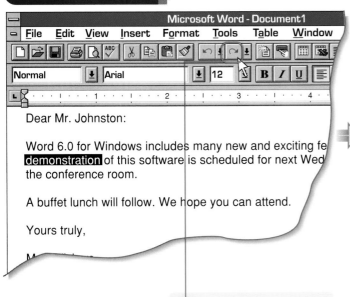

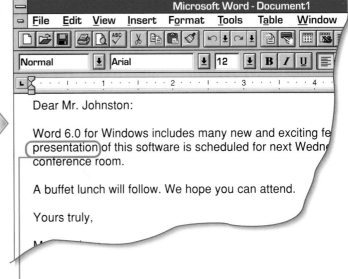

If you are not satisfied with the results of the Undo feature, you can use the Redo feature to return the document to the way it was.

1 To reverse the results of using the Undo feature, move the mouse ↳ over ⟳ and then press the left button.

◆ Word reverses the results of the last undo command.

2 Repeat step **1** until you reverse the results of all the undo commands you regret.

*Note: For the following pages, the word **presentation** was returned to **demonstration**.*

37

CHANGE THE CASE OF TEXT

You can change the case of text in your document without having to retype the text. Word offers five case options.

CHANGE THE CASE OF TEXT

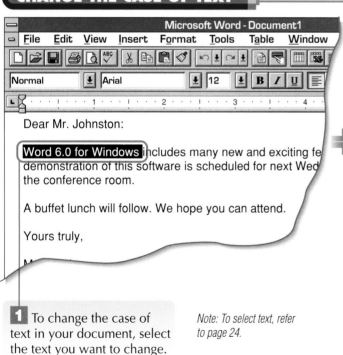

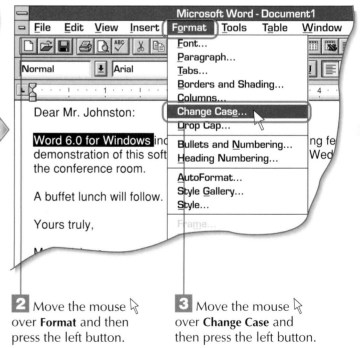

1 To change the case of text in your document, select the text you want to change.

Note: To select text, refer to page 24.

2 Move the mouse over **Format** and then press the left button.

3 Move the mouse over **Change Case** and then press the left button.

- Insert Text
- Delete Text
- Replace Selected Text
- Undo Changes
- Redo Changes
- **Change the Case of Text**
- Move Text
- Copy Text
- Change Views

SHORTCUT

1 To quickly change the case of text in your document, select the text you want to change.

2 Press `Shift` + `F3` to change the case of the text. Continue pressing `Shift` + `F3` until the text appears in the case you want.

◆ Each time you press `Shift` + `F3`, your text appears in one of three cases:

UPPERCASE

lowercase

Title Case

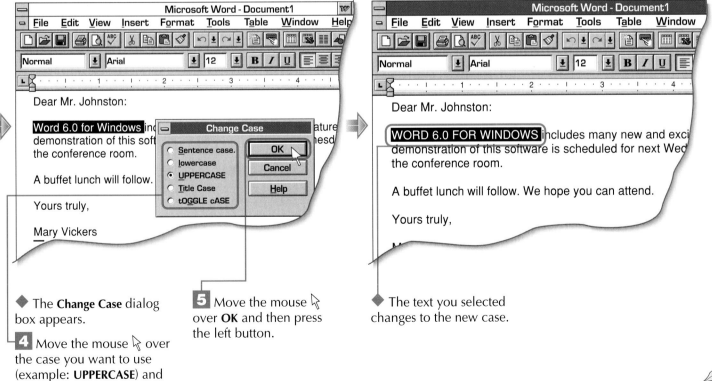

◆ The **Change Case** dialog box appears.

4 Move the mouse ⬧ over the case you want to use (example: **UPPERCASE**) and then press the left button (○ changes to ◉).

5 Move the mouse ⬧ over **OK** and then press the left button.

◆ The text you selected changes to the new case.

MOVE TEXT

You can move text from one location in your document to another.

MOVE TEXT

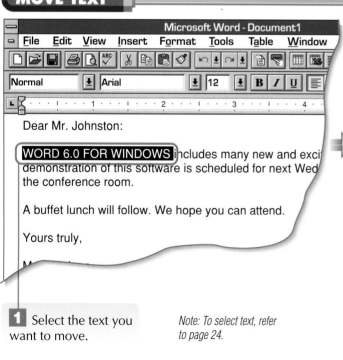

Dear Mr. Johnston:

WORD 6.0 FOR WINDOWS includes many new and exci demonstration of this software is scheduled for next Wed the conference room.

A buffet lunch will follow. We hope you can attend.

Yours truly,

1 Select the text you want to move.

Note: To select text, refer to page 24.

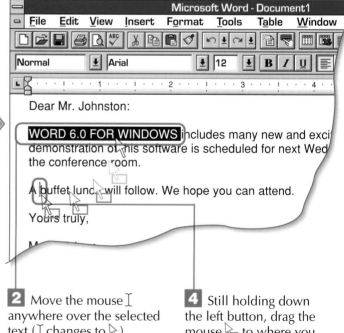

Dear Mr. Johnston:

WORD 6.0 FOR WINDOWS includes many new and exci demonstration of this software is scheduled for next Wed the conference room.

A buffet lunch will follow. We hope you can attend.

Yours truly,

2 Move the mouse I anywhere over the selected text (I changes to ⇗).

3 Press and hold down the left button (⇗ changes to ⬚).

4 Still holding down the left button, drag the mouse ⬚ to where you want to place the text.

Note: The text will appear where you position the dotted insertion point on your screen.

40

- Insert Text
- Delete Text
- Replace Selected Text

- Undo Changes
- Redo Changes
- Change the Case of Text

- **Move Text**
- Copy Text
- Change Views

You can also use these buttons to move text.

1 Select the text you want to move.

2 Move the mouse ⟶ over ✂ and then press the left button. The text you selected disappears from your screen.

3 Position the insertion point where you want to move the text.

4 Move the mouse ⟶ over 📋 and then press the left button. The text appears in the new location.

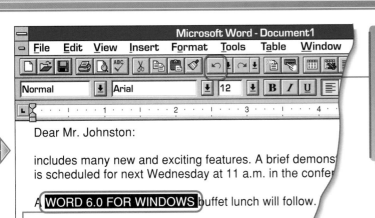

Microsoft Word - Document1

File   Edit   View   Insert   Format   Tools   Table   Window

Normal   Arial   12   B   I   U

Dear Mr. Johnston:

includes many new and exciting features. A brief demons
is scheduled for next Wednesday at 11 a.m. in the confer

A WORD 6.0 FOR WINDOWS buffet lunch will follow.

Yours truly,

Mary Vickers

You can cancel the last change you made to your document.

◆ To move the text back to its original location, position the mouse ⟶ over ↺ and then press the left button.

Note: For more information on canceling changes made to your document, refer to page 36.

5 Release the button and the text moves to the new location.

COPY TEXT

You can place a copy of text in a different location in your document. This will save you time since you do not have to retype the text.

COPY TEXT

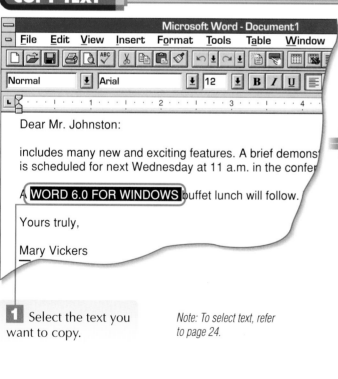

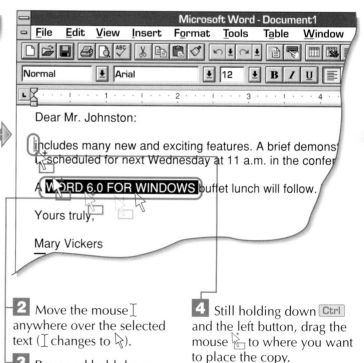

1 Select the text you want to copy.

Note: To select text, refer to page 24.

2 Move the mouse I anywhere over the selected text (I changes to ⬧).

3 Press and hold down `Ctrl` and press and hold down the left button (⬧ changes to ⬧₊).

4 Still holding down `Ctrl` and the left button, drag the mouse to where you want to place the copy.

Note: The text will appear where you position the dotted insertion point on your screen.

42

- Insert Text
- Delete Text
- Replace Selected Text

- Undo Changes
- Redo Changes
- Change the Case of Text

- Move Text
- Copy Text
- Change Views

You can also use these buttons to copy text.

1 Select the text you want to copy.

2 Move the mouse over and then press the left button. The text you selected remains on your screen.

3 Position the insertion point where you want to place the copy.

4 Move the mouse over and then press the left button. A copy of the text appears in the new location.

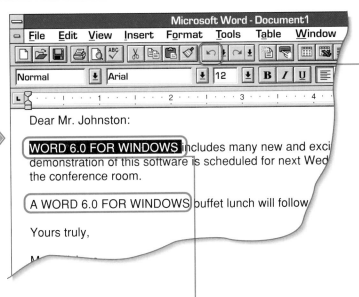

You can cancel the last change you made to your document.

◆ To remove the copy, move the mouse over and then press the left button.

Note: For more information on canceling changes made to your document, refer to page 36.

5 Release the button and then release Ctrl.

◆ A copy of the text appears in the new location.

Word offers three ways to display your document. You can choose the view that best suits your needs.

CHANGE VIEWS

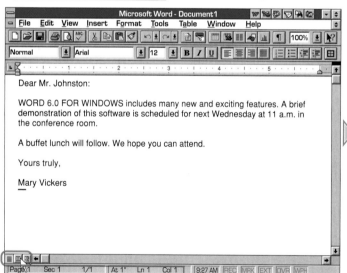

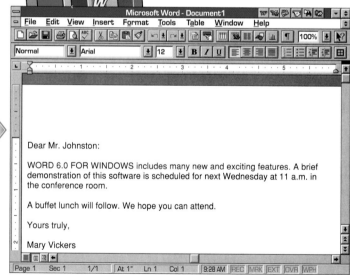

When you first start Word, your document appears in the Normal view.

1 To change to another view, move the mouse ⌖ over one of the options listed below (example: ▤) and then press the left button.

▤ Normal view

▤ Page Layout view

▤ Outline view

◆ Your document appears in the new view (example: **Page Layout**).

44

- Insert Text
- Delete Text
- Replace Selected Text

- Undo Changes
- Redo Changes
- Change the Case of Text

- Move Text
- Copy Text
- **Change Views**

THREE WAYS TO VIEW YOUR DOCUMENT

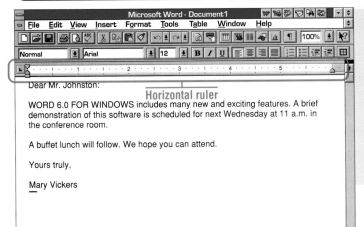

1 NORMAL VIEW

◆ The Normal view simplifies the page layout so you can type and edit the document quickly.

◆ This view does not display top or bottom margins, headers, footers or page numbers.

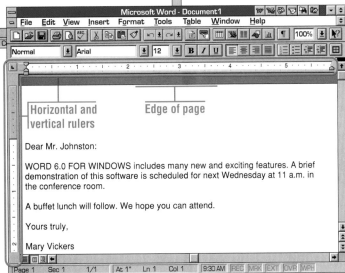

2 PAGE LAYOUT VIEW

◆ The Page Layout view displays your document exactly the way it will appear on a printed page.

◆ This view displays all features in your document, including top and bottom margins, headers, footers and page numbers.

3 OUTLINE VIEW

◆ The Outline view lets you create an outline of your document, similar to a Table of Contents. You can display the headings and subheadings and hide the body text. This view helps you work more efficiently with longer documents.

You can use the Find feature to locate a word or phrase in your document.

FIND TEXT

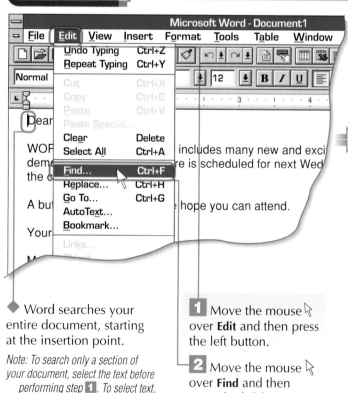

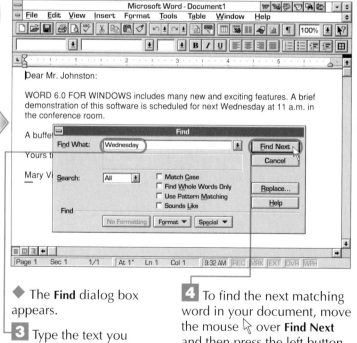

◆ Word searches your entire document, starting at the insertion point.

Note: To search only a section of your document, select the text before performing step 1. To select text, refer to page 24.

1 Move the mouse ⟋ over **Edit** and then press the left button.

2 Move the mouse ⟋ over **Find** and then press the left button.

◆ The **Find** dialog box appears.

3 Type the text you want to find (example: **Wednesday**).

4 To find the next matching word in your document, move the mouse ⟋ over **Find Next** and then press the left button.

46

- **Find Text**
- Replace Text
- Check Spelling
- Using AutoCorrect

- Using AutoText
- Using the Thesaurus
- Check Grammar

The **Sounds Like** option finds words that sound the same but are spelled differently. For example, if you search for **there**, Word will also find **their** and **they're**.

☐ Match **C**ase
☐ Find **W**hole Words Only
☐ Use Pattern **M**atching
☒ Sounds **L**ike

◆ To select the **Sounds Like** option, move the mouse ⟍ over the option and then press the left button (☐ changes to ☒).

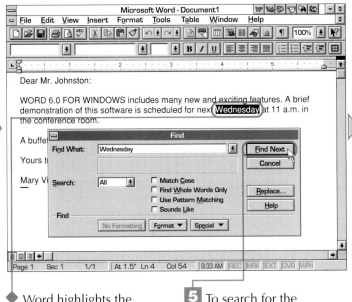

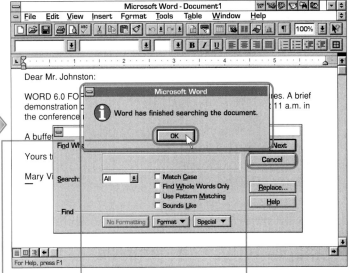

◆ Word highlights the first matching word it finds.

5 To search for the next matching word, repeat step **4**.

Note: To cancel the search at any time, press **Esc** *.*

◆ This dialog box appears when there are no more matching words in your document.

6 To close the dialog box, move the mouse ⟍ over **OK** and then press the left button.

7 To close the **Find** dialog box, move the mouse ⟍ over **Cancel** and then press the left button.

You can use the Replace feature to locate every occurrence of a word or phrase in your document. You can then replace the word or phrase with new text. This is ideal if you have frequently misspelled a name.

REPLACE TEXT

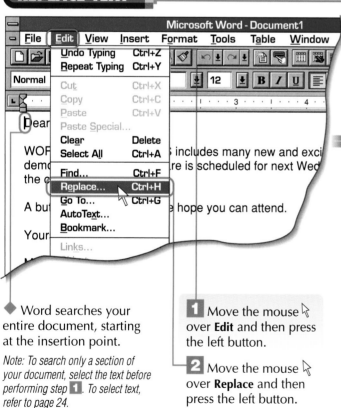

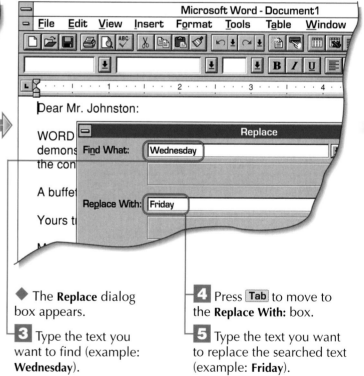

◆ Word searches your entire document, starting at the insertion point.

Note: To search only a section of your document, select the text before performing step **1**. *To select text, refer to page 24.*

1 Move the mouse over **Edit** and then press the left button.

2 Move the mouse over **Replace** and then press the left button.

◆ The **Replace** dialog box appears.

3 Type the text you want to find (example: **Wednesday**).

4 Press **Tab** to move to the **Replace With:** box.

5 Type the text you want to replace the searched text (example: **Friday**).

48

- Find Text
- Replace Text
- Check Spelling
- Using AutoCorrect
- Using AutoText
- Using the Thesaurus
- Check Grammar

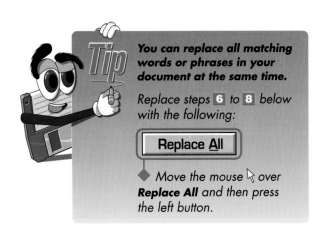

Tip

You can replace all matching words or phrases in your document at the same time.

Replace steps 6 *to* 8 *below with the following:*

Replace All

◆ *Move the mouse ♪ over* **Replace All** *and then press the left button.*

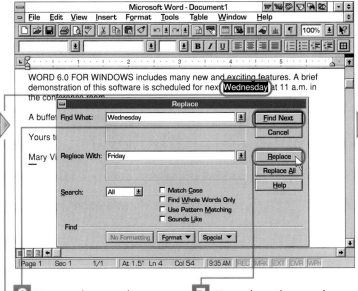

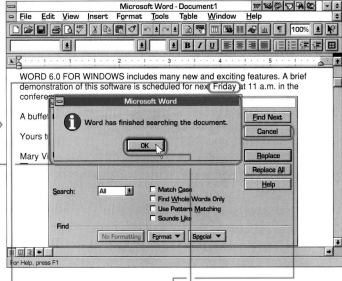

6 To start the search, move the mouse ♪ over **Find Next** and then press the left button.

◆ Word highlights the first matching word it finds.

7 To replace the word, move the mouse ♪ over **Replace** and then press the left button.

Note: If you do not want to replace the word, repeat step 6 *to find the next matching word in your document.*

◆ Word replaces the word and searches for the next matching word.

8 Repeat step 7 for each word you want to replace.

◆ This dialog box appears when there are no more matching words in your document.

9 To close this dialog box, move the mouse ♪ over **OK** and then press the left button.

10 To close the **Replace** dialog box, move the mouse ♪ over **Cancel** or **Close** and then press the left button.

CHECK SPELLING

You can use the Spelling feature to find and correct spelling errors in your document.
Sciense
Science
Word Dictionary
Expanded 6.0 Version

CHECK SPELLING

The spell check will find:	Example:
Misspelled words	The girl is six **yeers** old.
Duplicate words	The girl is **six six** years old.

The spell check will not find:	Example:
A correctly spelled word used in the wrong context.	The girl is **sit** years old.

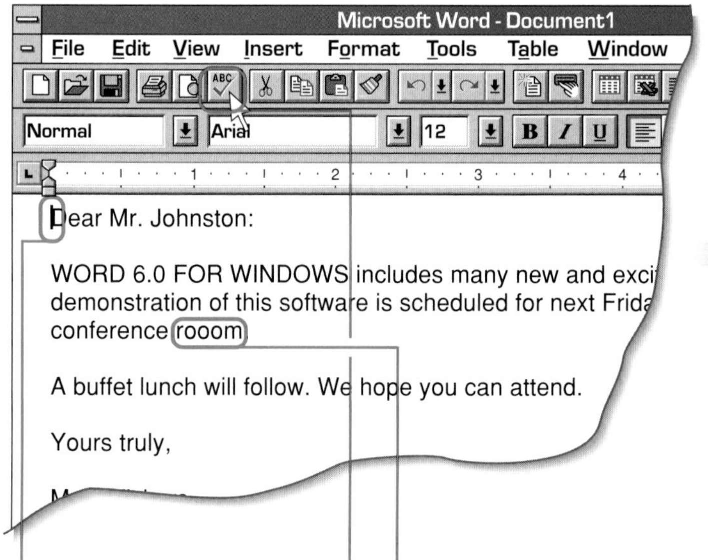
Microsoft Word - Document1
File Edit View Insert Format Tools Table Window
Normal
Arial
12
Dear Mr. Johnston:
WORD 6.0 FOR WINDOWS includes many new and exci
demonstration of this software is scheduled for next Frida
conference rooom.
A buffet lunch will follow. We hope you can attend.
Yours truly,

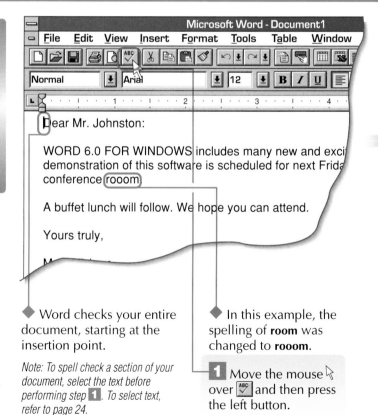

◆ Word checks your entire document, starting at the insertion point.

Note: To spell check a section of your document, select the text before performing step 1. To select text, refer to page 24.

◆ In this example, the spelling of **room** was changed to **rooom.**

1 Move the mouse over the spelling button and then press the left button.

- Find Text
- Replace Text
- **Check Spelling**
- Using AutoCorrect
- Using AutoText
- Using the Thesaurus
- Check Grammar

IMPORTANT!

You should save your document to store it for future use. If you do not save your document, it will disappear when you turn off your computer.

Note: To save your document, refer to page 64.

Once you have stored your document, save it every 5 to 10 minutes to reduce the possibility of work loss due to system or power failure.

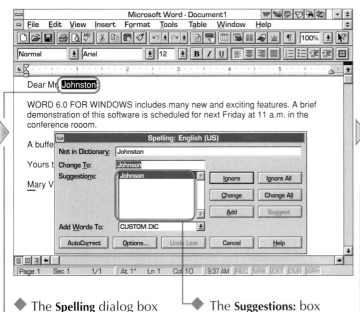

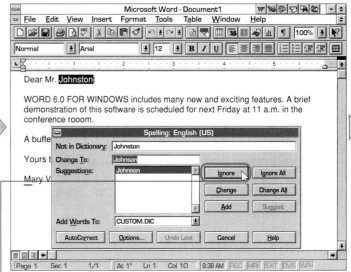

◆ The **Spelling** dialog box appears.

◆ Word highlights the first word it does not recognize (example: **Johnston**).

◆ The **Suggestions:** box displays alternative spellings.

IGNORE MISSPELLED WORD

2 If you do not want to change the spelling of the highlighted word, move the mouse ᐅ over **Ignore** and then press the left button.

CONTINUED

51

CHECK SPELLING

Word compares every word in your document to words in its dictionary. If a word does not exist in the dictionary, Word considers it misspelled.

CHECK SPELLING (CONTINUED)

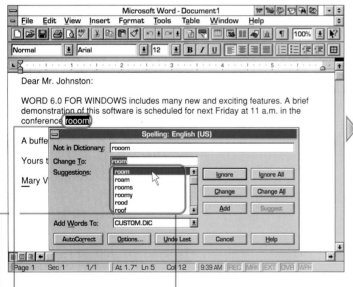

◆ Word highlights the next word it does not recognize (example: **rooom**).

◆ The **Suggestions:** box displays alternative spellings.

CORRECT MISSPELLED WORD

3 To select the correct spelling, move the mouse ⍚ over the word you want to use (example: **room**) and then press the left button.

◆ If you want to have Word automatically correct the misspelled word every time you type it in your document, move the mouse ⍚ over **AutoCorrect** and then press the left button.

Note: For more information on the AutoCorrect feature, refer to page 54.

4 To replace the misspelled word in your document with the correct spelling, move the mouse ⍚ over **Change** and then press the left button.

52

- Find Text
- Replace Text
- **Check Spelling**
- Using AutoCorrect
- Using AutoText
- Using the Thesaurus
- Check Grammar

You can cancel the spell check at any time.

◆ To cancel the spell check, move the mouse ⬚ over **Cancel** or **Close** and then press the left button.

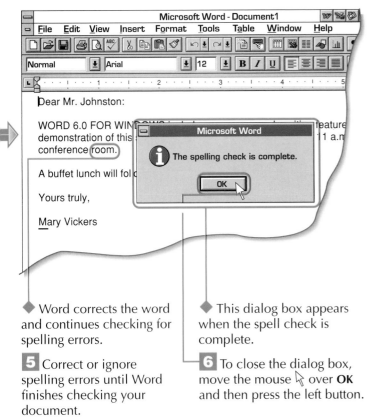

◆ Word corrects the word and continues checking for spelling errors.

5 Correct or ignore spelling errors until Word finishes checking your document.

◆ This dialog box appears when the spell check is complete.

6 To close the dialog box, move the mouse ⬚ over **OK** and then press the left button.

DUPLICATE WORDS

If you accidentally typed a word twice in your document, Word will find this error during the spell check.

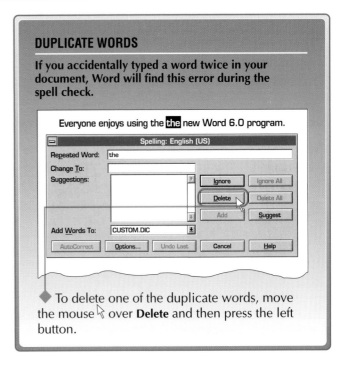

◆ To delete one of the duplicate words, move the mouse ⬚ over **Delete** and then press the left button.

USING AUTOCORRECT

Word automatically corrects common spelling errors as you type. You can customize the AutoCorrect list to include words you often misspell or words you frequently use.

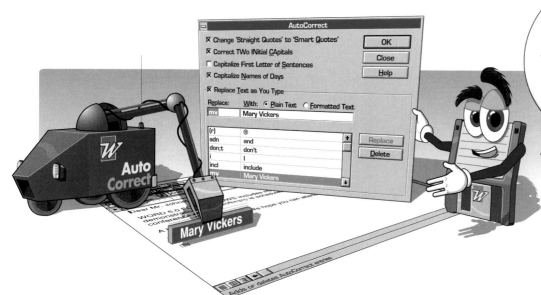

ADD TEXT TO AUTOCORRECT

If you type one of the following words and then press the Spacebar, Word will automatically change the word for you.

Text You Type	Replace With
(r)	®
adn	and
don;t	don't
i	I
incl	include
occurence	occurrence
recieve	receive
seperate	separate
teh	the

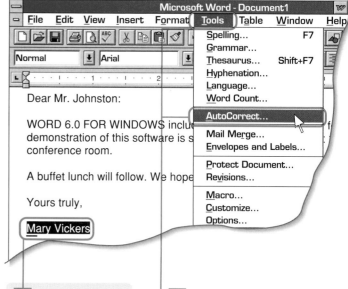

1 Select the text you want Word to automatically place in your documents.

Note: To select text, refer to page 24.

2 Move the mouse ⌖ over **Tools** and then press the left button.

3 Move the mouse ⌖ over **AutoCorrect** and then press the left button.

54

- Find Text
- Replace Text
- Check Spelling
- **Using AutoCorrect**

- Using AutoText
- Using the Thesaurus
- Check Grammar

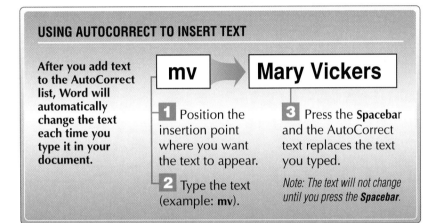

USING AUTOCORRECT TO INSERT TEXT

After you add text to the AutoCorrect list, Word will automatically change the text each time you type it in your document.

mv ➡ **Mary Vickers**

1 Position the insertion point where you want the text to appear.

2 Type the text (example: **mv**).

3 Press the **Spacebar** and the AutoCorrect text replaces the text you typed.

*Note: The text will not change until you press the **Spacebar**.*

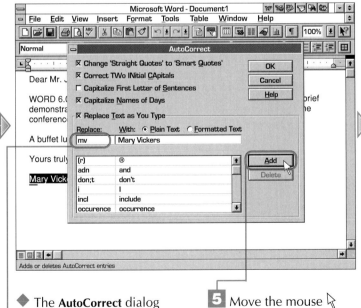

◆ The **AutoCorrect** dialog box appears.

4 Type the text you want Word to automatically replace every time you type it in a document (example: **mv**).

Note: This text cannot contain any spaces. Also, do not use a real word.

5 Move the mouse ⌖ over **Add** and then press the left button.

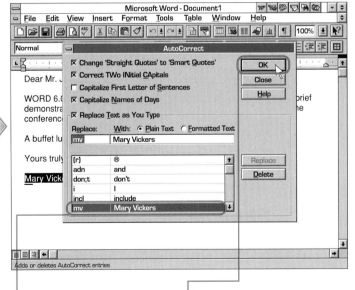

◆ The entry appears in the AutoCorrect list.

6 To close the **AutoCorrect** dialog box and return to your document, move the mouse ⌖ over **OK** and then press the left button.

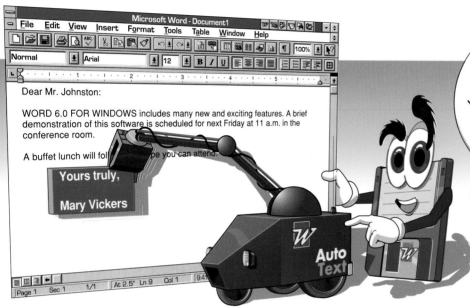

The AutoText feature lets you store frequently used words, phrases and sentences. You can then insert them into your document by typing an abbreviated version of the text.

ADD TEXT TO AUTOTEXT

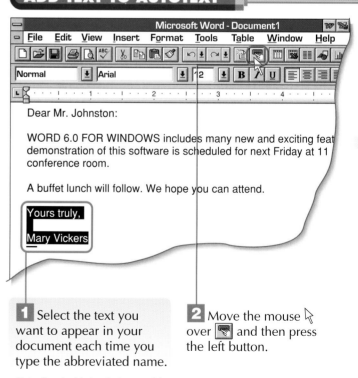

1 Select the text you want to appear in your document each time you type the abbreviated name.

2 Move the mouse ▷ over 📋 and then press the left button.

Note: To select text, refer to page 24.

- Find Text
- Replace Text
- Check Spelling
- Using AutoCorrect

• **Using AutoText**
- Using the Thesaurus
- Check Grammar

Tip

The AutoText and AutoCorrect features both insert text into your document. However, there are two distinct differences:

Note: For information on the AutoCorrect feature, refer to page 54.

AUTOTEXT

◆ *Use AutoText to insert groups of text or to insert text you use occasionally.*

◆ *Word inserts the text only when you instruct it to do so.*

AUTOCORRECT

◆ *Use AutoCorrect to correct your most common spelling errors or to insert text you use frequently (i.e., every day).*

◆ *Word automatically inserts the text as you type.*

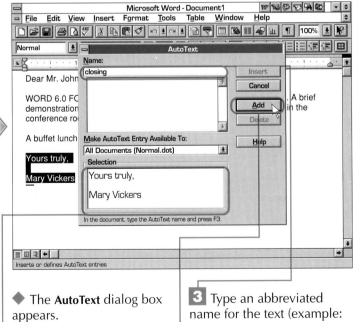

USING AUTOTEXT

After you add text to the AutoText list, you can insert the text into your document.

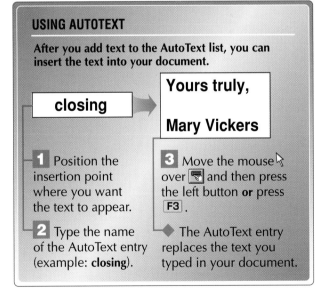

1 Position the insertion point where you want the text to appear.

2 Type the name of the AutoText entry (example: **closing**).

3 Move the mouse over and then press the left button **or** press **F3** .

◆ The AutoText entry replaces the text you typed in your document.

◆ The **AutoText** dialog box appears.

◆ The text you selected in your document appears in the **Selection** box.

3 Type an abbreviated name for the text (example: **closing**).

4 Move the mouse over **Add** and then press the left button.

USING THE THESAURUS

You can use the Thesaurus to add variety to your writing. This feature lets you replace a word in your document with one that is more suitable.

USING THE THESAURUS

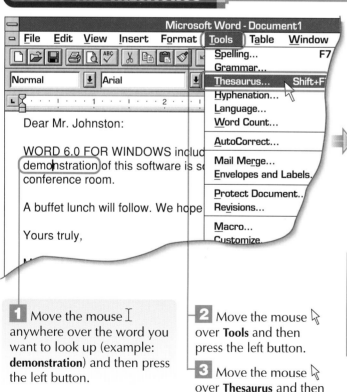

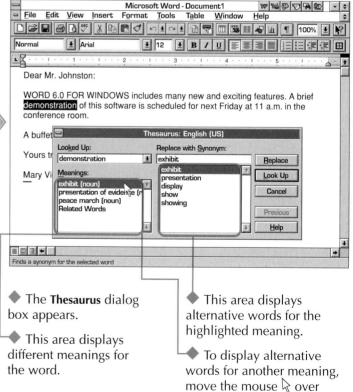

1 Move the mouse I anywhere over the word you want to look up (example: **demonstration**) and then press the left button.

2 Move the mouse ⊾ over **Tools** and then press the left button.

3 Move the mouse ⊾ over **Thesaurus** and then press the left button.

◆ The **Thesaurus** dialog box appears.

◆ This area displays different meanings for the word.

◆ This area displays alternative words for the highlighted meaning.

◆ To display alternative words for another meaning, move the mouse ⊾ over the meaning and then press the left button.

58

- Find Text
- Replace Text
- Check Spelling
- Using AutoCorrect

- Using AutoText
- • **Using the Thesaurus**
- Check Grammar

LOOK UP A WORD

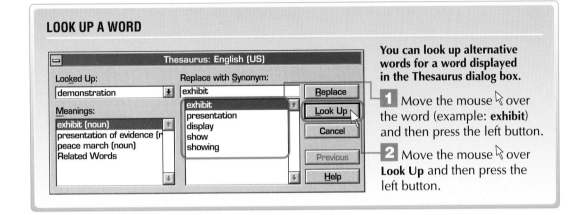

You can look up alternative words for a word displayed in the Thesaurus dialog box.

1 Move the mouse 🖱 over the word (example: **exhibit**) and then press the left button.

2 Move the mouse 🖱 over **Look Up** and then press the left button.

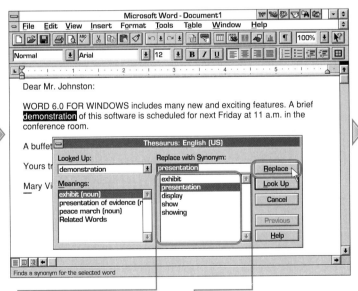

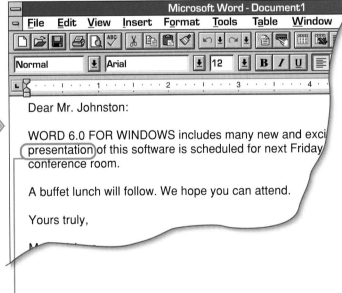

4 To select the word you want to use, move the mouse 🖱 over the word (example: **presentation**) and then press the left button.

5 Move the mouse 🖱 over **Replace** and then press the left button.

◆ The word from the Thesaurus replaces the word in your document.

CHECK GRAMMAR

You can use the Grammar feature to find and correct grammar and spelling errors in your document.

CHECK GRAMMAR

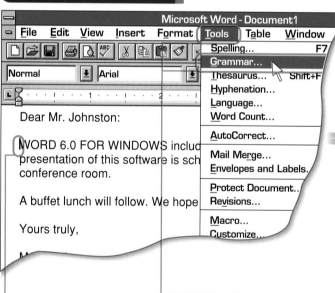

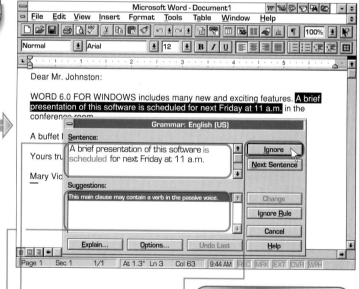

◆ Word checks your entire document, starting at the insertion point.

Note: To check only a section of your document, select the text before performing step **1**. *To select text, refer to page 24.*

1 Move the mouse over **Tools** and then press the left button.

2 Move the mouse over **Grammar** and then press the left button.

◆ If Word finds a grammatical error, the **Grammar** dialog box appears. This area displays the sentence containing the error.

◆ This area tells you what is wrong with the sentence and may offer a suggestion to correct the error.

IGNORE GRAMMATICAL ERROR

3 If you want to ignore the error and continue checking your document, move the mouse over **Ignore** and then press the left button.

- Find Text
- Replace Text
- Check Spelling
- Using AutoCorrect
- Using AutoText
- Using the Thesaurus
- **Check Grammar**

Tip

If Word finds a spelling error during a grammar check, the **Spelling** dialog box appears.

For more information on using the **Spelling** dialog box to correct a misspelled word, refer to page 52.

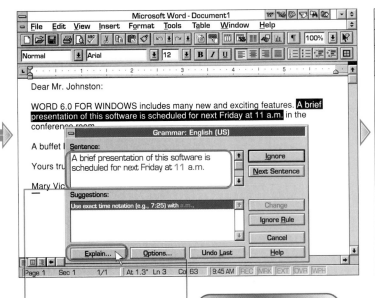

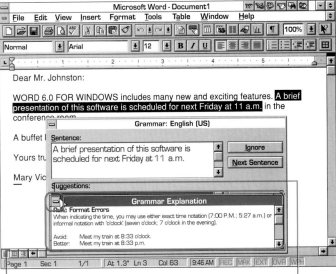

◆ If Word discovers another grammatical error, this area displays the sentence containing the error.

DISPLAY EXPLANATION

4 To display an explanation of the error, move the mouse ⌖ over **Explain** and then press the left button.

◆ An explanation of the error appears.

5 When you finish reading the explanation, move the mouse ⌖ over ⊟ and then quickly press the left button twice.

CONTINUED

CHECK GRAMMAR

The Grammar feature will improve the accuracy of your document.

I did not buy no books.

I did not buy any books.

CHECK GRAMMAR (CONTINUED)

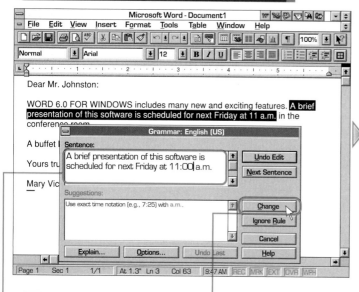

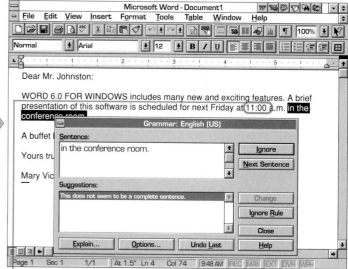

CORRECT GRAMMATICAL ERROR

6 Edit the text in the dialog box as you would any text in your document (example: change **11** to **11:00**).

Note: To insert and delete text, refer to pages 28 to 35.

7 Move the mouse over **Change** and then press the left button.

◆ The change appears in your document and Word continues checking for grammatical and spelling errors.

8 Correct or ignore grammatical errors until Word finishes checking your document.

- Find Text
- Replace Text
- Check Spelling
- Using AutoCorrect

- Using AutoText
- Using the Thesaurus
- Check Grammar

You can cancel the grammar check at any time.

	Ignore **R**ule
	Cancel
Undo Last	Help

◆ To cancel the grammar check, move the mouse ⌖ over **Cancel** or **Close** and then press the left button.

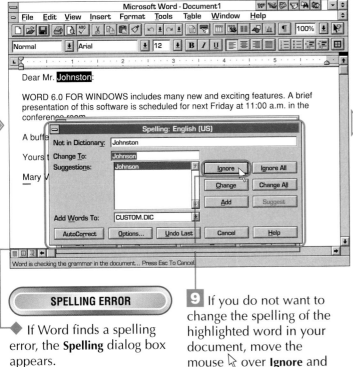

SPELLING ERROR

◆ If Word finds a spelling error, the **Spelling** dialog box appears.

9 If you do not want to change the spelling of the highlighted word in your document, move the mouse ⌖ over **Ignore** and then press the left button.

Note: For more information on checking your document for spelling errors, refer to pages 50 to 53.

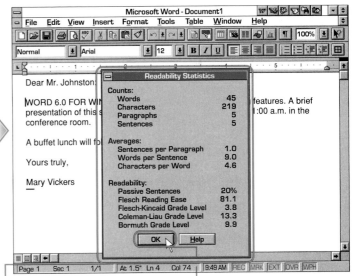

READABILITY STATISTICS

◆ The **Readability Statistics** dialog box appears when Word finishes checking your document.

10 To close this dialog box and return to your document, move the mouse ⌖ over **OK** and then press the left button.

SAVE A NEW DOCUMENT

You should save your document to store it for future use. This enables you to later retrieve the document for reviewing or editing purposes.

SAVE A NEW DOCUMENT

When you save a document for the first time, you must give it a name. The name of a document consists of two parts: a name and an extension. You must separate these parts with a period.

notice . doc

◆ **Name**

The name describes the contents of a document. It can have up to eight characters.

◆ **Period**

A period separates the name and the extension.

◆ **Extension**

The extension describes the type of information a document contains. It can have up to three characters.

*Note: **doc** stands for **document**.*

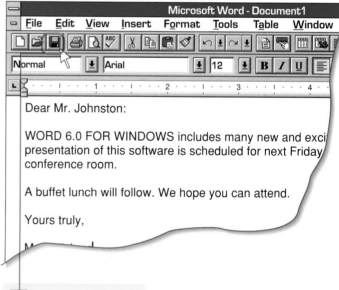

Dear Mr. Johnston:

WORD 6.0 FOR WINDOWS includes many new and exci presentation of this software is scheduled for next Friday conference room.

A buffet lunch will follow. We hope you can attend.

Yours truly,

1 Move the mouse over 🖫 and then press the left button.

◆ The **Save As** dialog box appears.

*Note: If you previously saved your document, the **Save As** dialog box will not appear since you have already named the document.*

64

- • **Save a New Document**
- • Save a Document to a Diskette
- • Close a Document
- • Exit Word
- • Open a Document

Rules for Naming a Document

The name of a document *can* contain the following characters:

◆ The letters A to Z

◆ The numbers 0 to 9

◆ The symbols
_ ^ $ ~ ! # % & { } @ ( )

The name of a document *cannot* contain the following characters:

◆ A comma (,)

◆ A blank space

◆ The symbols
* ? ; [ ] + = \ / : < >

Each document in a directory must have a unique name.

letter.doc
note1q.doc
test.doc
training.doc

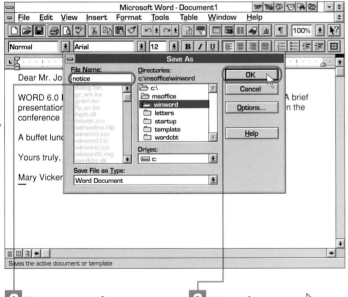

2 Type a name for your document (example: **notice**).

*Note: To make it easier to find your document later on, do not type an extension. Word will then automatically add the **doc** extension to the name.*

3 Move the mouse ⌐ over **OK** and then press the left button.

◆ Word saves your document and displays the name at the top of your screen.

◆ You should save your document every 5 to 10 minutes to store any changes made since the last time you saved the document. To save changes, move the mouse ⌐ over 🖫 and then press the left button.

SAVE A DOCUMENT TO A DISKETTE

If you want to give your colleagues a copy of a document, you can save the document to a diskette. They can then review the document on their own computers.

SAVE A DOCUMENT TO A DISKETTE

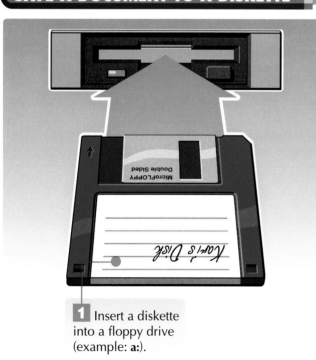

1 Insert a diskette into a floppy drive (example: **a:**).

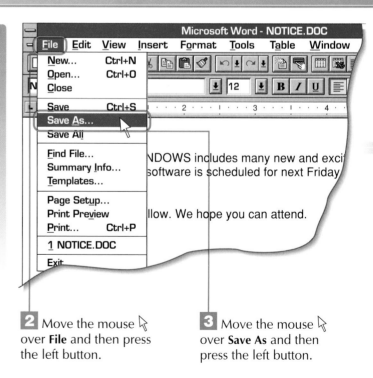

2 Move the mouse over **File** and then press the left button.

3 Move the mouse over **Save As** and then press the left button.

- Save a New Document
- Save a Document to a Diskette
- Close a Document
- Exit Word
- Open a Document

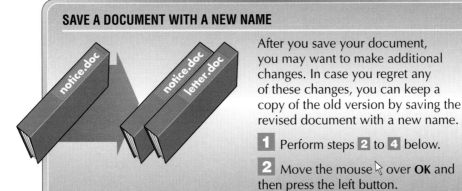

SAVE A DOCUMENT WITH A NEW NAME

After you save your document, you may want to make additional changes. In case you regret any of these changes, you can keep a copy of the old version by saving the revised document with a new name.

1 Perform steps **2** to **4** below.

2 Move the mouse ⬚ over **OK** and then press the left button.

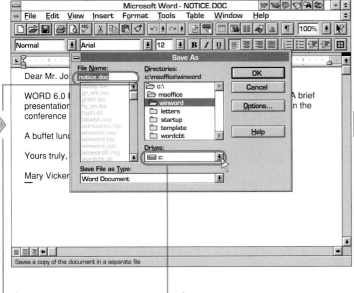

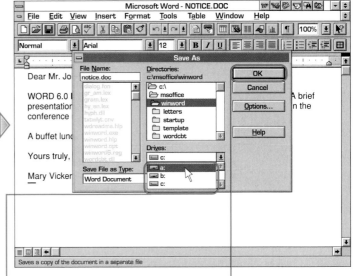

◆ The **Save As** dialog box appears.

4 The **File Name:** box displays the current file name. To save your document with a different name, type a new name.

◆ The **Drives:** box displays the current drive (example: **c:**).

5 To save the document to a diskette, move the mouse ⬚ over ⬛ in the **Drives:** box and then press the left button.

◆ A list of the available drives for your computer appears.

6 Move the mouse ⬚ over the drive that contains the diskette (example: **a:**) and then press the left button.

7 To save your document, move the mouse ⬚ over **OK** and then press the left button.

67

When you finish working with a document, you can close the document to remove it from your screen.

CLOSE A DOCUMENT

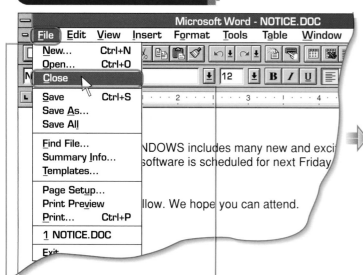

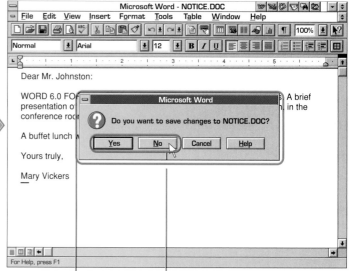

1 To close the document displayed on your screen, move the mouse ⌖ over **File** and then press the left button.

2 Move the mouse ⌖ over **Close** and then press the left button.

◆ This dialog box appears if you have not saved changes made to your document.

Note: For information on saving a document, refer to page 64.

3 To close the document without saving the changes, move the mouse ⌖ over **No** and then press the left button.

◆ To save the changes, move the mouse ⌖ over **Yes** and then press the left button.

- Save a New Document
- Save a Document to a Diskette
- Close a Document
- Exit Word
- Open a Document

When you finish using Word, you can easily exit the program.

EXIT WORD

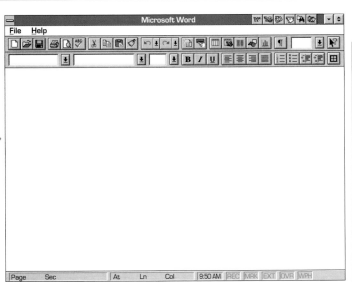

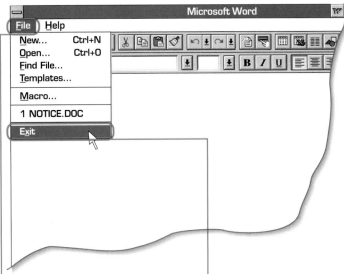

◆ Word removes the document from your screen.

1 To exit Word, move the mouse over **File** and then press the left button.

2 Move the mouse over **Exit** and then press the left button.

Note: To restart Word, refer to page 19.

OPEN A DOCUMENT

You can open a saved document and display it on your screen. This lets you review and edit the document.

OPEN A DOCUMENT

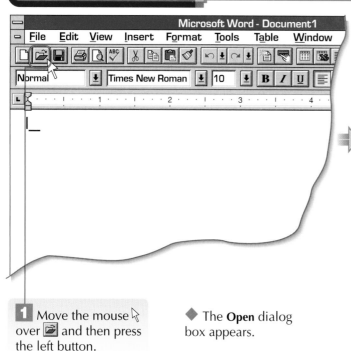

1 Move the mouse over 📂 and then press the left button.

◆ The **Open** dialog box appears.

◆ The **Drives:** box displays the current drive (example: **c:**).

2 To open a document on a different drive, move the mouse over ⬇ in the **Drives:** box and then press the left button.

◆ A list of the available drives for your computer appears.

3 Move the mouse over the drive containing the document you want to open and then press the left button.

70

- Save a New Document
- Save a Document to a Diskette
- Close a Document
- Exit Word
- **Open a Document**

SHORTCUT

The File menu displays the names of the last four documents you opened.

Note: In this example, only one document has been opened.

File

New...	Ctrl+N
Open...	Ctrl+O
Close	
Save	Ctrl+S
Save As...	
Save All	
Find File...	
Summary Info...	
Templates...	
Page Setup...	
Print Preview	
Print...	Ctrl+P
1 NOTICE.DOC	
Exit	

To open one of the documents listed:

1 Move the mouse over **File** and then press the left button.

2 Move the mouse over the name of the document you want to open (example: **NOTICE.DOC**) and then press the left button.

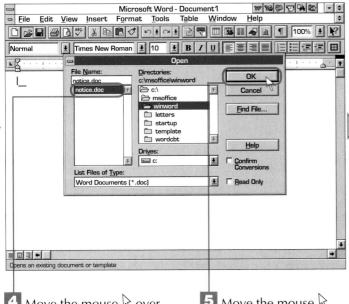

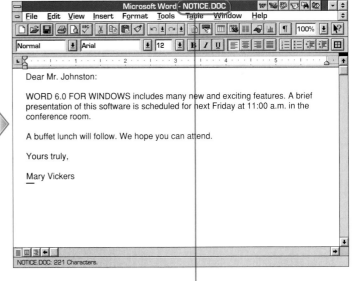

4 Move the mouse over the name of the document you want to open (example: **notice.doc**) and then press the left button.

5 Move the mouse over **OK** and then press the left button.

◆ Word opens the document and displays it on your screen. You can now make changes to the document.

◆ The name of the document appears at the top of your screen.

You can create a document to start a new letter, report or memo. Word lets you have several documents open at the same time.

CREATE A NEW DOCUMENT

Dear Mr. Johnston:

WORD 6.0 FOR WINDOWS includes many new and exci
presentation of this software is scheduled for next Friday
conference room.

A buffet lunch will follow. We hope you can attend.

Yours truly,

1 Move the mouse ⌖ over ▯ and then press the left button.

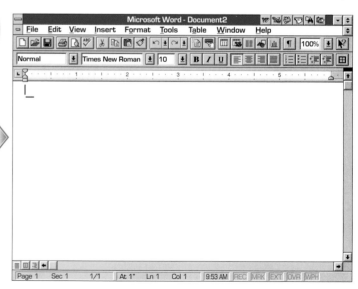

◆ A new document appears.

Note: The previous document is now hidden behind the new document.

◆ Think of each document as a separate piece of paper. When you create a document, you are placing a new piece of paper on your screen.

- **Create a New Document**
- **Arrange Open Documents**
- Copy or Move Text Between Documents
- Maximize a Document
- Switch Between Documents

If you have several documents open, some of them may be hidden from view. To view the contents of each document, you can use the Arrange All command.

ARRANGE OPEN DOCUMENTS

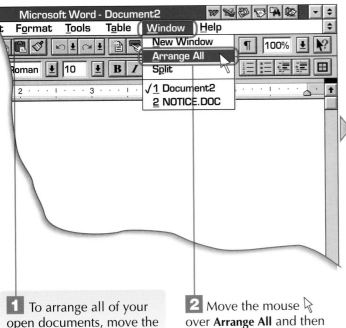

1 To arrange all of your open documents, move the mouse over **Window** and then press the left button.

2 Move the mouse over **Arrange All** and then press the left button.

◆ You can now view the contents of all your open documents at the same time.

◆ You can only work in the current document, which displays a highlighted title bar.

Note: To make another document current, move the mouse anywhere over the document and then press the left button.

73

COPY OR MOVE TEXT BETWEEN DOCUMENTS

Copying or moving text between documents saves you time when you are working in one document and want to use text from another.

COPY OR MOVE TEXT BETWEEN DOCUMENTS

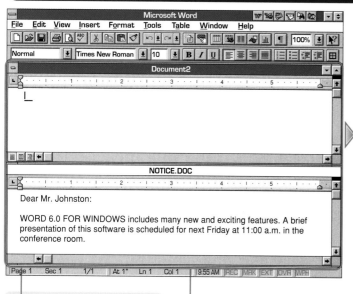

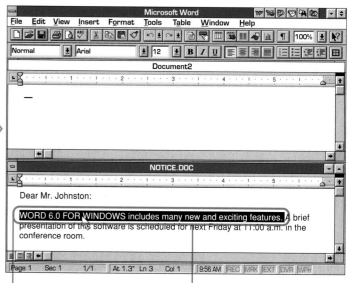

1 Open the documents you want to copy or move text between.

Note: To open a saved document, refer to page 70. To create a new document, refer to page 72.

2 Display the contents of both documents by using the **Arrange All** command.

*Note: For information on the **Arrange All** command, refer to page 73.*

3 Select the text you want to copy or move to another document.

Note: To select text, refer to page 24.

4 Move the mouse I anywhere over the selected text and I changes to ⍽.

- Create a New Document
- Arrange Open Documents
- Copy or Move Text Between Documents
- Maximize a Document
- Switch Between Documents

The Copy and Move features both place text in a new location, but they have one distinct difference.

COPY TEXT

When you copy text, the original text remains in its place.

MOVE TEXT

When you move text, the original text disappears.

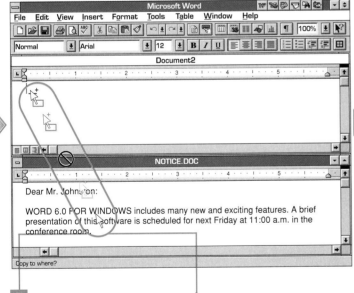

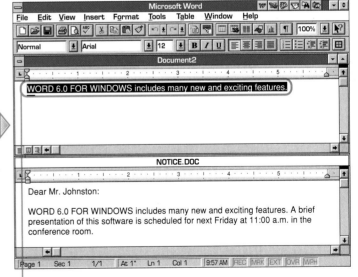

5 To copy the text, press and hold down Ctrl. Still holding down Ctrl, press and hold down the left button as you drag the mouse to where you want to place the copy.

◆ To move the text, press and hold down the left button as you drag the mouse to where you want to move the text.

6 Release the button (and Ctrl) and the text appears in the new location.

Note: To deselect text, move the mouse I outside the selected area and then press the left button.

75

You can enlarge a document to fill your screen. This lets you view more of its contents.

MAXIMIZE A DOCUMENT

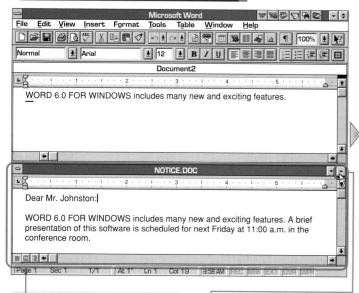

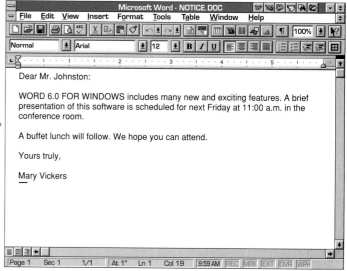

1 To select the document you want to maximize, move the mouse ⟍ anywhere over the document and then press the left button.

2 Move the mouse ⟍ over ▲ in the document you want to maximize and then press the left button.

◆ The document enlarges to fill your screen.

Note: The document you maximized covers all of your open documents.

- Create a New Document
- Arrange Open Documents
- Copy or Move Text Between Documents

- Maximize a Document
- Switch Between Documents

You can easily switch between all of your open documents.

SWITCH BETWEEN DOCUMENTS

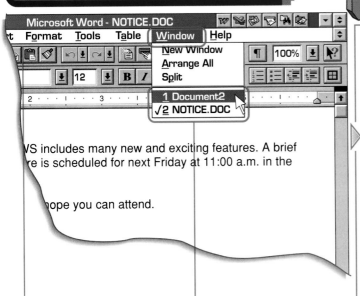

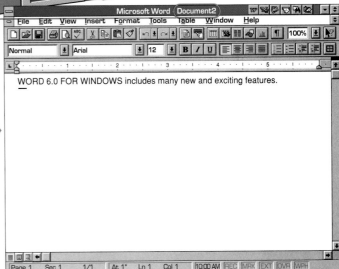

1 To display a list of all your open documents, move the mouse ⃗ over **Window** and then press the left button.

2 Move the mouse ⃗ over the document you want to switch to and then press the left button.

◆ The document appears. Word displays its name at the top of your screen.

Note: When you finish working with a document, you can close the document to remove it from your screen. For more information, refer to page 68.

The Print Preview feature lets you see on screen what your document will look like when printed.

PREVIEW A DOCUMENT

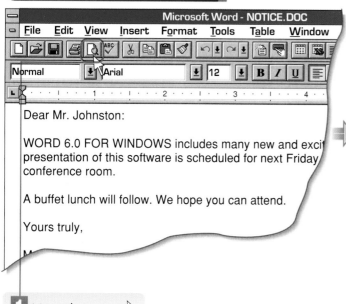

1 Move the mouse over 🔍 and then press the left button.

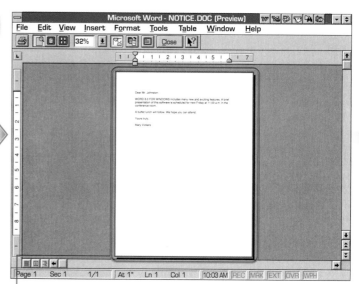

◆ The page you are currently working on appears in the Print Preview window.

◆ If your document contains more than one page, press **PageDown** on your keyboard to display the next page. Press **PageUp** to display the previous page.

78

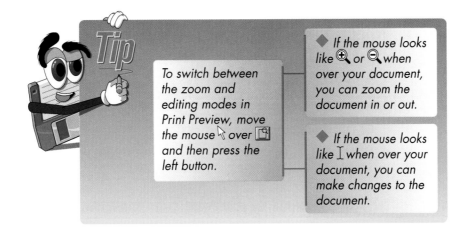

To switch between the zoom and editing modes in Print Preview, move the mouse ⟋ over 🔲 and then press the left button.

◆ If the mouse looks like ⊕ or ⊖ when over your document, you can zoom the document in or out.

◆ If the mouse looks like I when over your document, you can make changes to the document.

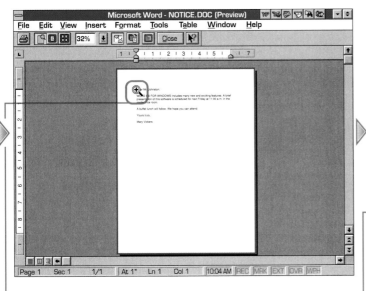

ZOOM IN OR OUT

1 To magnify a section of the page, move the mouse ⟋ over the section (⟋ changes to ⊕) and then press the left button.

*Note: If the mouse looks like I when over your document, refer to the **Tip** above to change to the zoom mode.*

◆ A magnified view of the page appears and the mouse ⊕ changes to ⊖ .

2 To again display the entire page, move the mouse ⊖ anywhere over the page and then press the left button.

In Print Preview, Word can display more than one page at a time. This lets you view the overall style of multiple pages at once.

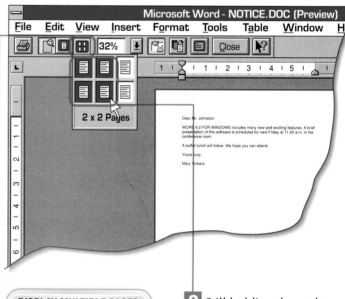

PREVIEW A DOCUMENT

DISPLAY MULTIPLE PAGES

1 Move the mouse ⌖ over ⊞ and then press and hold down the left button.

2 Still holding down the button, move the mouse ⌖ over the number of pages you want to display at once.

Note: If you drag the mouse ⌖ down or to the right, more choices appear.

SHRINK TO FIT

The Shrink to Fit feature is useful if the last page in your document contains only a few lines of text and you want it to fit on one less page.

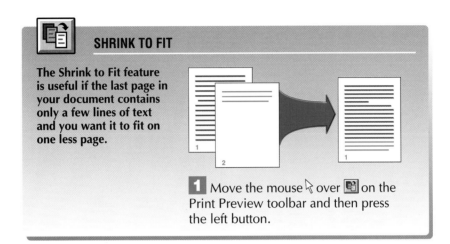

1 Move the mouse ❇ over 🖻 on the Print Preview toolbar and then press the left button.

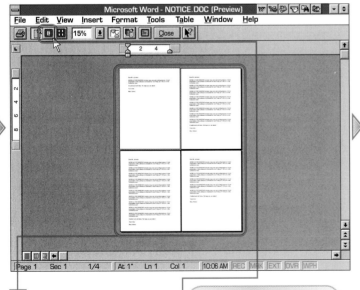

3 Release the button and the number of pages you specified appears on your screen.

Note: In this example, the document contains four pages.

DISPLAY ONE PAGE

1 To display a single page, move the mouse ❇ over 🖻 and then press the left button.

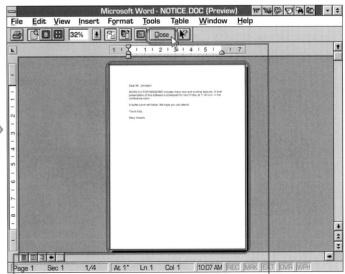

◆ A single page appears on your screen.

◆ Press **PageDown** on your keyboard to display the next page. Press **PageUp** to display the previous page.

CLOSE PRINT PREVIEW

1 To close Print Preview and return to your document, move the mouse ❇ over **Close** and then press the left button.

You can print a single page, specific pages or your entire document. Before printing, make sure your printer is on and contains paper.

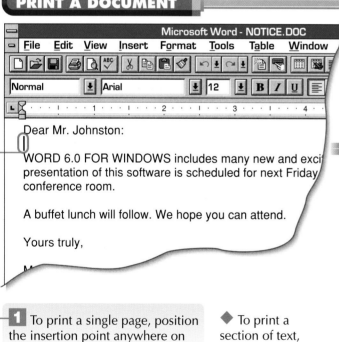

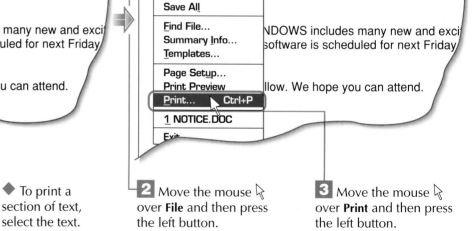

1 To print a single page, position the insertion point anywhere on the page you want to print.

◆ To print your entire document or specific pages, position the insertion point anywhere in the document.

◆ To print a section of text, select the text.

Note: To select text, refer to page 24.

2 Move the mouse over **File** and then press the left button.

3 Move the mouse over **Print** and then press the left button.

- Preview a Document
- **Print a Document**
- Print an Envelope

SHORTCUT

PRINT YOUR ENTIRE DOCUMENT

◆ To quickly print your entire document, move the mouse � over 🖶 and then press the left button.

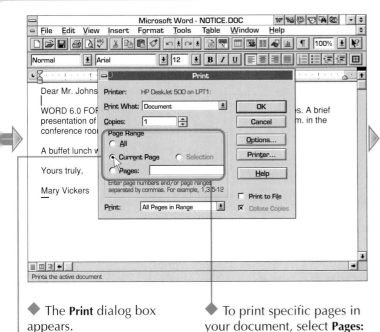

◆ The **Print** dialog box appears.

4 Move the mouse � over the range you want to print (example: **Current Page**) and then press the left button.

◆ To print specific pages in your document, select **Pages:** in step **4**. Then type the page numbers separated by commas (example: **1,3,5**) or type the first and last page numbers separated by a dash (example: **3-5**).

5 Move the mouse � over **OK** and then press the left button.

You can use the Envelope feature to create and print an envelope.

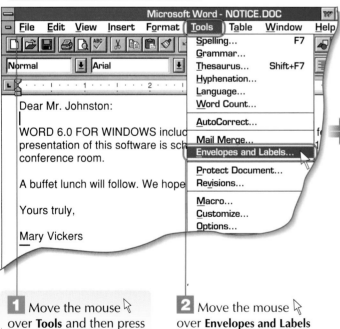

1 Move the mouse ⟍ over **Tools** and then press the left button.

2 Move the mouse ⟍ over **Envelopes and Labels** and then press the left button.

◆ The **Envelopes and Labels** dialog box appears.

3 Move the mouse ⟍ over the **Envelopes** tab and then press the left button.

◆ A delivery address appears in this area if Word found one in your document.

4 If a delivery address did not appear, move the mouse I over this area and then press the left button. Then type the address.

84

This dialog box appears if you made changes to the return address.

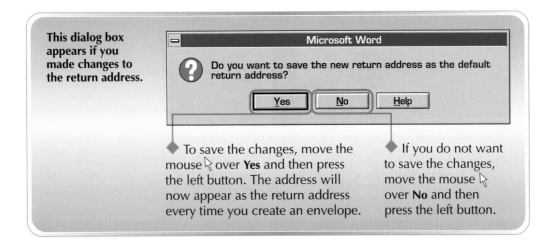

◆ To save the changes, move the mouse ⍩ over **Yes** and then press the left button. The address will now appear as the return address every time you create an envelope.

◆ If you do not want to save the changes, move the mouse ⍩ over **No** and then press the left button.

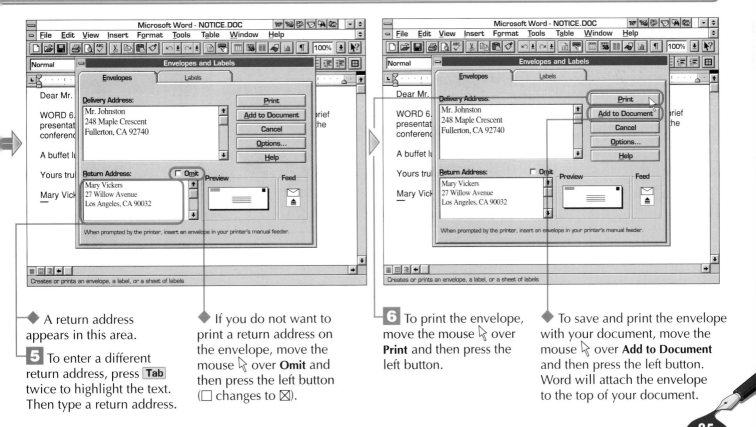

◆ A return address appears in this area.

5 To enter a different return address, press **Tab** twice to highlight the text. Then type a return address.

◆ If you do not want to print a return address on the envelope, move the mouse ⍩ over **Omit** and then press the left button (□ changes to ⊠).

6 To print the envelope, move the mouse ⍩ over **Print** and then press the left button.

◆ To save and print the envelope with your document, move the mouse ⍩ over **Add to Document** and then press the left button. Word will attach the envelope to the top of your document.

85

BOLD, UNDERLINE AND ITALICS

You can use the Bold, Underline and Italic features to emphasize important information. This will improve the overall appearance of your document.

bold   underline   *italic*

BOLD TEXT

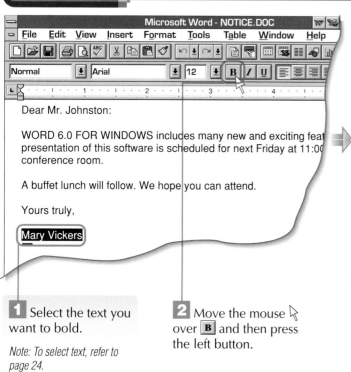

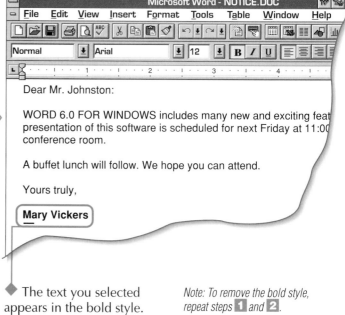

1 Select the text you want to bold.

Note: To select text, refer to page 24.

2 Move the mouse over **B** and then press the left button.

◆ The text you selected appears in the bold style.

Note: To deselect text, move the mouse I outside the selected area and then press the left button.

Note: To remove the bold style, repeat steps **1** and **2**.

- **Bold, Underline and Italics**
- Change Fonts
- Insert a Symbol

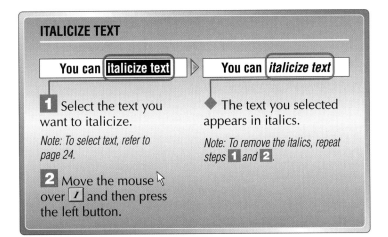

ITALICIZE TEXT

You can *italicize text* ▷ You can *italicize text*

1 Select the text you want to italicize.

Note: To select text, refer to page 24.

2 Move the mouse ⏳ over *I* and then press the left button.

◆ The text you selected appears in italics.

Note: To remove the italics, repeat steps 1 and 2.

UNDERLINE TEXT

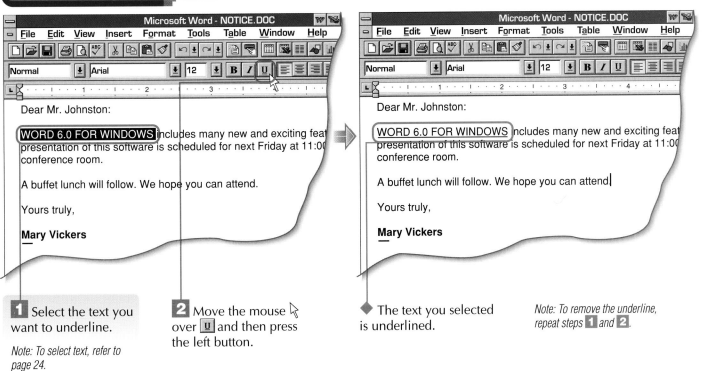

1 Select the text you want to underline.

Note: To select text, refer to page 24.

2 Move the mouse ⏳ over *U* and then press the left button.

◆ The text you selected is underlined.

Note: To remove the underline, repeat steps 1 and 2.

You can change the design and size of characters in your document to emphasize headings and make text easier to read.

CHANGE FONTS

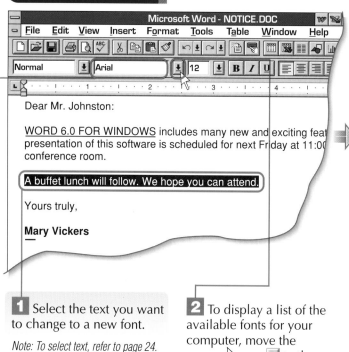

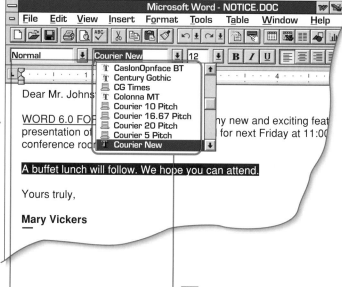

1 Select the text you want to change to a new font.

Note: To select text, refer to page 24.

◆ The **Font** box displays the font of the text you selected (example: **Arial**).

2 To display a list of the available fonts for your computer, move the mouse ⌖ over ⬇ to the right of the **Font** box and then press the left button.

◆ A list of the available fonts appears.

3 Press ⬇ or ⬆ on your keyboard until you highlight the font you want to use (example: **Courier New**).

4 To select the highlighted font, press **Enter**.

REMOVE ALL CHARACTER FORMATTING

You can instantly remove all character formatting from text in your document.

1 Select the text that displays the character formatting you want to remove.

2 Press `Ctrl` + **Spacebar** on your keyboard.

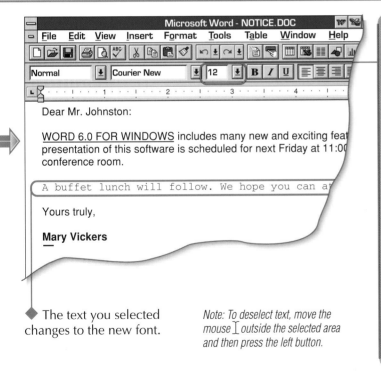

Dear Mr. Johnston:

WORD 6.0 FOR WINDOWS includes many new and exciting feat presentation of this software is scheduled for next Friday at 11:00 conference room.

A buffet lunch will follow. We hope you can a

Yours truly,

Mary Vickers

◆ The text you selected changes to the new font.

Note: To deselect text, move the mouse ⌶ outside the selected area and then press the left button.

CHANGE FONT SIZE

You can increase or decrease the size of text in your document.

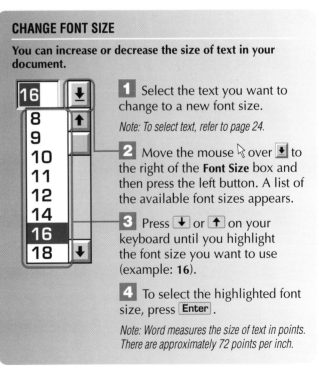

1 Select the text you want to change to a new font size.

Note: To select text, refer to page 24.

2 Move the mouse ⌖ over ▼ to the right of the **Font Size** box and then press the left button. A list of the available font sizes appears.

3 Press ▼ or ▲ on your keyboard until you highlight the font size you want to use (example: **16**).

4 To select the highlighted font size, press `Enter`.

Note: Word measures the size of text in points. There are approximately 72 points per inch.

You can use the Font dialog box to change the design and size of characters at the same time.

CHANGE FONTS

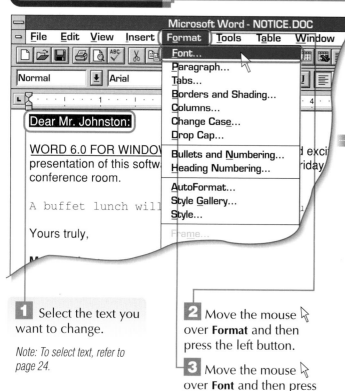

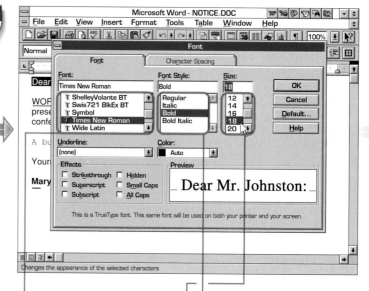

1 Select the text you want to change.

Note: To select text, refer to page 24.

2 Move the mouse ↖ over **Format** and then press the left button.

3 Move the mouse ↖ over **Font** and then press the left button.

4 Move the mouse ↖ over the font you want to use (example: **Times New Roman**) and then press the left button.

Note: To view all of the available font options, use the scroll bar. To use the scroll bar, refer to page 23.

5 Move the mouse ↖ over the font style you want to use (example: **Bold**) and then press the left button.

6 Move the mouse ↖ over the font size you want to use (example: **18**) and then press the left button.

- Bold, Underline and Italics
- **Change Fonts**
- Insert a Symbol

TEXT EFFECTS

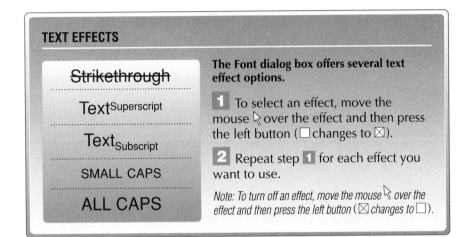

~~Strikethrough~~

Text^{Superscript}

Text_{Subscript}

SMALL CAPS

ALL CAPS

The Font dialog box offers several text effect options.

1 To select an effect, move the mouse over the effect and then press the left button (☐ changes to ☒).

2 Repeat step **1** for each effect you want to use.

Note: To turn off an effect, move the mouse over the effect and then press the left button (☒ changes to ☐).

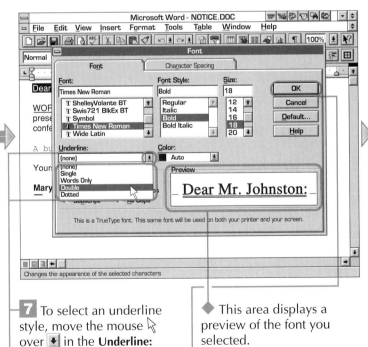

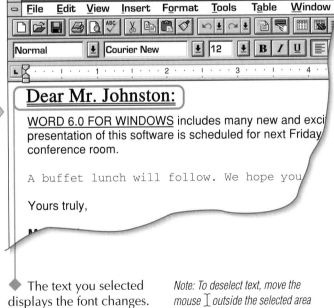

7 To select an underline style, move the mouse over ▼ in the **Underline:** box and then press the left button.

8 Move the mouse over the underline style you want to use (example: **Double**) and then press the left button.

◆ This area displays a preview of the font you selected.

9 Move the mouse over **OK** and then press the left button.

◆ The text you selected displays the font changes.

Note: To deselect text, move the mouse I outside the selected area and then press the left button.

INSERT A SYMBOL

Word lets you insert symbols into your document that do not appear on your keyboard.

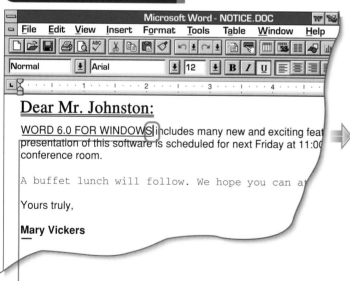

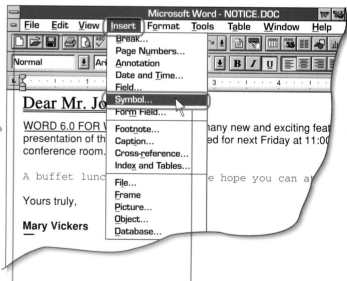

1 Position the insertion point where you want a symbol to appear in your document.

2 Move the mouse over **Insert** and then press the left button.

3 Move the mouse over **Symbol** and then press the left button.

• Bold, Underline and Italics
• Change Fonts
• **Insert a Symbol**

DISPLAY MORE SYMBOLS

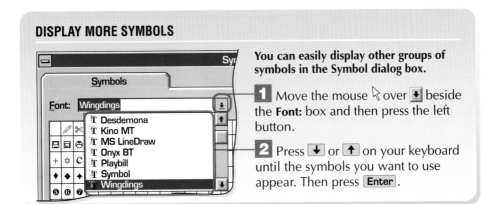

Symbols

Font: Wingdings

T Desdemona
T Kino MT
T MS LineDraw
T Onyx BT
T Playbill
T Symbol
T Wingdings

You can easily display other groups of symbols in the Symbol dialog box.

1 Move the mouse ⬚ over ⬇ beside the **Font:** box and then press the left button.

2 Press ⬇ or ⬆ on your keyboard until the symbols you want to use appear. Then press **Enter**.

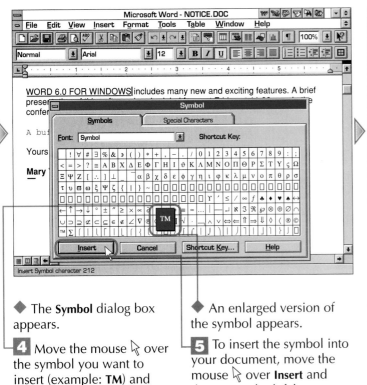

◆ The **Symbol** dialog box appears.

4 Move the mouse ⬚ over the symbol you want to insert (example: **TM**) and then press the left button.

◆ An enlarged version of the symbol appears.

5 To insert the symbol into your document, move the mouse ⬚ over **Insert** and then press the left button.

◆ The symbol appears in your document.

6 To close the **Symbol** dialog box, move the mouse ⬚ over **Close** and then press the left button.

CHANGE LINE SPACING

Single line spacing
This is the initial (or default) setting.

1.5 line spacing

Double line spacing

You can make your document easier to read by changing the amount of space between the lines of text.

CHANGE LINE SPACING

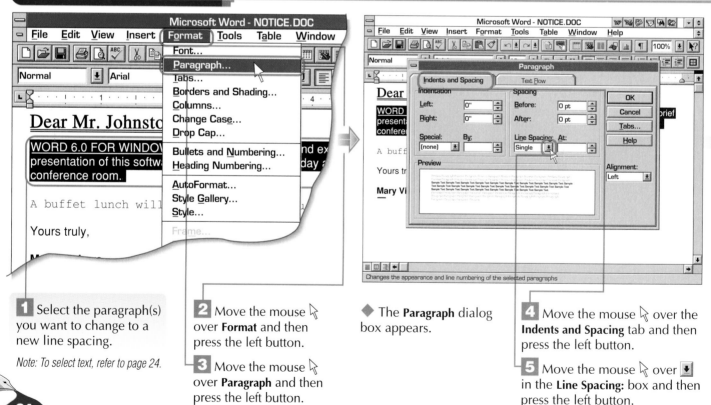

1 Select the paragraph(s) you want to change to a new line spacing.

Note: To select text, refer to page 24.

2 Move the mouse ⟩ over **Format** and then press the left button.

3 Move the mouse ⟩ over **Paragraph** and then press the left button.

◆ The **Paragraph** dialog box appears.

4 Move the mouse ⟩ over the **Indents and Spacing** tab and then press the left button.

5 Move the mouse ⟩ over ⬇ in the **Line Spacing:** box and then press the left button.

- • Change Line Spacing
- • Change Paragraph Alignment
- • Display or Hide the Ruler
- • Change Tab Settings
- • Indent Paragraphs
- • Create Numbered and Bulleted Lists

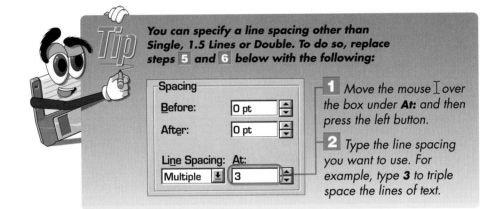

Tip

You can specify a line spacing other than Single, 1.5 Lines or Double. To do so, replace steps 5 and 6 below with the following:

Spacing

Before: 0 pt

After: 0 pt

Line Spacing: At:
Multiple | 3

1 Move the mouse I over the box under **At:** and then press the left button.

2 Type the line spacing you want to use. For example, type **3** to triple space the lines of text.

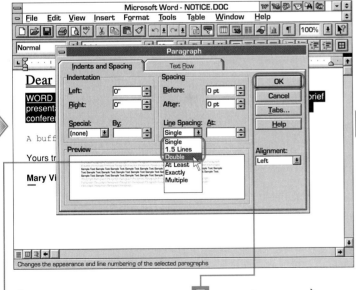

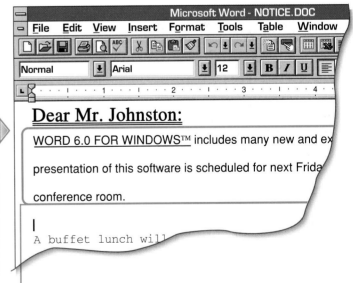

◆ A list of the available line spacing options appears.

6 Move the mouse ⬓ over the line spacing you want to use (example: **Double**) and then press the left button.

7 Move the mouse ⬓ over **OK** and then press the left button.

◆ Word changes the line spacing of the paragraph(s) you selected.

Note: To deselect text, move the mouse I outside the selected area and then press the left button.

95

You can enhance the appearance of your document by aligning text in different ways. Word offers four alignment options.

Right

Center

Left

Full

Wendy Johnston

CHANGE PARAGRAPH ALIGNMENT

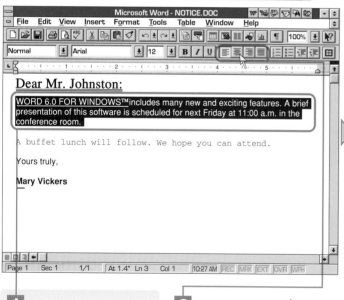

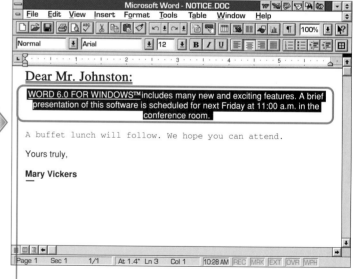

1 Select the paragraph(s) you want to change.

Note: To select text, refer to page 24.

2 Move the mouse ⌖ over the alignment option you want to use (example: **Center**) and then press the left button.

▤ Left
▤ Center
▤ Right
▤ Full

◆ The paragraph displays the new alignment.

*Note: To return to the original alignment, repeat steps **1** and **2**, selecting **Left** in step **2**.*

96

- Change Line Spacing
- **Change Paragraph Alignment**
- **Display or Hide the Ruler**
- Change Tab Settings
- Indent Paragraphs
- Create Numbered and Bulleted Lists

The ruler lets you indent paragraphs and change margin and tab settings. If you are not using the ruler, you can hide it to provide a larger and less cluttered working area.

DISPLAY OR HIDE THE RULER

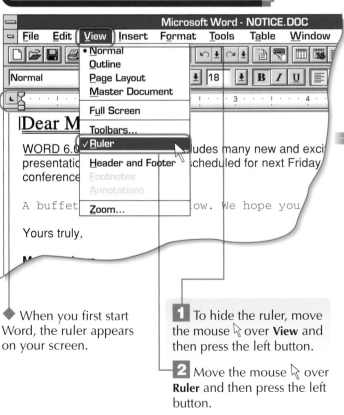

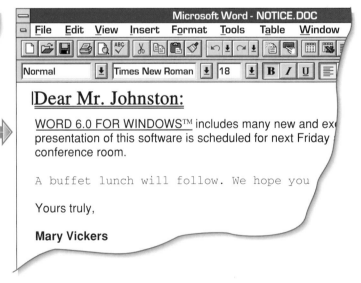

◆ When you first start Word, the ruler appears on your screen.

1 To hide the ruler, move the mouse ⌖ over **View** and then press the left button.

2 Move the mouse ⌖ over **Ruler** and then press the left button.

◆ The ruler disappears from your screen.

Note: To again display the ruler, repeat steps 1 and 2.

You can use tabs to line up columns of information in your document. Word offers four types of tabs.

Left tab

Right tab

Center tab

123.45 (Decimal tab)

Tab stop position

ADD A TAB STOP

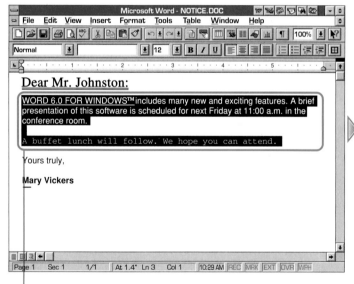

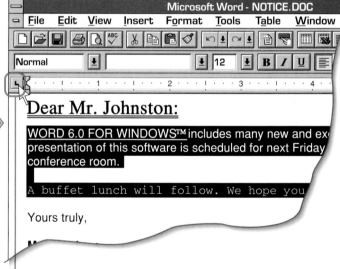

1 Select the paragraph(s) you want to contain the new tab stops.

Note: To select text, refer to page 24.

◆ To add tab stops to text you are about to type, position the insertion point where you want to begin typing the text.

2 Move the mouse over this box and then press the left button. Repeat this step until the type of tab you want to add appears (example: ⌊).

Note: If the ruler is not displayed on your screen, refer to page 97.

⌊ **Left tab**

⊥ **Center tab**

⌐ **Right tab**

⊥ **Decimal tab**

98

- Change Line Spacing
- Change Paragraph Alignment
- Display or Hide the Ruler
- **Change Tab Settings**
- Indent Paragraphs
- Create Numbered and Bulleted Lists

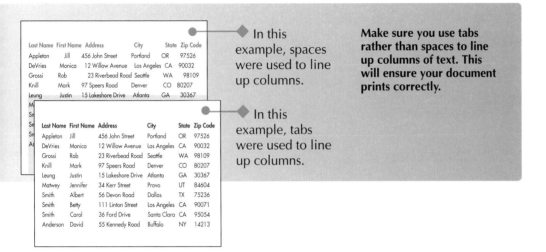

◆ In this example, spaces were used to line up columns.

Make sure you use tabs rather than spaces to line up columns of text. This will ensure your document prints correctly.

◆ In this example, tabs were used to line up columns.

USING TABS

3 Move the mouse ⏺ over the position on the ruler where you want to add a tab stop and then press the left button.

Note: Make sure you position the mouse ⏺ over the lower half of the ruler.

◆ The new tab stop appears on the ruler.

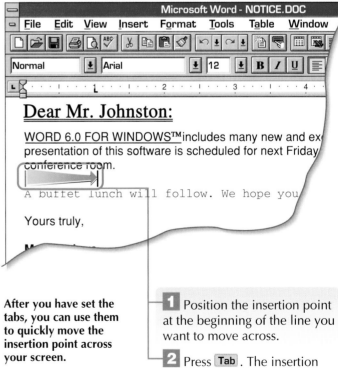

After you have set the tabs, you can use them to quickly move the insertion point across your screen.

1 Position the insertion point at the beginning of the line you want to move across.

2 Press **Tab**. The insertion point and any text that follows move to the first tab stop.

You can easily move a tab stop to a different location on the ruler.

MOVE A TAB STOP

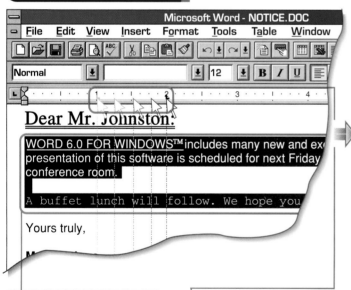

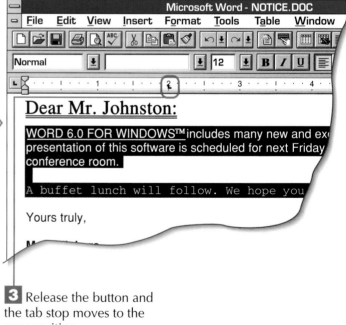

1 Select the paragraph(s) containing the tab stop you want to move.

Note: To select text, refer to page 24.

2 Move the mouse ▷ over the tab stop and then press and hold down the left button as you drag the tab stop to a new position.

◆ A dotted line indicates the new tab stop position.

3 Release the button and the tab stop moves to the new position.

- Change Line Spacing
- Change Paragraph Alignment
- Display or Hide the Ruler
- **Change Tab Settings**
- Indent Paragraphs
- Create Numbered and Bulleted Lists

Word lets you remove a tab stop from the ruler.

REMOVE A TAB STOP

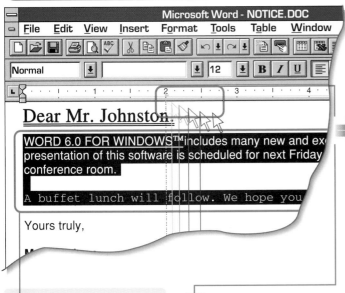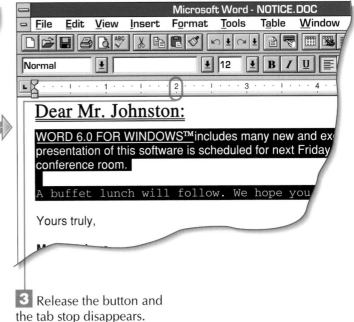

1 Select the paragraph(s) containing the tab stop you want to remove.

Note: To select text, refer to page 24.

2 Move the mouse ⌖ over the tab stop and then press and hold down the left button as you drag the tab stop downward off the ruler.

3 Release the button and the tab stop disappears.

INDENT
PARAGRAPHS

You can use the Indent feature to emphasize paragraphs in your document. Word offers several indent options.

Indent first line of paragraph

Indent left edge of paragraph

Indent right edge of paragraph

INDENT PARAGRAPHS

You can move these symbols on the ruler to indent paragraphs in your document.

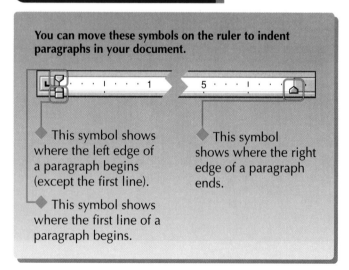

◆ This symbol shows where the left edge of a paragraph begins (except the first line).

◆ This symbol shows where the right edge of a paragraph ends.

◆ This symbol shows where the first line of a paragraph begins.

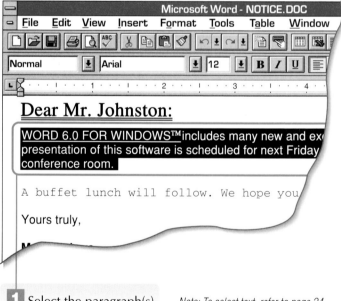

1 Select the paragraph(s) you want to indent.

Note: To select text, refer to page 24.

- Change Line Spacing
- Change Paragraph Alignment
- Display or Hide the Ruler
- Change Tab Settings
- **Indent Paragraphs**
- Create Numbered and Bulleted Lists

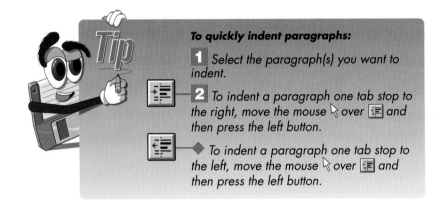

To quickly indent paragraphs:

1 Select the paragraph(s) you want to indent.

2 To indent a paragraph one tab stop to the right, move the mouse ⤢ over ⊞ and then press the left button.

◆ To indent a paragraph one tab stop to the left, move the mouse ⤢ over ⊞ and then press the left button.

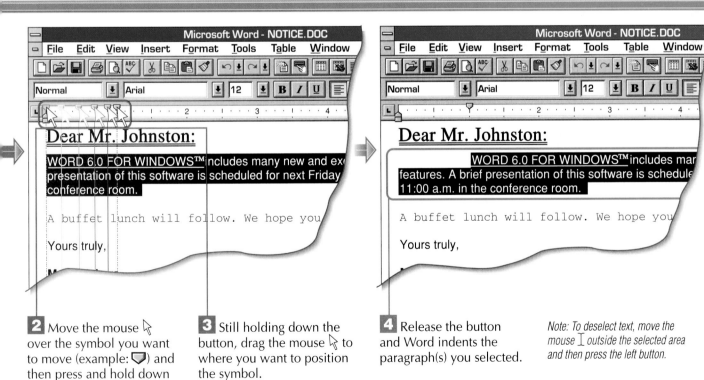

2 Move the mouse ⤢ over the symbol you want to move (example: ▽) and then press and hold down the left button.

3 Still holding down the button, drag the mouse ⤢ to where you want to position the symbol.

4 Release the button and Word indents the paragraph(s) you selected.

Note: To deselect text, move the mouse ⫯ outside the selected area and then press the left button.

103

CREATE NUMBERED AND BULLETED LISTS

You can separate items in a list by beginning each item with a bullet or number.

◆ **Numbers** are useful for items in a specific order, such as a recipe.

◆ **Bullets** are useful for items in no particular order, such as a list of goals.

CREATE NUMBERED AND BULLETED LISTS

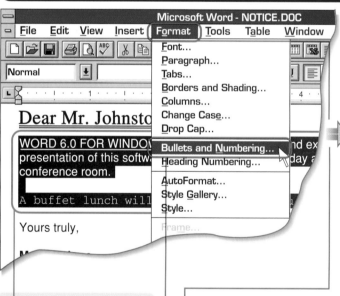

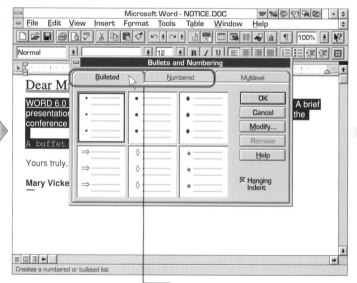

1 Select the paragraph(s) you want to display bullets or numbers.

Note: To select text, refer to page 24.

2 Move the mouse ⓘ over **Format** and then press the left button.

3 Move the mouse ⓘ over **Bullets and Numbering** and then press the left button.

◆ The **Bullets and Numbering** dialog box appears.

4 To create a bulleted list, move the mouse ⓘ over the **Bulleted** tab and then press the left button.

◆ To create a numbered list, move the mouse ⓘ over the **Numbered** tab and then press the left button.

104

- Change Line Spacing
- Change Paragraph Alignment
- Display or Hide the Ruler
- Change Tab Settings
- Indent Paragraphs
- **Create Numbered and Bulleted Lists**

Tips

To quickly create a bulleted or numbered list:

1 Select the paragraph(s) you want to display bullets or numbers.

2 To create a bulleted list, move the mouse ⤐ over 📇 and then press the left button.

◆ To create a numbered list, move the mouse ⤐ over 📇 and then press the left button.

To remove bullets or numbers:

1 Select the paragraph(s) displaying the bullets or numbers you want to remove.

2 To remove bullets, move the mouse ⤐ over 📇 and then press the left button.

◆ To remove numbers, move the mouse ⤐ over 📇 and then press the left button.

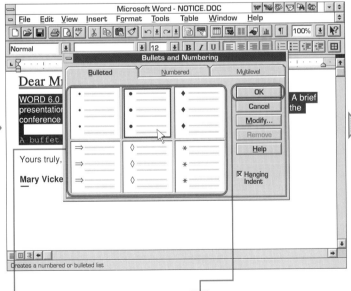

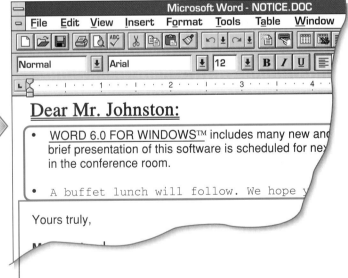

5 Move the mouse ⤐ over the style you want to use and then press the left button.

6 Move the mouse ⤐ over **OK** and then press the left button.

◆ The bullets or numbers appear in your document.

Note: To deselect text, move the mouse ⟂ outside the selected area and then press the left button.

INSERT A PAGE BREAK

If you want to start a new page at a specific place in your document, you can insert a page break. A page break defines where one page ends and another begins.

A page break you inserted.

When you fill an entire page with text, Word automatically starts a new one by inserting a page break.

A page break Word inserted.

INSERT A PAGE BREAK

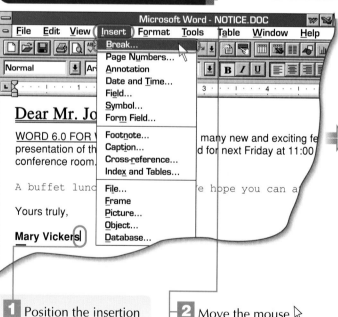

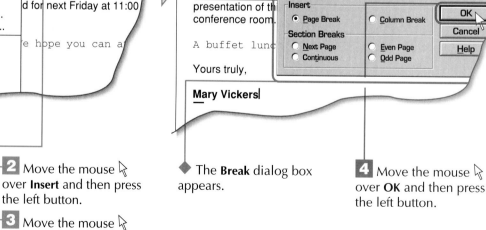

1 Position the insertion point where you want to start a new page.

2 Move the mouse ⌖ over **Insert** and then press the left button.

3 Move the mouse ⌖ over **Break** and then press the left button.

◆ The **Break** dialog box appears.

4 Move the mouse ⌖ over **OK** and then press the left button.

106

- **Insert a Page Break**
- Create a New Section
- Change Margins
- Add Headers or Footers
- Add Footnotes
- Add Page Numbers
- Center a Page

To quickly insert a page break:

1 Position the insertion point where you want to start a new page.

2 Press Ctrl + Enter.

DELETE A PAGE BREAK

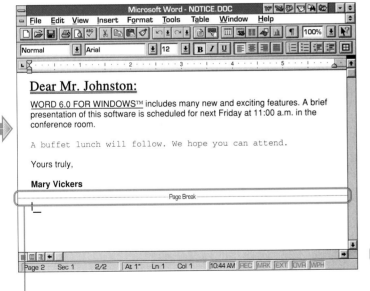

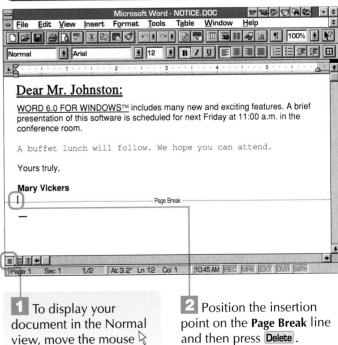

◆ If your document is in the Normal view, a dotted line with the words **Page Break** appears across your screen. This line defines where one page ends and another begins.

*Note: The **Page Break** line will not appear when you print your document.*

1 To display your document in the Normal view, move the mouse over ▤ and then press the left button.

2 Position the insertion point on the **Page Break** line and then press Delete.

CREATE A NEW SECTION

> If you want to change the page formatting of a part of your document, you must divide the document into separate sections. Otherwise, the changes will affect your entire document.

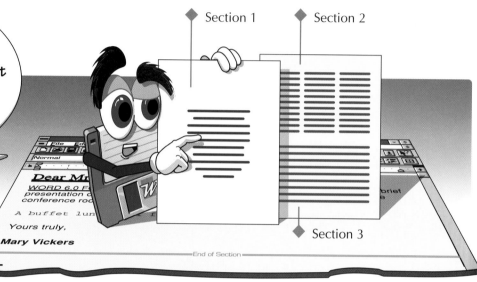

Section 1   Section 2

Section 3

End of Section

CREATE A NEW SECTION

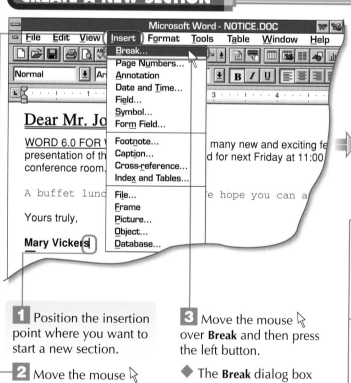

1 Position the insertion point where you want to start a new section.

2 Move the mouse ⇧ over **Insert** and then press the left button.

3 Move the mouse ⇧ over **Break** and then press the left button.

◆ The **Break** dialog box appears.

4 To start a new section at the top of the next page, move the mouse ⇧ over **Next Page** and then press the left button.

◆ To start a new section on the same page, move the mouse ⇧ over **Continuous** and then press the left button.

5 Move the mouse ⇧ over **OK** and then press the left button.

108

- Insert a Page Break
- **Create a New Section**
- Change Margins
- Add Headers or Footers
- Add Footnotes
- Add Page Numbers
- Center a Page

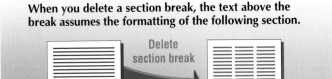

When you delete a section break, the text above the break assumes the formatting of the following section.

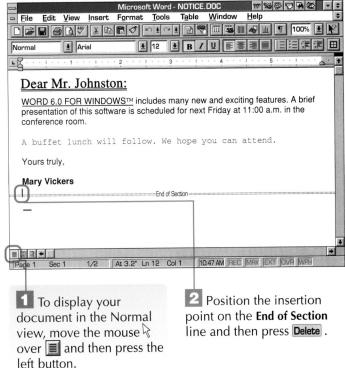

Delete section break

End of Section

DELETE A SECTION BREAK

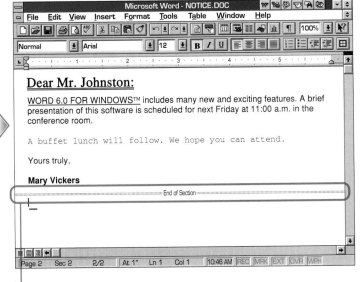

Microsoft Word - NOTICE.DOC

File   Edit   View   Insert   Format   Tools   Table   Window   Help

Normal   Arial   12   **B** *I* U

Dear Mr. Johnston:

WORD 6.0 FOR WINDOWS™ includes many new and exciting features. A brief presentation of this software is scheduled for next Friday at 11:00 a.m. in the conference room.

A buffet lunch will follow. We hope you can attend.

Yours truly,

Mary Vickers

End of Section

Page 2   Sec 2   2/2   At 1"   Ln 1   Col 1   10:46 AM   REC   MRK   EXT   OVR   WPH

Microsoft Word - NOTICE.DOC

File   Edit   View   Insert   Format   Tools   Table   Window   Help

Normal   Arial   12   **B** *I* U

Dear Mr. Johnston:

WORD 6.0 FOR WINDOWS™ includes many new and exciting features. A brief presentation of this software is scheduled for next Friday at 11:00 a.m. in the conference room.

A buffet lunch will follow. We hope you can attend.

Yours truly,

Mary Vickers

End of Section

Page 1   Sec 1   1/2   At 3.2" Ln 12 Col 1   10:47 AM   REC   MRK   EXT   OVR   WPH

◆ If your document is in the Normal view, a dotted line with the words **End of Section** appears across your screen. This line defines where one section ends and another begins.

*Note: The **End of Section** line will not appear when you print your document.*

1 To display your document in the Normal view, move the mouse over ▤ and then press the left button.

2 Position the insertion point on the **End of Section** line and then press **Delete** .

109

A margin is the amount of space between text and an edge of your paper.

◆ When you create a document, the top and bottom margins are set at 1 inch. You can change these settings to accommodate letterhead or other specialty paper.

◆ The left and right margins are set at 1.25 inches. You can change these settings to increase or decrease the amount of text on a page.

CHANGE MARGINS

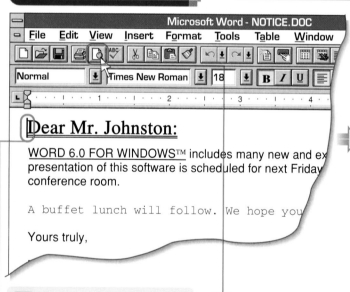

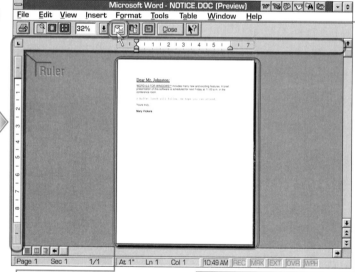

1 To change the margins for your entire document, position the insertion point anywhere in the document.

◆ To change the margins for a part of your document, position the insertion point in the section you want to change.

Note: For information on sections, refer to page 108.

2 Move the mouse ⌖ over [🔍] and then press the left button.

◆ The page you were working on appears in the Print Preview window.

Note: For more information on using Print Preview, refer to pages 78 to 81.

3 If the ruler is not displayed, move the mouse ⌖ over [🖼] and then press the left button.

• Insert a Page Break
• Create a New Section
• **Change Margins**
• Add Headers or Footers

• Add Footnotes
• Add Page Numbers
• Center a Page

If you want to change the left and right margins for a part of your document, it is much easier to change the indentation.

Note: To indent paragraphs, refer to page 102.

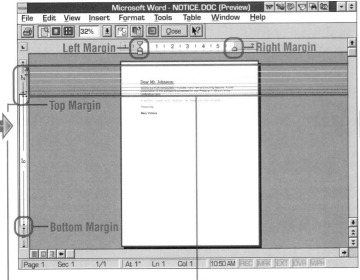

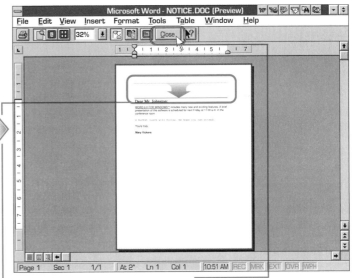

4 Move the mouse over the margin boundary you want to move and changes to ↕ or ↔.

5 To display the page measurements as you drag the margin boundary, press and hold down **Alt**.

6 Still holding down **Alt**, press and hold down the left button as you drag the margin boundary to a new location. A dotted line shows the location of the new margin.

7 Release the button and then **Alt** to display the margin changes.

8 Repeat steps **4** to **7** for each margin you want to change.

9 To close Print Preview and return to your document, move the mouse over **Close** and then press the left button.

Note: The top and bottom margins are not visible on your screen when in the Normal view.

ADD HEADERS OR FOOTERS

You can add a header or footer to your document to display such information as the date or your company name.

ABC Corporation

Header
A header appears at the top of a page.

October 10

Footer
A footer appears at the bottom of a page.

ADD HEADERS OR FOOTERS

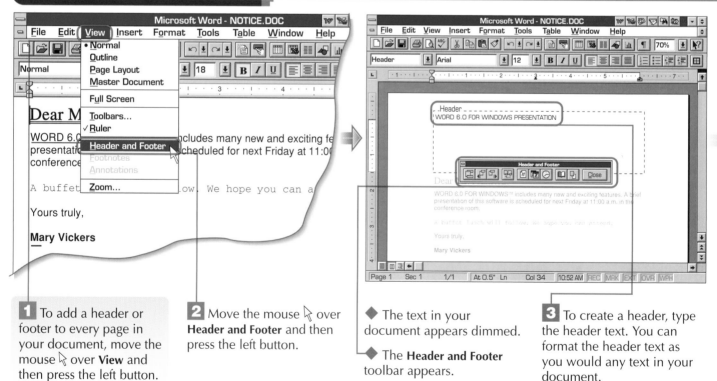

1 To add a header or footer to every page in your document, move the mouse ⬚ over **View** and then press the left button.

2 Move the mouse ⬚ over **Header and Footer** and then press the left button.

◆ The text in your document appears dimmed.

◆ The **Header and Footer** toolbar appears.

3 To create a header, type the header text. You can format the header text as you would any text in your document.

- Insert a Page Break
- Create a New Section
- Change Margins
- **Add Headers or Footers**

- Add Footnotes
- Add Page Numbers
- Center a Page

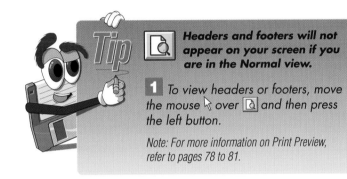

Tip

Headers and footers will not appear on your screen if you are in the Normal view.

1 *To view headers or footers, move the mouse over and then press the left button.*

Note: For more information on Print Preview, refer to pages 78 to 81.

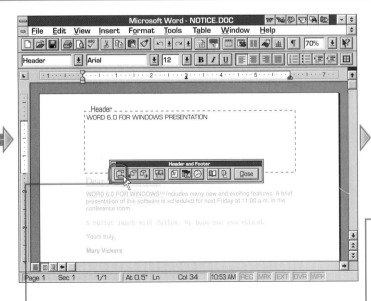

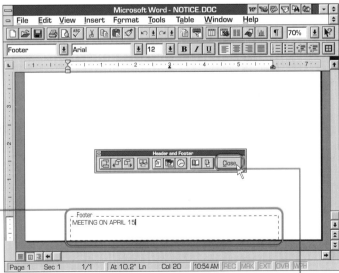

4 To create a footer, move the mouse over and then press the left button.

Note: You can return to the header area at any time by repeating step 4.

◆ The **Footer** area appears.

5 Type the footer text. You can format the footer text as you would any text in your document.

6 To return to your document, move the mouse over **Close** and then press the left button.

ADD FOOTNOTES

A footnote appears at the bottom of a page to provide additional information about text in your document.

Word automatically numbers a footnote and places the footnote on the same page as the text it refers to.

① H. Smith, *Aeronautical Refrigeration Repair* (California: Quest Publishing, 1989) 10.

② R. Anderson, *Volatile Cold Gases* (Alaska: Inert Publishing, 1992) 31.

ADD FOOTNOTES

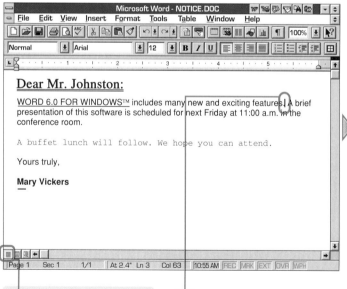

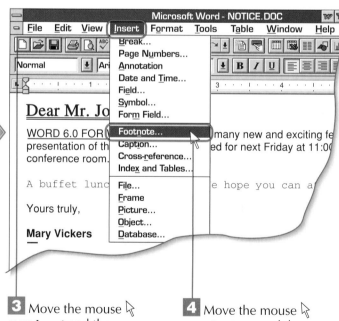

1 To display your document in the Normal view, move the mouse over ▤ and then press the left button.

2 Position the insertion point where you want the number for the footnote to appear in your document.

3 Move the mouse over **Insert** and then press the left button.

4 Move the mouse over **Footnote** and then press the left button.

114

- Insert a Page Break
- Create a New Section
- Change Margins
- Add Headers or Footers
- Add Footnotes
- Add Page Numbers
- Center a Page

EDIT A FOOTNOTE

1 To edit a footnote, move the mouse ⌶ over the footnote number in your document and then quickly press the left button twice. The footnote appears.

2 Edit the footnote as you would any text in your document.

3 When you finish editing the footnote, move the mouse ⌖ over **Close** and then press the left button.

DELETE A FOOTNOTE

1 To delete a footnote, select the footnote number in your document and then press Delete.

Note: To select text, refer to page 24.

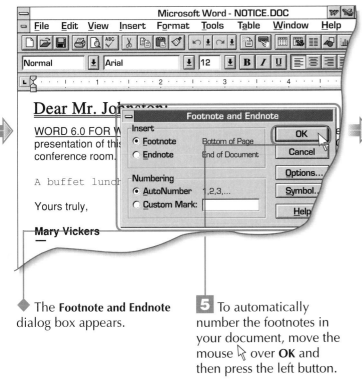

◆ The **Footnote and Endnote** dialog box appears.

5 To automatically number the footnotes in your document, move the mouse ⌖ over **OK** and then press the left button.

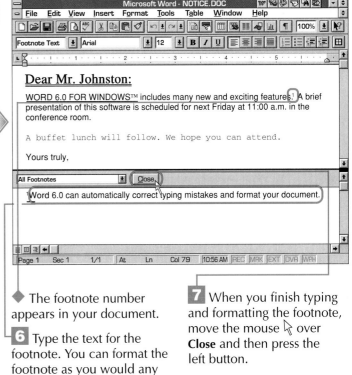

◆ The footnote number appears in your document.

6 Type the text for the footnote. You can format the footnote as you would any text in your document.

7 When you finish typing and formatting the footnote, move the mouse ⌖ over **Close** and then press the left button.

ADD PAGE NUMBERS

You can have Word number the pages in your document.

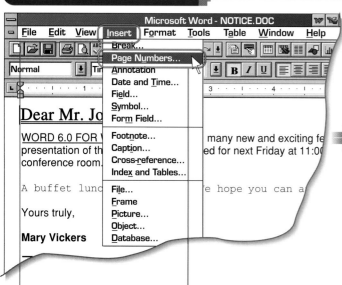

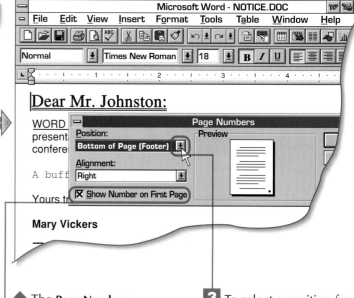

1 Move the mouse 🔓 over **Insert** and then press the left button.

2 Move the mouse 🔓 over **Page Numbers** and then press the left button.

◆ The **Page Numbers** dialog box appears.

◆ To hide the page number on the first page of your document, move the mouse 🔓 over **Show Number on First Page** and then press the left button (⊠ changes to ☐).

3 To select a position for the page numbers, move the mouse 🔓 over ⬇ in the **Position:** box and then press the left button.

- Insert a Page Break
- Create a New Section
- Change Margins
- Add Headers or Footers
- Add Footnotes
- **Add Page Numbers**
- Center a Page

Page numbers will not appear on your screen if you are in the Normal view.

1 To view the page numbers, move the mouse ⊩ over 🔍 and then press the left button.

Note: For more information on Print Preview, refer to pages 78 to 81.

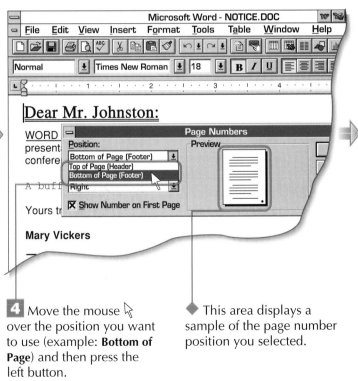

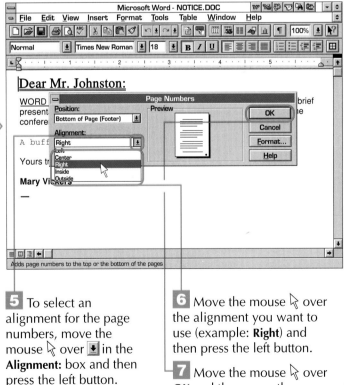

4 Move the mouse ⊩ over the position you want to use (example: **Bottom of Page**) and then press the left button.

◆ This area displays a sample of the page number position you selected.

5 To select an alignment for the page numbers, move the mouse ⊩ over ⬇ in the **Alignment:** box and then press the left button.

6 Move the mouse ⊩ over the alignment you want to use (example: **Right**) and then press the left button.

7 Move the mouse ⊩ over **OK** and then press the left button.

CENTER A PAGE

You can vertically center text on a page. This is useful when creating title pages or short memos.

CENTER A PAGE

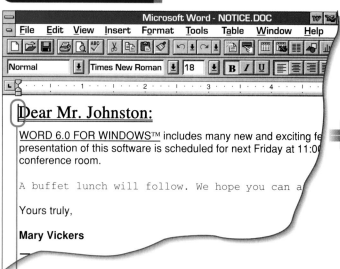

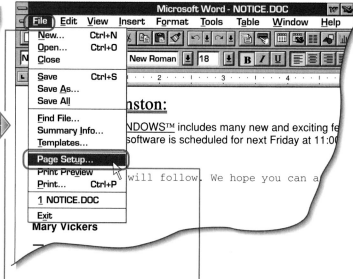

1 To center the text on all pages in your document, position the insertion point anywhere in the document.

◆ To center the text for a part of your document, position the insertion point in the section you want to change.

Note: For information on sections, refer to page 108.

2 Move the mouse � over **File** and then press the left button.

3 Move the mouse � over **Page Setup** and then press the left button.

- Insert a Page Break
- Create a New Section
- Change Margins
- Add Headers or Footers
- Add Footnotes
- Add Page Numbers
- Center a Page

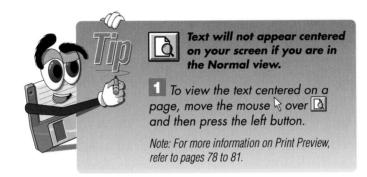

Text will not appear centered on your screen if you are in the Normal view.

1 To view the text centered on a page, move the mouse ⊠ over 🔲 and then press the left button.

Note: For more information on Print Preview, refer to pages 78 to 81.

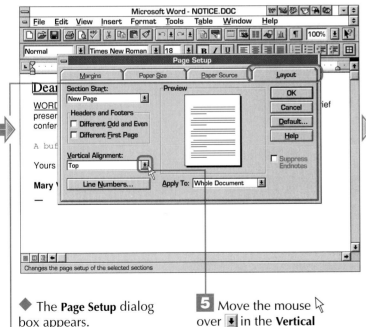

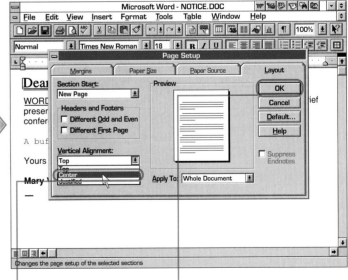

◆ The **Page Setup** dialog box appears.

4 Move the mouse ⊠ over the **Layout** tab and then press the left button.

5 Move the mouse ⊠ over ▾ in the **Vertical Alignment:** box and then press the left button.

6 Move the mouse ⊠ over **Center** and then press the left button.

7 Move the mouse ⊠ over **OK** and then press the left button.

119

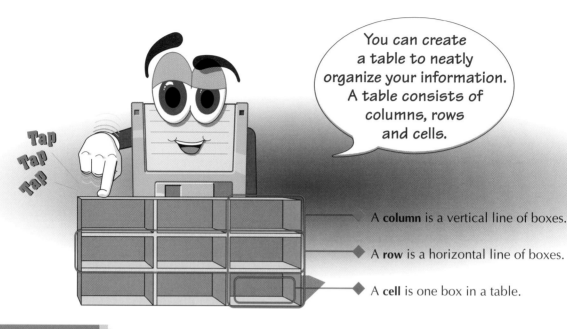

You can create a table to neatly organize your information. A table consists of columns, rows and cells.

A **column** is a vertical line of boxes.

A **row** is a horizontal line of boxes.

A **cell** is one box in a table.

CREATE A TABLE

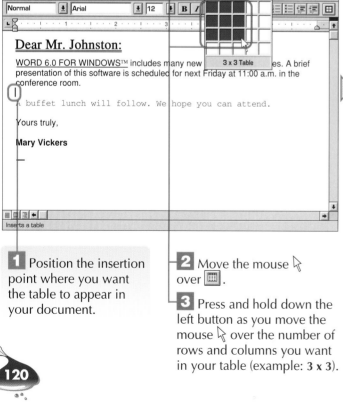

1 Position the insertion point where you want the table to appear in your document.

2 Move the mouse over ▦.

3 Press and hold down the left button as you move the mouse over the number of rows and columns you want in your table (example: **3 x 3**).

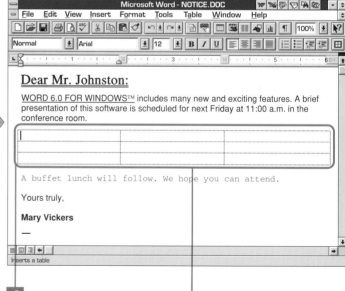

4 Release the button and the table appears.

◆ The dotted lines around the cells in the table will not appear when you print your document. To print table lines, you can add borders using the **Table AutoFormat** feature. For more information, refer to page 128.

120

- **Create a Table**
- **Type Text**
- Add a Row or Column
- Delete a Row or Column
- Change Column Width
- Format a Table
- Merge Cells

MOVE IN A TABLE (Using the Keyboard)

↓ Press this key to move **down** one cell.	Tab Press this key to move **right** one cell.
↑ Press this key to move **up** one cell.	Shift + Tab Press these keys to move **left** one cell.

TYPE TEXT IN A TABLE

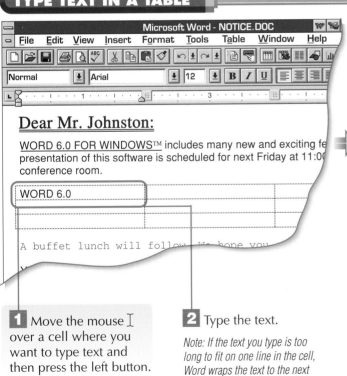

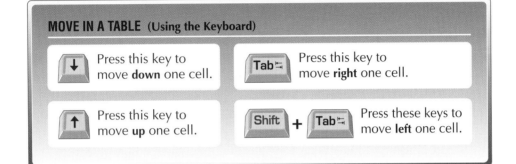

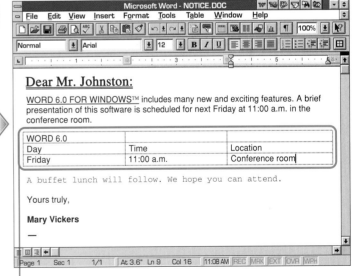

1 Move the mouse I over a cell where you want to type text and then press the left button.

2 Type the text.

Note: If the text you type is too long to fit on one line in the cell, Word wraps the text to the next line. To keep the text on the same line, refer to page 126 to change the column width.

3 Repeat steps **1** and **2** until you have typed all the text.

◆ Pressing **Enter** after typing text in a cell will begin a new line and increase the row height. If you accidentally press **Enter**, immediately press **◆Backspace** to cancel the action.

121

ADD A ROW OR COLUMN

You can add a row or column to your table if you want to insert new information.

ADD A ROW

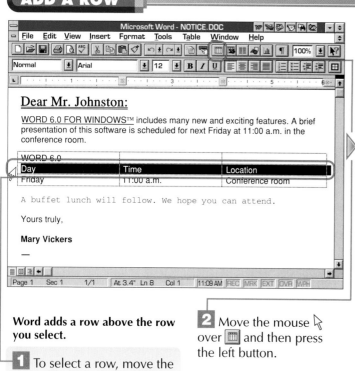

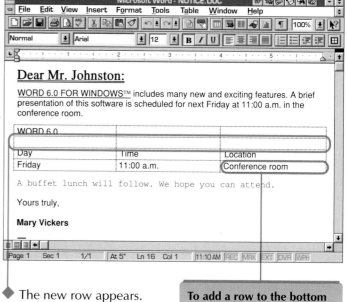

Word adds a row above the row you select.

1 To select a row, move the mouse I to the left edge of the row (I changes to ⇗) and then press the left button.

2 Move the mouse ⇗ over ▥ and then press the left button.

◆ The new row appears.

Note: To deselect a row, move the mouse I outside the table and then press the left button.

To add a row to the bottom of your table:

1 Position the insertion point in the bottom right cell of your table.

2 Press **Tab** and the new row appears.

122

- Create a Table
- Type Text
- **Add a Row or Column**
- Delete a Row or Column

- Change Column Width
- Format a Table
- Merge Cells

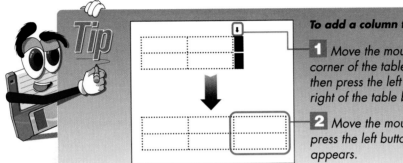

To add a column to the end of your table:

1 Move the mouse I over the top right corner of the table (I changes to ↓) and then press the left button. The area to the right of the table becomes highlighted.

2 Move the mouse ↕ over ▦ and then press the left button. A new column appears.

ADD A COLUMN

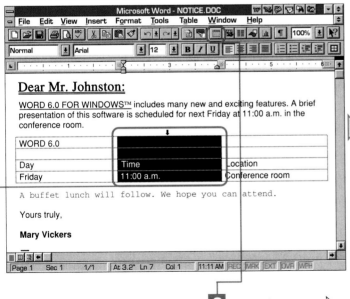

Word adds a column to the left of the column you select.

1 To select a column, move the mouse I to the top edge of the column (I changes to ↓) and then press the left button.

2 Move the mouse ↕ over ▦ and then press the left button.

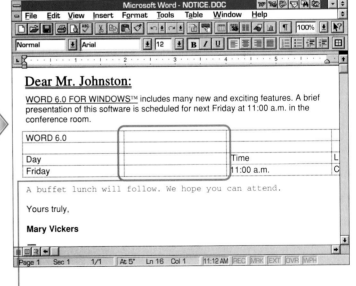

◆ The new column appears.

Note: To deselect a column, move the mouse I outside the table and then press the left button.

123

DELETE A ROW OR COLUMN

> You can delete a row or column from your table. This lets you remove information or cells you no longer need.

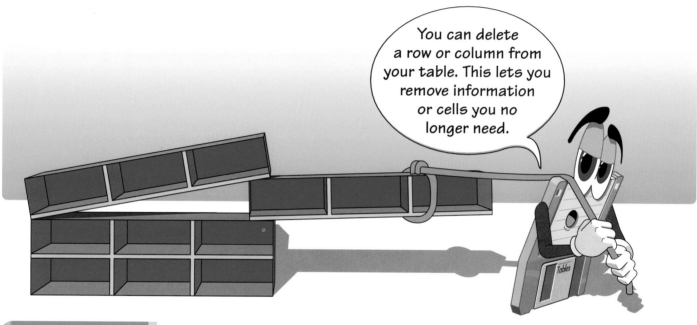

DELETE A ROW

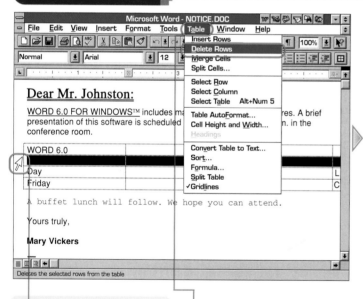

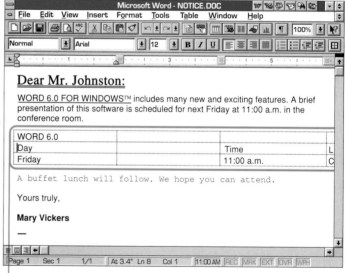

1 To select the row you want to delete, move the mouse I to the left edge of the row (I changes to ⇗) and then press the left button.

2 Move the mouse ⇗ over **Table** and then press the left button.

3 Move the mouse ⇗ over **Delete Rows** and then press the left button.

◆ The row disappears from your screen.

- Create a Table
- Type Text
- Add a Row or Column
- **Delete a Row or Column**
- Change Column Width
- Format a Table
- Merge Cells

DELETE A TABLE

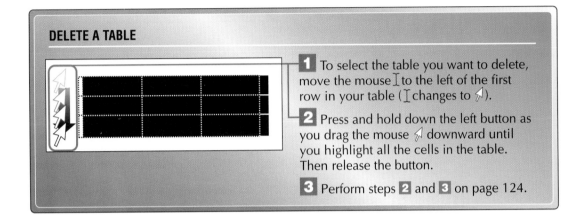

1 To select the table you want to delete, move the mouse I to the left of the first row in your table (I changes to ⇗).

2 Press and hold down the left button as you drag the mouse ⇗ downward until you highlight all the cells in the table. Then release the button.

3 Perform steps **2** and **3** on page 124.

DELETE A COLUMN

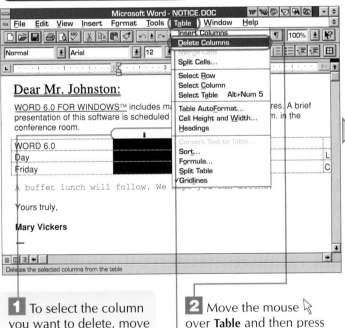

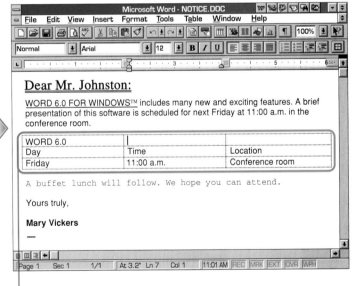

1 To select the column you want to delete, move the mouse I to the top edge of the column (I changes to ↓) and then press the left button.

2 Move the mouse ⇗ over **Table** and then press the left button.

3 Move the mouse ⇗ over **Delete Columns** and then press the left button.

◆ The column disappears from your screen.

125

CHANGE COLUMN WIDTH

You can adjust the columns in your table to make them wider or narrower.

CHANGE COLUMN WIDTH

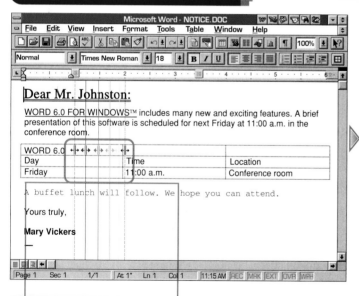

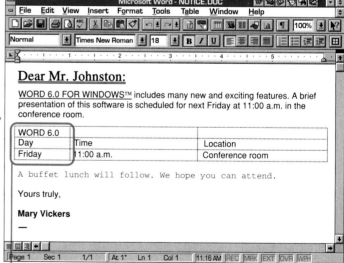

1 Move the mouse I over the right edge of the column you want to adjust (I changes to +||+).

2 Press and hold down the left button as you drag the edge of the column to a new position.

◆ The dotted line indicates the new position.

3 Release the button and the new column width appears.

Note: The width of the entire table remains the same.

- Create a Table
- Type Text
- Add a Row or Column
- Delete a Row or Column
- **Change Column Width**
- Format a Table
- Merge Cells

You can have Word adjust a column width to fit the longest item in the column.

CHANGE COLUMN WIDTH AUTOMATICALLY

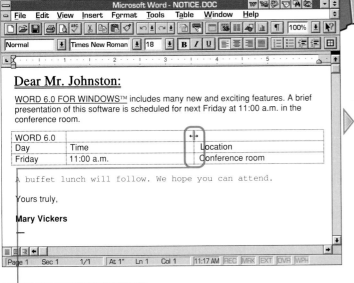

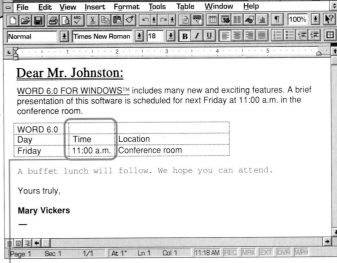

1 Move the mouse I over the right edge of the column you want to adjust (I changes to +‖+).

2 Quickly press the left button twice.

◆ The column width changes to fit the longest item in the column.

Note: The width of the entire table changes.

127

FORMAT A TABLE

You can use the Table AutoFormat feature to emphasize information and enhance the appearance of your table.

FORMAT A TABLE

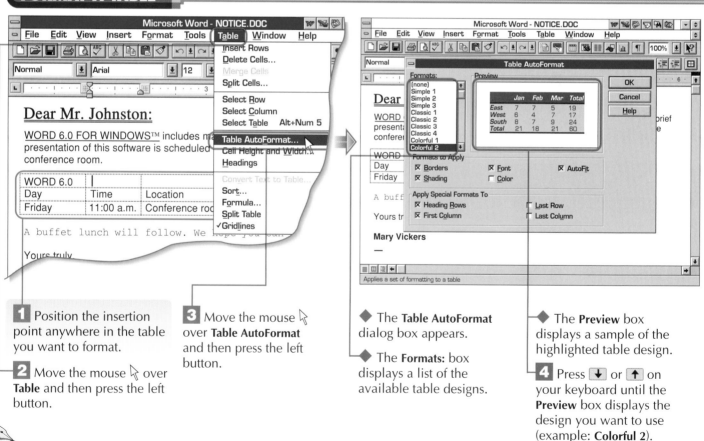

1 Position the insertion point anywhere in the table you want to format.

2 Move the mouse ↖ over **Table** and then press the left button.

3 Move the mouse ↖ over **Table AutoFormat** and then press the left button.

◆ The **Table AutoFormat** dialog box appears.

◆ The **Formats:** box displays a list of the available table designs.

◆ The **Preview** box displays a sample of the highlighted table design.

4 Press ↓ or ↑ on your keyboard until the **Preview** box displays the design you want to use (example: **Colorful 2**).

- Create a Table
- Type Text
- Add a Row or Column
- Delete a Row or Column
- Change Column Width
- **Format a Table**
- Merge Cells

When you create a table, Word places dotted lines around the cells. These lines will not appear when you print your document. To print table lines, you must use the Table AutoFormat feature to add borders to the table.

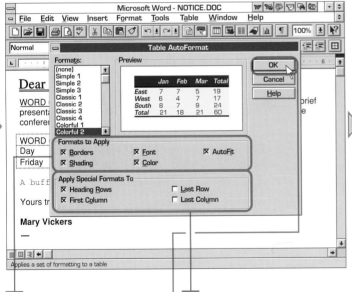

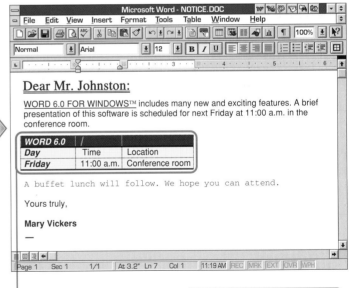

5 To apply or remove a format such as shading or color, move the mouse ☒ over an option (example: **Color**) and then press the left button.

Note: ☒ *indicates an option is on.*
☐ *indicates an option is off.*

6 To apply or remove a format from specific rows or columns, move the mouse ☒ over an option and then press the left button.

7 When the **Preview** box displays the table appearance you want, move the mouse ☒ over **OK** and then press the left button.

◆ Word applies the formats you selected to the table.

REMOVE FORMATS

To remove the formats from the table, perform steps **1** to **3**, select (**none**) in step **4** and then perform step **7**.

MERGE CELLS

You can combine two or more cells in your table to create one large cell. This is useful if you want to display a title at the top of your table.

MERGE CELLS

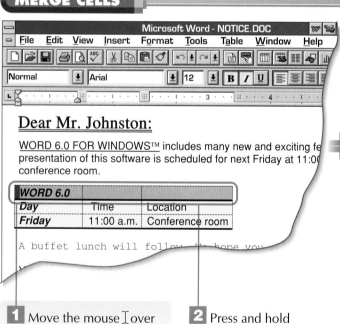

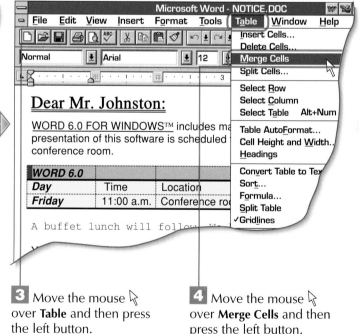

1 Move the mouse I over the first cell you want to join with other cells.

Note: You can only join cells in the same row. You cannot join cells in the same column.

2 Press and hold down the left button as you move the mouse I to highlight the cells you want to join. Then release the button.

3 Move the mouse ⇗ over **Table** and then press the left button.

4 Move the mouse ⇗ over **Merge Cells** and then press the left button.

WORD

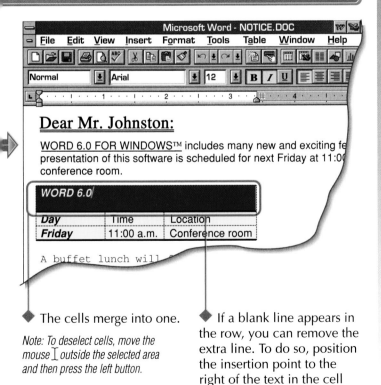

◆ The cells merge into one.

Note: To deselect cells, move the mouse I outside the selected area and then press the left button.

◆ If a blank line appears in the row, you can remove the extra line. To do so, position the insertion point to the right of the text in the cell and then press Delete.

SPLIT CELLS

You can split one cell into two or more cells.

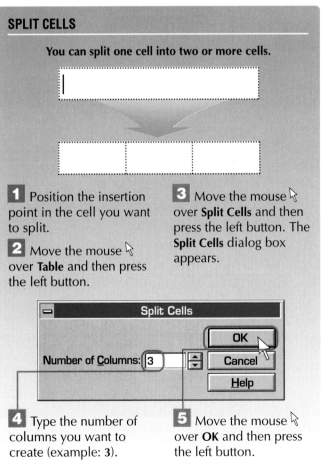

1 Position the insertion point in the cell you want to split.

2 Move the mouse over **Table** and then press the left button.

3 Move the mouse over **Split Cells** and then press the left button. The **Split Cells** dialog box appears.

4 Type the number of columns you want to create (example: **3**).

5 Move the mouse over **OK** and then press the left button.

131

EXCEL

In this section you will learn how to use Excel to manage, analyze and present financial information.

Excel helps you manage, analyze and present financial information.

HOW YOU CAN USE EXCEL

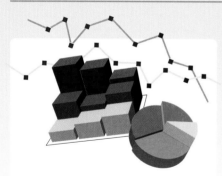

CHARTS

You can create charts from your worksheet data. A chart illustrates the relationship between different items.

PERSONAL FINANCES

Excel can help you keep track of your personal finances. You can use Excel to:

- balance your checkbook
- create a budget
- keep track of your mortgage
- compare investments
- prepare your taxes

FINANCIAL REPORTS

Businesses of all sizes use Excel to analyze and present financial information. Formatting and charting features help you present your results in professional-looking documents.

- ● **Introduction**
- ● **Start Excel**
- ● Excel Basics
- ● Enter Data
- ● Select Cells
- ● Using AutoFill
- ● Move Through a Worksheet
- ● Getting Help

When you start Excel, a blank worksheet appears. You can enter data into this worksheet.

START EXCEL

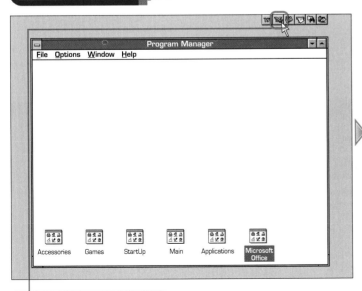

1 To start Excel, move the mouse ⃗ over ⬛ and then press the left button.

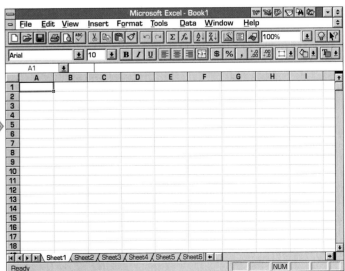

◆ The **Microsoft Excel** window appears, displaying a blank worksheet.

135

EXCEL BASICS

A worksheet consists of columns, rows and cells.

COLUMNS, ROWS AND CELLS

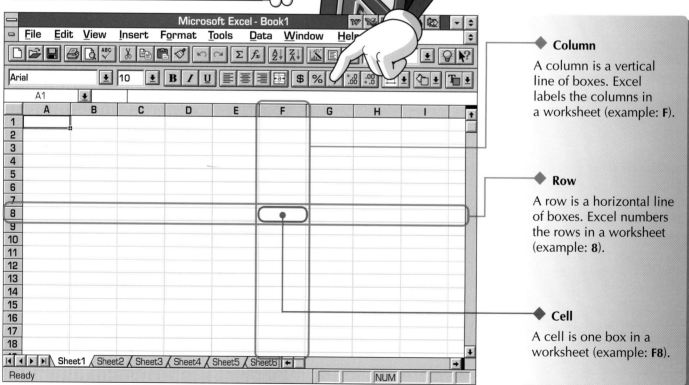

◆ **Column**

A column is a vertical line of boxes. Excel labels the columns in a worksheet (example: **F**).

◆ **Row**

A row is a horizontal line of boxes. Excel numbers the rows in a worksheet (example: **8**).

◆ **Cell**

A cell is one box in a worksheet (example: **F8**).

- Introduction
- Start Excel
- **Excel Basics**
- Enter Data
- Select Cells
- Using AutoFill
- Move Through a Worksheet
- Getting Help

THE ACTIVE CELL

ACTIVE CELL

◆ The active cell displays a thick border. You can only enter data into the active cell.

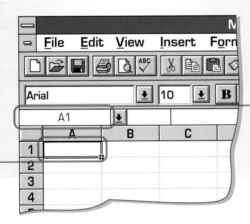

CELL REFERENCE

◆ A cell reference defines the location of each cell. It consists of a column letter followed by a row number (example: **A1**).

The cell reference of the active cell appears at the top of your worksheet.

CHANGE THE ACTIVE CELL

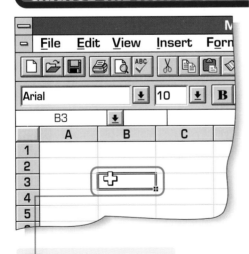

1 To make another cell on your screen the active cell, move the mouse ⌖ over the cell and then press the left button.

◆ The cell now displays a thick border.

USING THE KEYBOARD

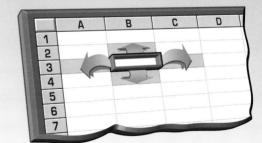

← Press this key to move **left** one cell.

→ Press this key to move **right** one cell.

↓ Press this key to move **down** one cell.

↑ Press this key to move **up** one cell.

ENTER DATA

You enter data into the cells of your worksheet using your keyboard.

ENTER DATA

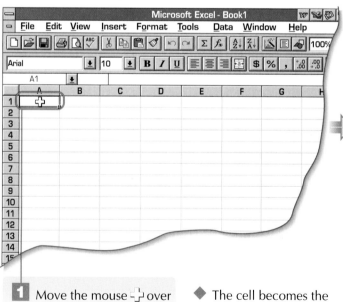

1 Move the mouse ⬚ over the cell where you want to enter data (example: **A1**) and then press the left button.

◆ The cell becomes the active cell and displays a thick border.

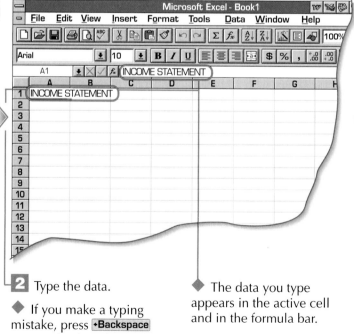

2 Type the data.

◆ If you make a typing mistake, press **←Backspace** on your keyboard to remove the incorrect data and then retype.

◆ The data you type appears in the active cell and in the formula bar.

138

- Introduction
- Start Excel
- Excel Basics
- **Enter Data**
- Select Cells
- Using AutoFill
- Move Through a Worksheet
- Getting Help

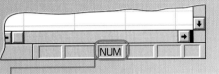

Tip

You can press Num Lock to switch the keys on the right side of your keyboard between number and movement keys.

When **NUM** is visible at the bottom of your screen, you can use the number keys 0 through 9 to quickly enter numbers.

When **NUM** is not visible at the bottom of your screen, you can use the movement keys to move through your worksheet.

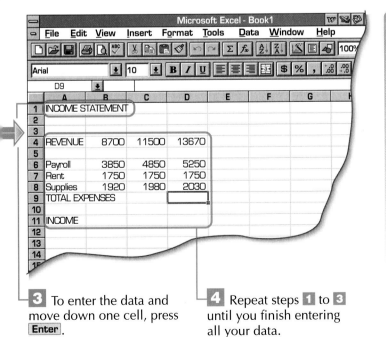

3 To enter the data and move down one cell, press **Enter**.

or

To enter the data and move one cell in any direction, press →, ←, ↓ or ↑.

4 Repeat steps **1** to **3** until you finish entering all your data.

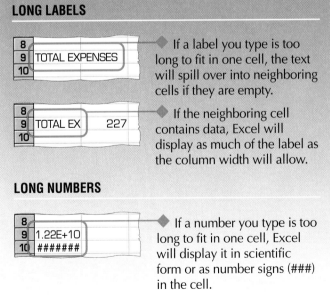

LONG LABELS

If a label you type is too long to fit in one cell, the text will spill over into neighboring cells if they are empty.

If the neighboring cell contains data, Excel will display as much of the label as the column width will allow.

LONG NUMBERS

If a number you type is too long to fit in one cell, Excel will display it in scientific form or as number signs (###) in the cell.

Note: To display an entire label or number, you must increase the column width. For more information, refer to page 190.

SELECT CELLS

Before you can use many Excel features, you must first select the cells you want to work with. Selected cells appear highlighted on your screen.

SELECT A ROW

	A	B	C	D	E	F
1	INCOME STATEMENT					
2						
3						
4	REVENUE	**8700**	**11500**	**13670**		
5						
6	Payroll	3850	4850	5250		
7	Rent	1750	1750	1750		
8	Supplies	1920	1980	2030		
9	TOTAL EXPENSES					
10						
11	INCOME					

1 Move the mouse over the row number you want to select (example: **4**) and then press the left button.

◆ Make sure the mouse looks like (not) before pressing the button.

TO CANCEL A SELECTION

Move the mouse over any cell in your worksheet and then press the left button.

SELECT A COLUMN

	A	B	C	D	E	F
1	INCOME STATEMENT					
2						
3						
4	REVENUE	**8700**	11500	13670		
5						
6	Payroll	**3850**	4850	5250		
7	Rent	**1750**	1750	1750		
8	Supplies	**1920**	1980	2030		
9	TOTAL EXPENSES					
10						
11	INCOME					

1 Move the mouse over the column letter you want to select (example: **B**) and then press the left button.

◆ Make sure the mouse looks like (not) before pressing the button.

SELECT THE ENTIRE WORKSHEET

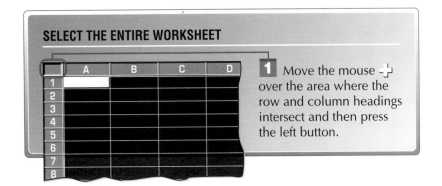

1 Move the mouse ✛ over the area where the row and column headings intersect and then press the left button.

SELECT A GROUP OF CELLS

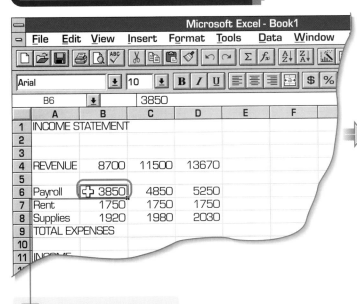

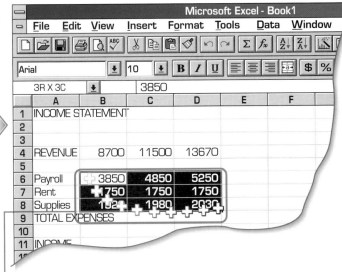

1 Move the mouse ✛ over the first cell you want to select (example: **B6**) and then press and hold down the left button.

2 Still holding down the button, drag the mouse ✛ until you highlight all the cells you want to select.

3 Release the button.

SELECT TWO GROUPS OF CELLS

To select another group of cells, press and hold down Ctrl while repeating steps **1** to **3**.

141

USING AUTOFILL

You can save time by using the AutoFill feature to complete a series of labels or numbers in your worksheet.

USING AUTOFILL TO COMPLETE A SERIES

Complete a Series of Labels

Monday	Tuesday	Wednesday	Thursday
Product 1	Product 2	Product 3	Product 4
Q1	Q2	Q3	Q4

◆ Excel completes a series of labels based on the label in the first cell.

Complete a Series of Numbers

1993	1994	1995	1996
1	2	3	4
5	10	15	20

◆ Excel completes a series of numbers based on the numbers in the first two cells. These numbers tell Excel how much to add to each number to complete the series.

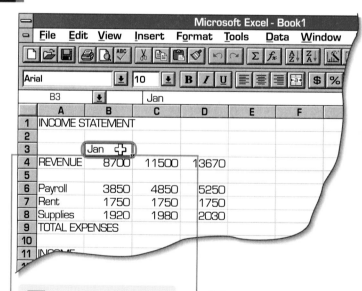

1 To create a series of labels, type and enter the first label in the series (example: **Jan**).

◆ To create a series of numbers, type and enter the first two numbers in the series.

2 Select the cell(s) containing the label or numbers you entered.

Note: To select cells, refer to page 140.

- Introduction
- Start Excel
- Excel Basics
- Enter Data
- Select Cells
- Using AutoFill
- Move Through a Worksheet
- Getting Help

Tip

January	March	May	July
Monday	Wednesday	Friday	Sunday

◆ *To create a series of labels that increases by more than one unit, type and enter the first two labels in the series. Then perform steps* **2** *to* **5** *below.*

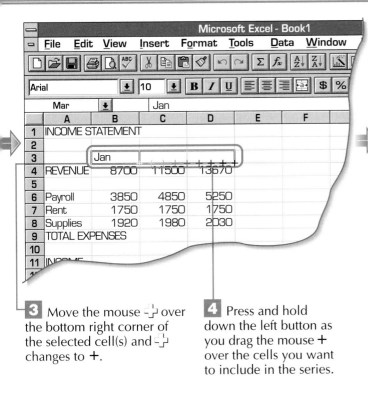

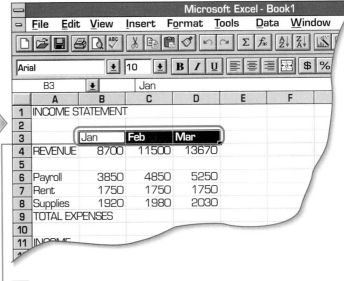

3 Move the mouse ⌖ over the bottom right corner of the selected cell(s) and ⌖ changes to +.

4 Press and hold down the left button as you drag the mouse + over the cells you want to include in the series.

5 Release the button and the cells display the series.

Note: You can also use the AutoFill feature to complete a series of labels or numbers in a column.

MOVE THROUGH A WORKSHEET

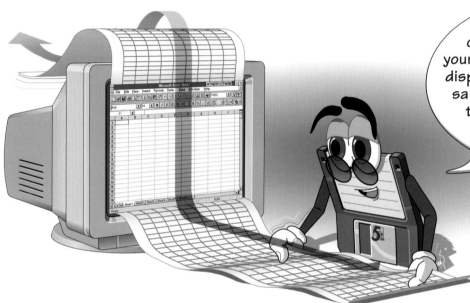

If your worksheet contains a lot of data, your computer screen cannot display all of the data at the same time. You must move through the worksheet to view other areas of data.

MOVE TO CELL A1

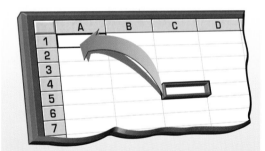

◆ Press **Ctrl** + **Home** to move to cell **A1** from any cell in your worksheet.

MOVE ONE SCREEN IN ANY DIRECTION

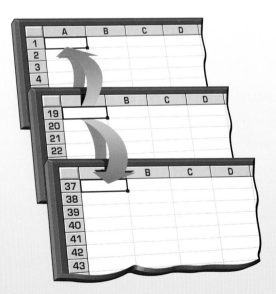

◆ Press **PageDown** to move **down** one screen.

◆ Press **PageUp** to move **up** one screen.

◆ Press **Alt** + **PageDown** to move **right** one screen.

◆ Press **Alt** + **PageUp** to move **left** one screen.

GETTING STARTED

- Introduction
- Start Excel
- Excel Basics
- Enter Data
- Select Cells
- Using AutoFill
- **Move Through a Worksheet**
- Getting Help

EXCEL

SCROLL UP OR DOWN

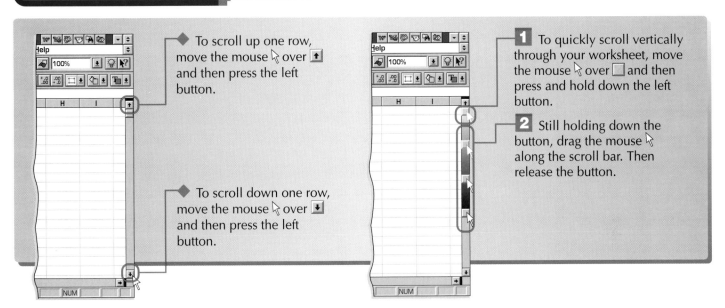

◆ To scroll up one row, move the mouse over ▲ and then press the left button.

◆ To scroll down one row, move the mouse over ▼ and then press the left button.

1 To quickly scroll vertically through your worksheet, move the mouse over □ and then press and hold down the left button.

2 Still holding down the button, drag the mouse along the scroll bar. Then release the button.

SCROLL LEFT OR RIGHT

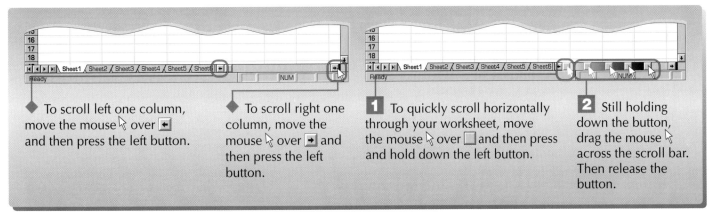

◆ To scroll left one column, move the mouse over ◄ and then press the left button.

◆ To scroll right one column, move the mouse over ► and then press the left button.

1 To quickly scroll horizontally through your worksheet, move the mouse over □ and then press and hold down the left button.

2 Still holding down the button, drag the mouse across the scroll bar. Then release the button.

If you forget how to perform a task, you can use the Help feature to obtain information. This can save you time by eliminating the need to refer to other sources.

GETTING HELP

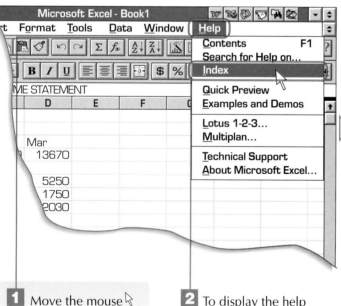

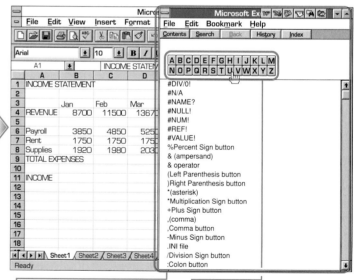

1 Move the mouse over **Help** and then press the left button.

2 To display the help index, move the mouse over **Index** and then press the left button.

◆ The **Microsoft Excel Help** window appears.

3 Move the mouse over the first letter of the topic you want information on (example: **U** for **Underlining**) and then press the left button.

- Introduction
- Start Excel
- Excel Basics
- Enter Data
- Select Cells
- Using AutoFill
- Move Through a Worksheet
- Getting Help

THE TIPWIZARD

If Excel knows a better way to accomplish a task you are performing, the TipWizard button will turn from white to yellow.

1 To display the tip, move the mouse ⬉ over 💡 and then press the left button. The tip appears.

*Note: To hide the tip, repeat step **1**.*

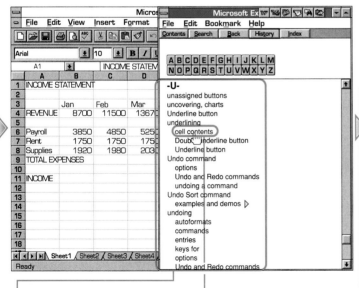

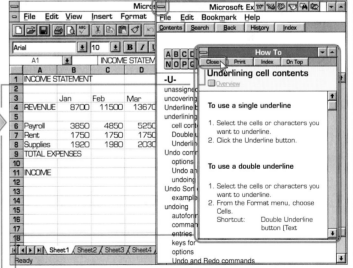

◆ Topics beginning with the letter you selected appear.

◆ To view more topics beginning with that letter, press **PageDown** on your keyboard.

4 Move the mouse 🖑 over the topic of interest and then press the left button.

◆ Information on the topic you selected appears.

5 To close the **How To** window, move the mouse ⬉ over **Close** and then press the left button.

6 To close the **Microsoft Excel Help** window, move the mouse ⬉ over ▬ and then quickly press the left button twice.

147

You should save your workbook to store it for future use. This lets you later retrieve the workbook for reviewing or editing purposes.

SAVE A WORKBOOK

When you save a workbook for the first time, you must give it a name. The name of a workbook consists of two parts: a name and an extension. You must separate these parts with a period.

INCOME.XLS

◆ **Name**

The name describes the contents of a workbook. It can have up to eight characters.

◆ **Period**

A period separates the name and the extension.

◆ **Extension**

The extension identifies the program you used to create the workbook. It can have up to three characters.

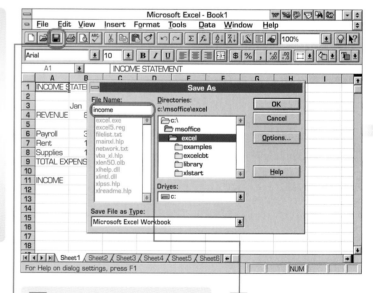

1 Move the mouse 🗅 over 🖫 and then press the left button.

◆ The **Save As** dialog box appears.

*Note: If you previously saved your workbook, the **Save As** dialog box will **not** appear since you have already named the workbook.*

2 Type a name for your workbook (example: **income**) and then press **Enter**.

*Note: To make it easier to find your workbook later on, do not type an extension. Excel will automatically add the **xls** extension to the name.*

- **Save a Workbook**
- Save a Workbook to a Diskette
- Close a Workbook
- Exit Excel

- Open a Workbook
- Create a New Workbook
- Switch Between Workbooks

Rules for Naming a Workbook

The name of a workbook *can* contain the following characters:

◆ The letters A to Z

◆ The numbers 0 to 9

◆ The symbols
_ ^ $ ~ ! # % & { } @ ( )

The name of a workbook *cannot* contain the following characters:

◆ A comma (,)

◆ A blank space

◆ The symbols
* ? ; [ ] + = \ / : < >

Each workbook in a directory must have a unique name.

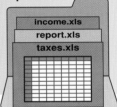

income.xls
report.xls
taxes.xls

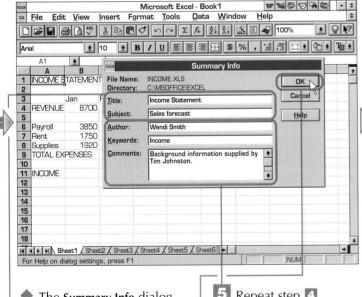

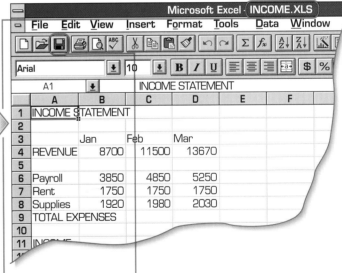

◆ The **Summary Info** dialog box appears.

3 Type a title for your workbook.

4 Press **Tab** to move to the next category. Type the corresponding information.

5 Repeat step **4** until you have typed all the information.

6 Move the mouse ⌖ over **OK** and then press the left button.

◆ Excel saves your workbook and displays the name at the top of your screen.

◆ You should save your workbook every 5 to 10 minutes to store any changes made since the last time you saved the workbook. To save changes, move the mouse ⌖ over 🖫 and then press the left button.

SAVE A WORKBOOK TO A DISKETTE

If you want to give your colleagues a copy of a workbook, you can save the workbook to a diskette. They can then review the workbook on their own computers.

SAVE A WORKBOOK TO A DISKETTE

1 Insert a diskette into a floppy drive (example: **a:**).

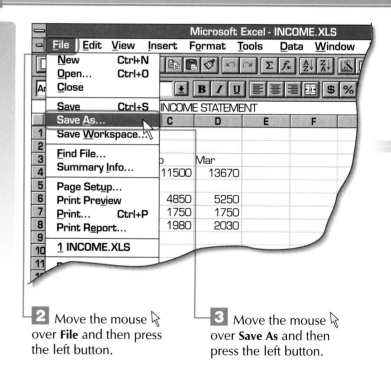

2 Move the mouse over **File** and then press the left button.

3 Move the mouse over **Save As** and then press the left button.

150

- Save a Workbook
- **Save a Workbook to a Diskette**
- Close a Workbook
- Exit Excel
- Open a Workbook
- Create a New Workbook
- Switch Between Workbooks

SAVE A WORKBOOK WITH A NEW NAME

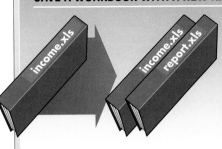

After you save your workbook, you may want to make additional changes. In case you regret any of these changes, you can keep a copy of the old version by saving the workbook with a new name.

1 Perform steps **2** to **4** below.

2 Move the mouse ⬉ over **OK** and then press the left button.

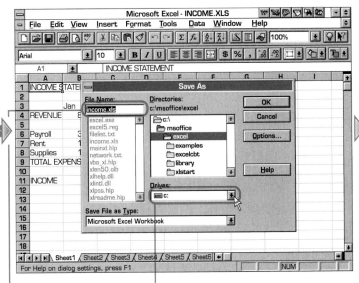

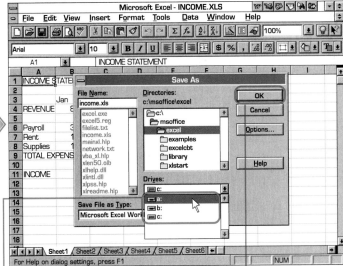

◆ The **Save As** dialog box appears.

4 The **File Name:** box displays the current file name. To save your workbook with a different name, type a new name.

◆ The **Drives:** box displays the current drive (example: **c:**).

5 To save the file to a diskette, move the mouse ⬉ over ⬇ in the **Drives:** box and then press the left button.

◆ A list of the available drives for your computer appears.

6 Move the mouse ⬉ over the drive that contains the diskette (example: **a:**) and then press the left button.

7 To save your workbook, move the mouse ⬉ over **OK** and then press the left button.

When you finish using a workbook, you can close the workbook to remove it from your screen.

CLOSE A WORKBOOK

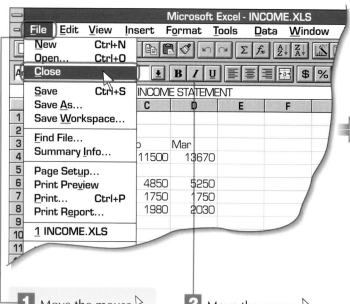

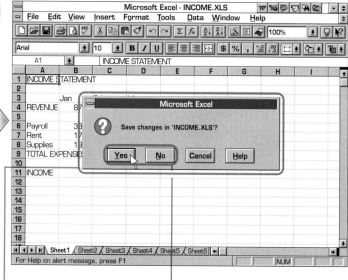

1 Move the mouse � over **File** and then press the left button.

2 Move the mouse � over **Close** and then press the left button.

◆ This dialog box appears if you have not saved changes made to your workbook.

3 To save the changes, move the mouse � over **Yes** and then press the left button.

◆ To close the workbook without saving the changes, move the mouse � over **No** and then press the left button.

152

- Save a Workbook
- Save a Workbook to a Diskette
- Close a Workbook
- Exit Excel

- Open a Workbook
- Create a New Workbook
- Switch Between Workbooks

When you finish using Excel, you can easily exit the program.

EXIT EXCEL

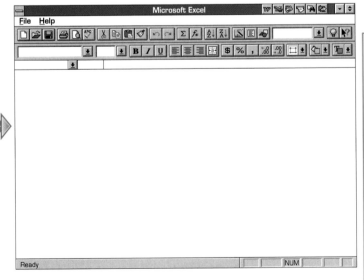

◆ The workbook disappears from your screen.

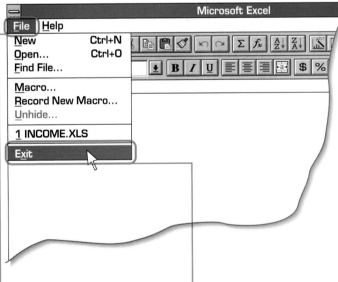

1 Move the mouse ⟍ over **File** and then press the left button.

2 Move the mouse ⟍ over **Exit** and then press the left button.

Note: To restart Excel, refer to page 135.

OPEN A WORKBOOK

You can open a saved workbook and display it on your screen. This lets you review and edit the workbook.

OPEN A WORKBOOK

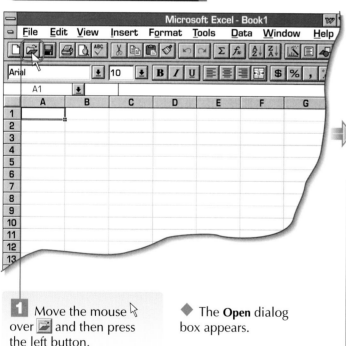

1 Move the mouse ⌖ over 📂 and then press the left button.

◆ The **Open** dialog box appears.

◆ The **Drives:** box displays the current drive (example: **c:**).

2 To open a workbook on a different drive, move the mouse ⌖ over ⯆ in the **Drives:** box and then press the left button.

◆ A list of the available drives for your computer appears.

3 Move the mouse ⌖ over the drive containing the workbook you want to open and then press the left button.

154

- Save a Workbook
- Save a Workbook to a Diskette
- Close a Workbook
- Exit Excel

- **Open a Workbook**
- Create a New Workbook
- Switch Between Workbooks

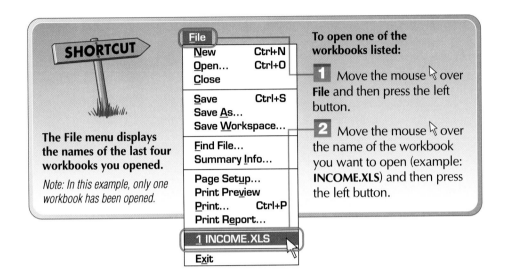

SHORTCUT

The File menu displays the names of the last four workbooks you opened.

Note: In this example, only one workbook has been opened.

To open one of the workbooks listed:

1 Move the mouse ⬚ over **File** and then press the left button.

2 Move the mouse ⬚ over the name of the workbook you want to open (example: **INCOME.XLS**) and then press the left button.

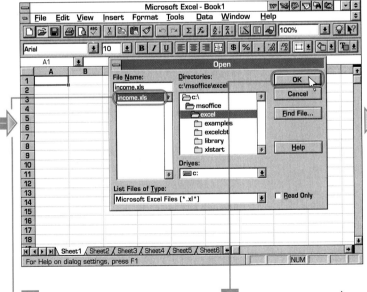

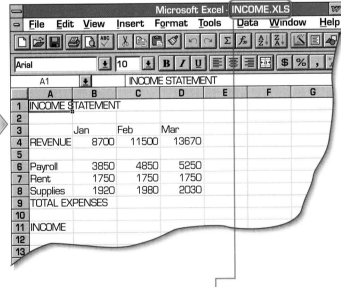

4 Move the mouse ⬚ over the name of the workbook you want to open (example: **income.xls**) and then press the left button.

5 Move the mouse ⬚ over **OK** and then press the left button.

◆ Excel opens the workbook and displays it on your screen. You can now make changes to the workbook.

◆ The name of the workbook appears at the top of your screen.

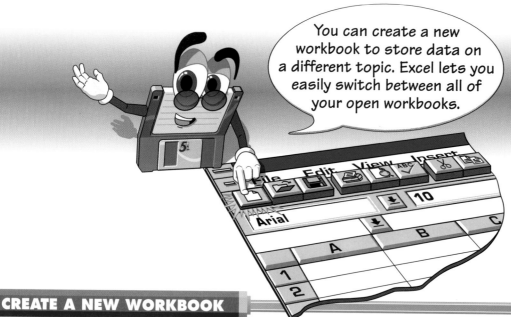

You can create a new workbook to store data on a different topic. Excel lets you easily switch between all of your open workbooks.

CREATE A NEW WORKBOOK

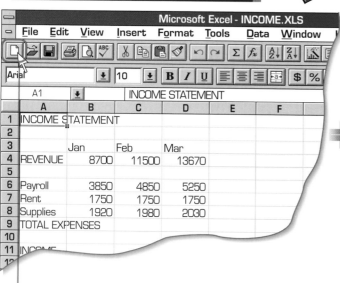

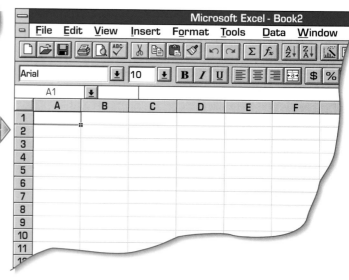

1 To create a new workbook, move the mouse ⌖ over ◻ and then press the left button.

◆ A new workbook appears.

Note: The previous workbook is now hidden behind the new workbook.

- Save a Workbook
- Save a Workbook to a Diskette
- Close a Workbook
- Exit Excel
- Open a Workbook
- **Create a New Workbook**
- **Switch Between Workbooks**

Think of each new workbook as a new 3-ring binder. Each workbook contains worksheets that you can use to organize your data.

Note: For information on using multiple worksheets in a workbook, refer to pages 216 to 221.

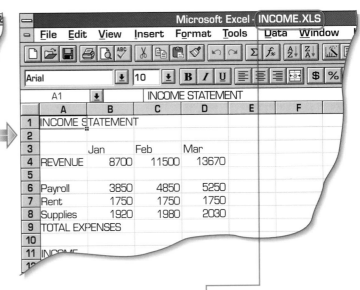

SWITCH BETWEEN WORKBOOKS

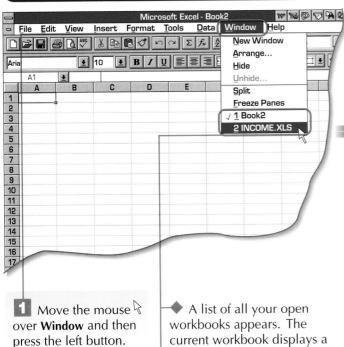

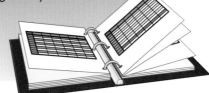

1 Move the mouse ⬚ over **Window** and then press the left button.

◆ A list of all your open workbooks appears. The current workbook displays a check mark (√) beside its name.

2 Move the mouse ⬚ over the workbook you want to switch to (example: **INCOME.XLS**) and then press the left button.

◆ The workbook appears.

◆ Excel displays the name of the workbook at the top of your screen.

EDIT DATA

After you enter data into your worksheet, you can correct a typing error or revise the data.

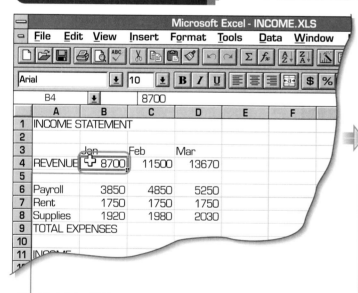

1 Move the mouse ✛ over the cell containing the data you want to change (example: **B4**) and then quickly press the left button twice.

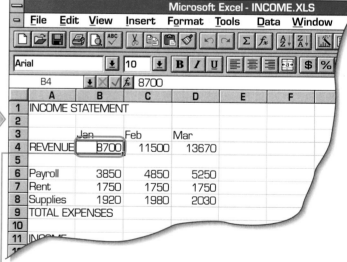

◆ A flashing insertion point appears in the cell.

2 Move the mouse I over the position where you want to add or delete characters and then press the left button.

Note: You can also press → or ← on your keyboard to move the insertion point.

- **Edit Data**
- Clear Data
- Undo Last Change
- Move Data
- Copy Data
- Check Spelling

EXCEL

REPLACE ENTIRE CELL CONTENTS

You can completely replace the contents of a cell with new data.

1 Move the mouse ✛ over the cell containing the data you want to replace with new data and then press the left button.

2 Type the new data and then press **Enter**.

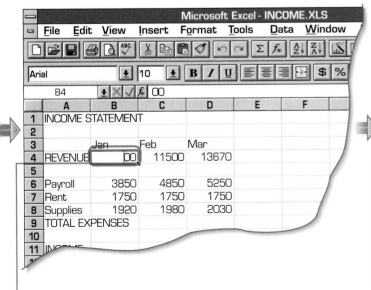

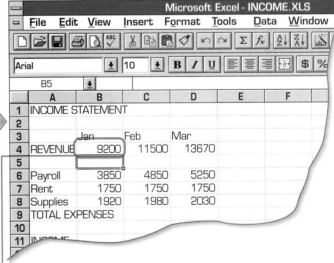

3 To remove the character to the right of the insertion point, press **Delete**.

◆ To remove the character to the left of the insertion point, press **←Backspace**.

4 To insert data where the insertion point flashes on your screen, type the data.

5 When you finish making the changes, press **Enter**.

You can completely erase the contents of cells in your worksheet.

CLEAR DATA

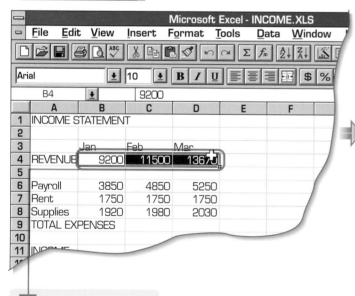

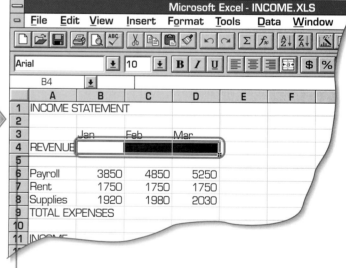

1 Select the cells containing the data you want to remove.

Note: To select cells, refer to page 140.

2 Press **Delete** and the contents of the cells you selected disappear.

160

- Edit Data
- **Clear Data**
- **Undo Last Change**
- Move Data
- Copy Data
- Check Spelling

> Excel remembers the last change you made to your worksheet. If you regret this change, you can cancel it by using the Undo feature.

UNDO YOUR LAST CHANGE

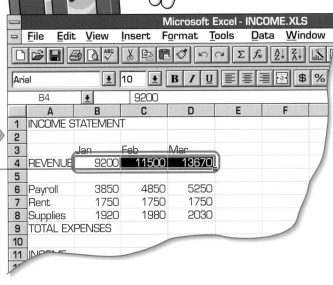

1 To cancel the last change made to your worksheet, move the mouse ⌖ over 🔄 and then press the left button.

◆ Excel cancels your last change.

You can move data from one location in your worksheet to another. Excel cuts the data and pastes it in a new location. The original data disappears.

MOVE DATA

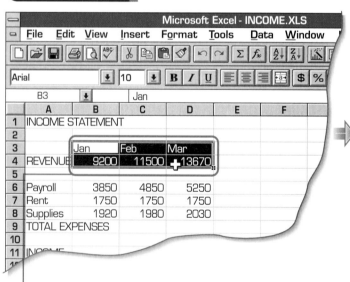

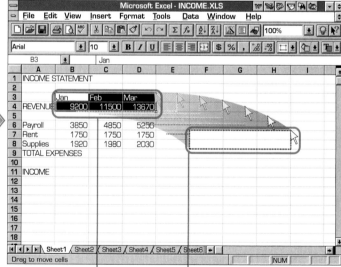

1 Select the cells containing the data you want to move to a new location.

Note: To select cells, refer to page 140.

2 Move the mouse ⊹ over any border of the selected cells and ⊹ changes to ⟋.

3 Press and hold down the left button and then drag the mouse ⟋ to where you want to place the data.

◆ A rectangular box indicates where the data will appear.

162

- Edit Data
- Clear Data
- Undo Last Change
- Move Data
- Copy Data
- Check Spelling

Tip

You can also move data to another worksheet.

Note: For more information, refer to page 218.

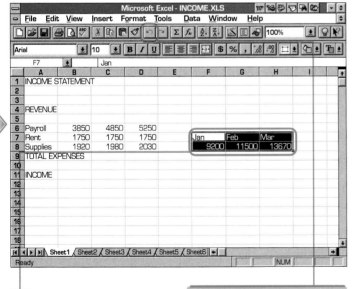

4 Release the left button and the data moves to the new location.

CANCEL THE MOVE

◆ To immediately cancel the move, position the mouse over and then press the left button.

You can also use these buttons to move data.

1 Select the cells containing the data you want to move to a new location.

2 Move the mouse over and then press the left button.

3 Select the cell where you want to place the data. This cell will become the top left cell of the new location.

4 Move the mouse over and then press the left button. The data appears in the new location.

COPY DATA

Like a photocopy machine, you can make an exact copy of data and then place the copy in a new location.

COPY DATA

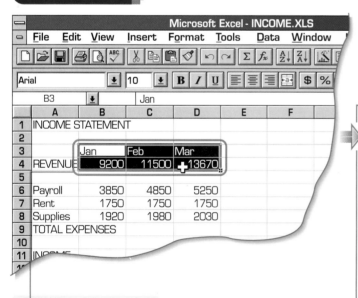

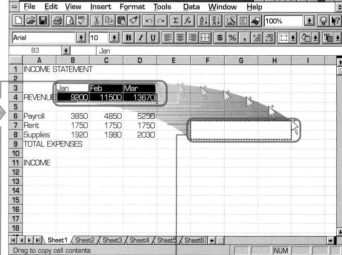

1 Select the cells containing the data you want to copy to a new location.

Note: To select cells, refer to page 140.

2 Move the mouse ⊹ over any border of the selected cells (⊹ changes to ↘).

3 Press and hold down Ctrl and the left button (↘ changes to ↖).

4 Still holding down Ctrl and the left button, drag the mouse ↖ to where you want to place the data.

◆ A rectangular box indicates where the data will appear.

EDIT YOUR WORKSHEETS

- Edit Data
- Clear Data
- Undo Last Change
- Move Data
- Copy Data
- Check Spelling

EXCEL

You can also copy data to another worksheet.

Note: For more information, refer to page 218.

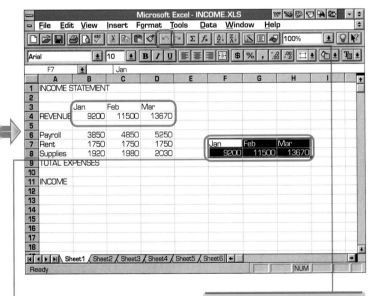

5 Release the left button and then release Ctrl.

◆ A copy of the data appears in the new location.

CANCEL THE COPY

◆ To immediately cancel the copy, position the mouse ▷ over ☒ and then press the left button.

You can also use these buttons to copy data.

1 Select the cells containing the data you want to copy to a new location.

2 Move the mouse over 🖹 and then press the left button.

3 Select the cell where you want to place the data. This cell will become the top left cell of the new location.

4 Move the mouse ▷ over 🖺 and then press the left button. A copy of the data appears in the new location.

Note: You can repeat steps **3** and **4** to place the data in multiple locations in your worksheet.

You can use Excel's spelling feature to find and correct spelling errors in your worksheet.

CHECK SPELLING

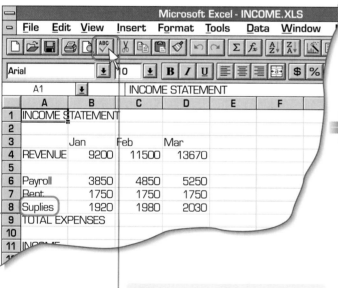

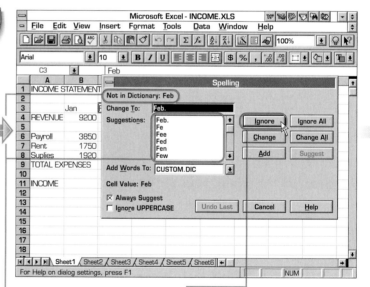

◆ In this example, the letter **p** was removed from **Supplies**.

1 To start the spell check at the beginning of your worksheet, press `Ctrl` + **Home** to move to cell **A1**.

Note: To spell check a section of your worksheet, select the cells before performing step 2. To select cells, refer to page 140.

2 Move the mouse ⤵ over 🖰 and then press the left button.

◆ If Excel finds a spelling error, the **Spelling** dialog box appears.

◆ Excel displays the word it does not recognize and suggestions to correct the error.

Ignore misspelled word

3 If you do not want to change the spelling of the word, move the mouse ⤵ over **Ignore** and then press the left button.

- Edit Data
- Clear Data
- Undo Last Change

- Move Data
- Copy Data
- **Check Spelling**

Excel compares every word in your worksheet to words in its own dictionary. If a word does not exist in the dictionary, Excel considers it misspelled.

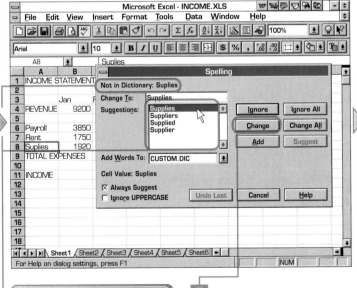

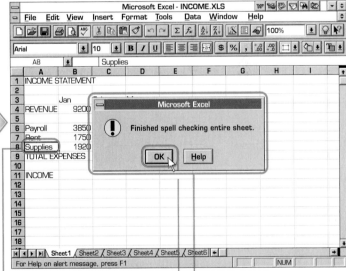

Correct misspelled word

◆ Excel displays the next word it does not recognize.

4 To correct the spelling, move the mouse ⌖ over the word you want to use and then press the left button.

5 To replace the misspelled word in your worksheet with the correct spelling, move the mouse ⌖ over **Change** and then press the left button.

◆ Excel corrects the word and continues checking for spelling errors.

6 Ignore or correct spelling errors until Excel finishes checking your worksheet.

◆ This dialog box appears when the spell check is complete.

7 To close the dialog box, move the mouse ⌖ over **OK** and then press the left button.

FORMULAS

You can use formulas to perform calculations on your worksheet data.

INTRODUCTION TO FORMULAS

◆ You must begin a formula with an equal sign (=).

◆ You should use cell references (example: **A1**) instead of actual numbers whenever possible. This way, if your data changes, Excel will automatically redo the calculations.

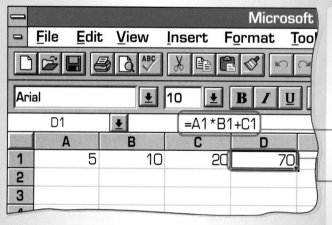

In this example, cell D1 contains the formula:

$$=A1*B1+C1$$

$$=5*10+20$$

$$=70$$

◆ The formula for the active cell appears in the formula bar.

◆ The result of the calculation appears in the cell containing the formula (example: **D1**).

- **Formulas**
- Enter a Formula
- Functions
- Enter a Function
- Add Numbers
- Errors in Formulas
- Copy Formulas

You can use these operators in your formulas:

+	Addition
-	Subtraction
*	Multiplication
/	Division
^	Exponentiation

Excel will perform calculations in the following order:

1 Exponentiation

2 Multiplication and Division

3 Addition and Subtraction

You can change the order that Excel calculates your formulas by using parentheses ( ).

◆ Excel will calculate the numbers in parentheses first.

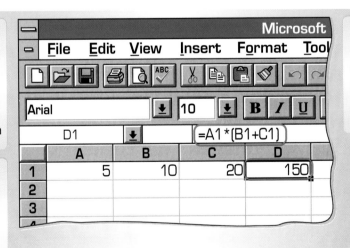

In this example, cell D1 contains the formula:

=A1*(B1+C1)

=5*(10+20)

=150

ENTER A FORMULA

You can enter a formula into any cell in your worksheet.

ENTER A FORMULA

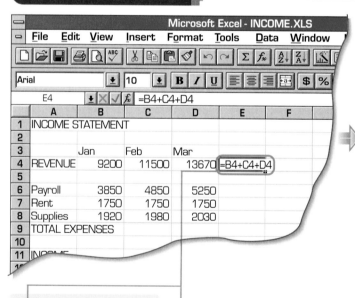

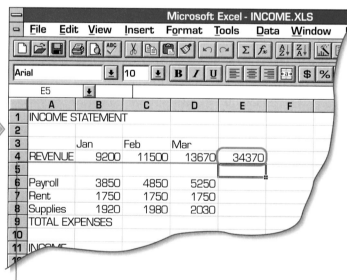

1 Move the mouse ⊹ over the cell where you want to enter a formula (example: **E4**) and then press the left button.

2 Type an equal sign (=) to begin the formula.

3 Type the calculation you want to perform (example: **B4+C4+D4**).

Note: This formula will calculate the total Revenue.

4 Press **Enter** and the result of the calculation appears in the cell (example: **34370**).

- Formulas
- **Enter a Formula**
- Functions
- Enter a Function
- Add Numbers
- Errors in Formulas
- Copy Formulas

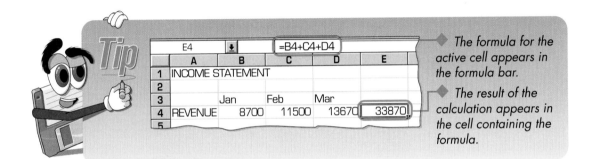

◆ The formula for the active cell appears in the formula bar.

◆ The result of the calculation appears in the cell containing the formula.

AUTOMATIC RECALCULATION

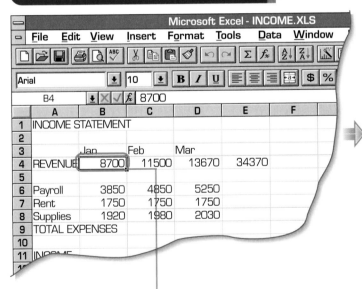

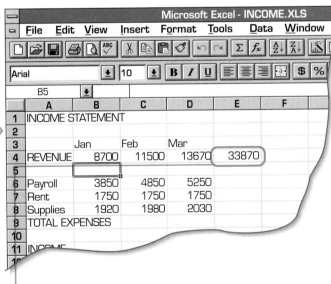

If you change a number used in a formula, Excel will automatically calculate a new result.

1 Move the mouse over the cell you want to change (example: **B4**) and then press the left button.

2 Type a new number (example: **8700**).

3 Press **Enter** and Excel automatically recalculates the formula using the new number.

171

FUNCTIONS

A function is a ready-to-use formula. Excel offers over 300 functions to perform specialized calculations on your worksheet data.

INTRODUCTION TO FUNCTIONS

You must tell Excel what data to use to calculate a function. This data is enclosed in parentheses ( ).

$=SUM(A1,A3,A5)$

◆ When there is a comma (,) between cell references in a function, Excel uses each cell to perform the calculation.

Example: =SUM(A1,A3,A5) is the same as the formula =A1+A3+A5.

$=SUM(A1:A4)$

◆ When there is a colon (:) between cell references in a function, Excel uses the displayed cells and all cells between them to perform the calculation.

Example: =SUM(A1:A4) is the same as the formula =A1+A2+A3+A4.

EXCEL

Common Functions

AVERAGE Calculates the average value of a list of numbers.
Example: =AVERAGE(B1:B6)

MIN Finds the smallest value in a list of numbers.
Example: =MIN(B1:B6)

COUNT Counts the number of values in a list of numbers.
Example: =COUNT(B1:B6)

ROUND Rounds a number to a specific number of digits.
Example: =ROUND(B6,2)

MAX Finds the largest value in a list of numbers.
Example: =MAX(B1:B6)

SUM Adds a list of numbers.
Example: =SUM(B1:B6)

◆ A function starts with an equal sign (=).

◆ You should use cell references (example: **A1**) instead of actual numbers whenever possible. This way, if your data changes, Excel will automatically redo the calculations.

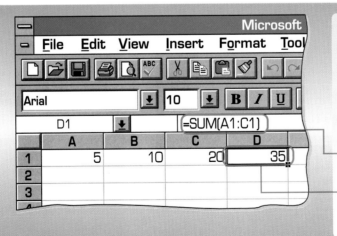

In this example, cell D1 contains the function:

=SUM(A1:C1)

=A1+B1+C1

=5+10+20

=35

◆ The function for the active cell appears in the formula bar.

◆ The result of the calculation appears in the cell containing the function (example: **D1**).

173

The Function Wizard lets you perform calculations without typing long, complex formulas.

ENTER A FUNCTION

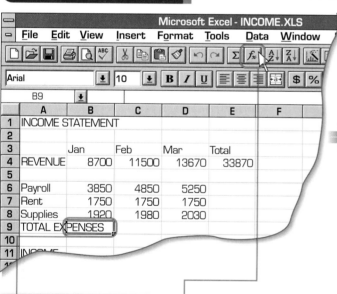

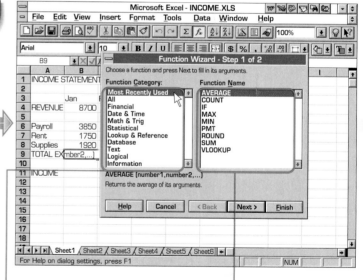

1 Move the mouse ⊹ over the cell where you want to enter a function (example: **B9**) and then press the left button.

2 Move the mouse ▹ over 𝑓𝑥 and then press the left button.

◆ The **Function Wizard** dialog box appears.

3 Move the mouse ▹ over the category containing the function you want to use and then press the left button.

*Note: If you do not know which category contains the function you want to use, select **All**. This will display a list of all the functions.*

◆ This area displays the functions in the category you selected.

USING FORMULAS AND FUNCTIONS

- Formulas
- Enter a Formula
- Functions
- Enter a Function

- Add Numbers
- Errors in Formulas
- Copy Formulas

EXCEL

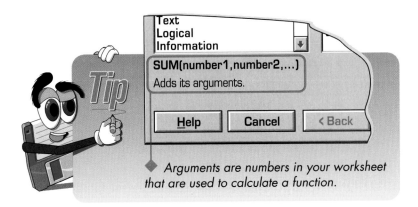

Text
Logical
Information

SUM(number1,number2,...)

Adds its arguments.

| Help | Cancel | < Back |

◆ Arguments are numbers in your worksheet that are used to calculate a function.

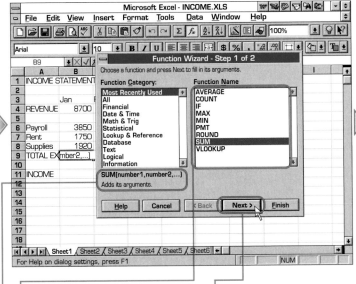

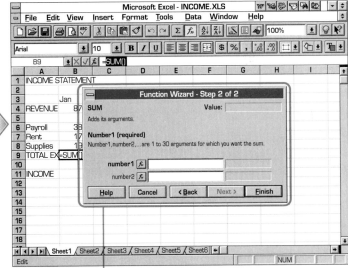

4 Move the mouse ↳ over the function you want to use (example: **SUM**) and then press the left button.

◆ A description of the function you selected appears.

5 To select the function, move the mouse ↳ over **Next** and then press the left button.

◆ This dialog box appears. The text in the dialog box depends on the function you selected in step **4**.

CONTINUED

175

ENTER A FUNCTION

> If the Function Wizard dialog box covers the data you want to use in the function, you can move the dialog box to another location on your screen.

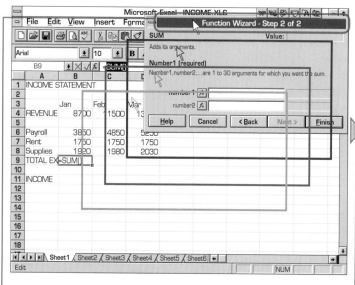

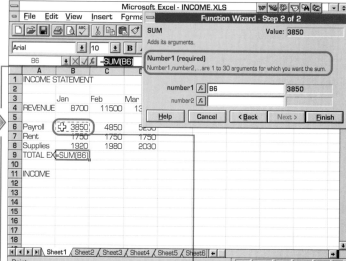

6 To move the **Function Wizard** dialog box, position the mouse ⌖ over the title bar and then press and hold down the left button.

7 Still holding down the button, drag the box to a new location.

8 Release the button and the dialog box moves to the new location.

◆ This area describes the first number Excel needs to perform the function.

9 To select a number, move the mouse ⌖ over the cell containing the data you want to use and then press the left button.

Note: If the number you want to enter does not appear in your worksheet, type the number.

176

- Formulas
- Enter a Formula
- Functions
- **Enter a Function**

- Add Numbers
- Errors in Formulas
- Copy Formulas

Tip

◆ *In the example below, you can quickly enter numbers in the **Function Wizard** dialog box. Replace steps* **9** *to* **11** *by selecting cells* **B6** *to* **B8**.

Note: To select cells, refer to page 140.

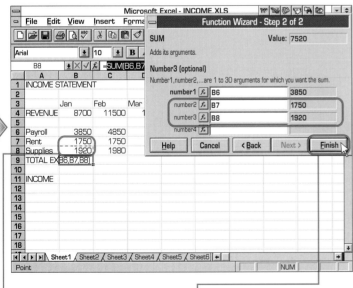

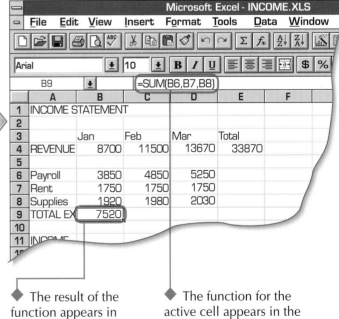

10 To display a description of the next number Excel needs to perform the function, press `Tab`.

11 Repeat steps **9** and **10** until you have selected all the cells you want to use in the function.

12 Move the mouse ⃗ over **Finish** and then press the left button.

◆ The result of the function appears in the cell.

◆ The function for the active cell appears in the formula bar.

ADD NUMBERS

You can use the AutoSum feature to quickly add a list of numbers in your worksheet.

ADD A LIST OF NUMBERS

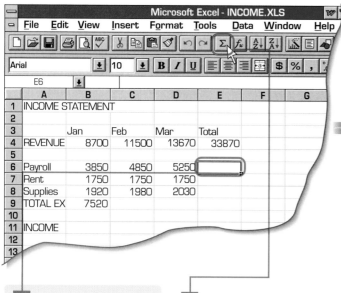

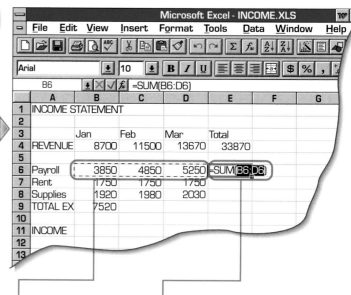

1 Move the mouse ⊹ over the cell you want to display the sum (example: **E6**) and then press the left button.

2 Move the mouse ↘ over Σ and then press the left button.

Note: Σ is the Greek symbol for sum.

◆ A moving border appears around the cells Excel will add together.

◆ The SUM function appears. It displays the first and last cells Excel will add together, separated by a colon (:).

◆ To add a different list of cells, select the cells.

Note: To select cells, refer to page 140.

USING FORMULAS AND FUNCTIONS

- Formulas
- Enter a Formula
- Functions
- Enter a Function

- **Add Numbers**
- Errors in Formulas
- Copy Formulas

EXCEL

You can sum rows and columns of data at the same time.

1 *Select the cells containing the numbers you want to sum and a blank row and column for the results.*

2 *Move the mouse over* Σ *and then press the left button.*

ADD SEVERAL LISTS OF NUMBERS

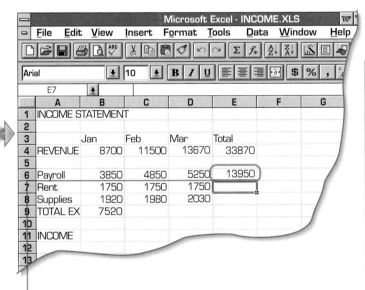

3 Press **Enter** and the result appears in the cell.

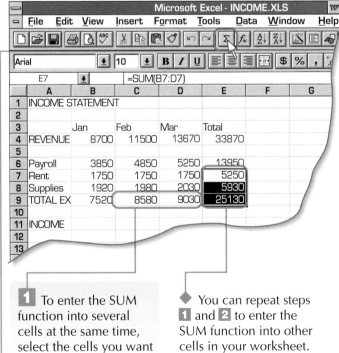

1 To enter the SUM function into several cells at the same time, select the cells you want to display the results.

2 Move the mouse over Σ and then press the left button.

◆ You can repeat steps **1** and **2** to enter the SUM function into other cells in your worksheet.

ERRORS IN FORMULAS

An error message appears when Excel cannot properly calculate a formula. You can correct an error by editing the cell displaying the error message.

COMMON ERRORS IN FORMULAS

#DIV/0!

This error message appears in a cell if the formula you entered divides a number by zero.

	A	B	C	D
1	50		35	
2	0			
3	#DIV/0!		#DIV/0!	
4				
5				

This cell contains the formula =A1/A2 = 50/0

The formula divides a number by 0.

This cell contains the formula =C1/C2 = 35/0

The formula divides a number by 0.

Note: Excel considers a blank cell to contain the zero value.

#NAME?

This error message appears in a cell if the formula you entered contains a name Excel does not recognize.

	A	B	C	D
1	5		30	
2	10		5	
3	20		10	
4	#NAME?		#NAME?	
5				

This cell contains the formula =A1+A2A3

The formula is missing a plus sign (+).

This cell contains the function =SUMM(C1:C3)

The name of the function is misspelled.

USING FORMULAS AND FUNCTIONS

- Formulas
- Enter a Formula
- Functions
- Enter a Function
- Add Numbers
- **Errors in Formulas**
- Copy Formulas

EXCEL

CORRECT AN ERROR

1 To correct an error, move the mouse 🔁 over the cell displaying the error message and then quickly press the left button twice.

2 Edit the formula as you would any data in your worksheet.

Note: To edit data, refer to page 158.

#REF!

This error message appears in a cell if the formula you entered refers to a cell that is not valid.

	A	B	
1	10		
2	20	Delete row 1	
3	30		
4	60		
5			

	A	B	
1	20		
2	30		
3	#REF!		
4			
5			

This cell contains the formula =A1+A2+A3

A cell used in the formula was deleted.

COPY FORMULAS

After entering a formula in your worksheet, you can copy the formula to other cells. This saves you time when entering the same formula into several cells.

COPY FORMULAS (USING RELATIVE REFERENCES)

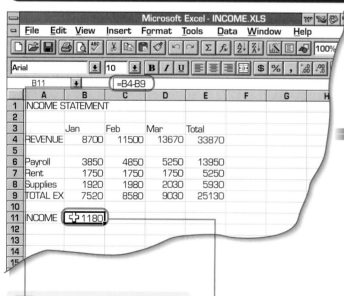

1 Enter the formula you want to copy to other cells (example: to calculate INCOME, enter **=B4-B9** in cell **B11**).

2 Move the mouse ⌖ over the cell containing the formula and then press the left button.

3 Move the mouse ⌖ over the bottom right corner of the cell and ⌖ changes to **+**.

4 Press and hold down the left button as you drag the mouse **+** over the cells you want to receive a copy of the formula.

USING FORMULAS AND FUNCTIONS

- Formulas
- Enter a Formula
- Functions
- Enter a Function
- Add Numbers
- Errors in Formulas
- Copy Formulas

EXCEL

When you copy a formula, Excel automatically changes the cell references in the formula.

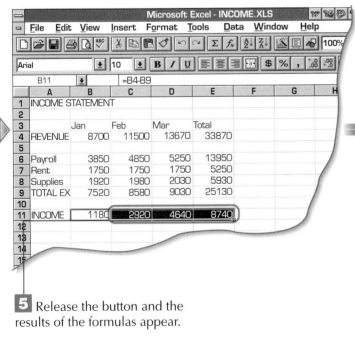

	A	B	C	
1	10	20	5	
2	20	30	10	
3	30	40	20	
4	60	90	35	
5				
6				

=A1+A2+A3 ➡ =B1+B2+B3   =C1+C2+C3

This cell contains the formula =A1+A2+A3

If you copy the formula to other cells in the worksheet, the cell references in the new formulas automatically change.

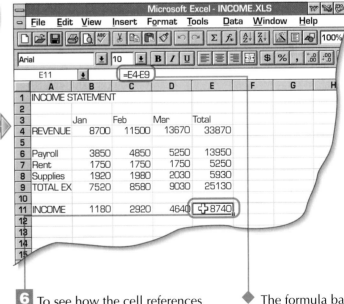

5 Release the button and the results of the formulas appear.

6 To see how the cell references changed, move the mouse ⌖ over a cell that received a copy of the formula (example: **E11**) and then press the left button.

◆ The formula bar displays the formula with the new cell references.

COPY FORMULAS

To save time, you can copy a formula to other cells in your worksheet. If you do not want Excel to change a cell reference when copying the formula, you must lock the cell. A locked cell reference is called an absolute reference.

COPY FORMULAS (USING ABSOLUTE REFERENCES)

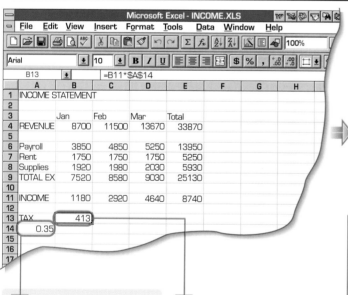

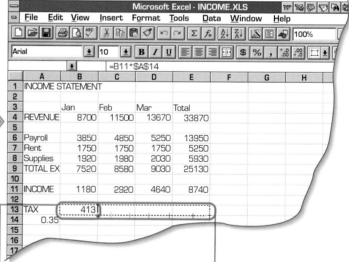

1 Enter the data you want to use as an absolute cell reference (example: **0.35** in cell **A14**).

2 Enter the formula you want to copy to other cells (example: to calculate TAX, enter **=B11*$A$14** in cell **B13**).

*Note: To lock a cell reference during the copy process, type a dollar sign (**$**) before both the column letter and row number (example: **$A$14**).*

3 Move the mouse ⇩ over the cell containing the formula you want to copy (example: **B13**) and then press the left button.

4 Move the mouse ⇩ over the bottom right corner of the cell and ⇩ changes to **+**.

5 Press and hold down the left button as you drag the mouse **+** over the cells you want to receive a copy of the formula.

USING FORMULAS AND FUNCTIONS

- Formulas
- Enter a Formula
- Functions
- Enter a Function
- Add Numbers
- Errors in Formulas
- **Copy Formulas**

EXCEL

To make a cell reference absolute, type a dollar sign ($) before both the column letter and row number (example: $B$1).

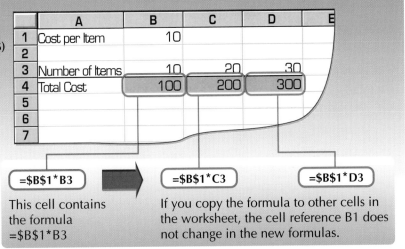

	A	B	C	D	E
1	Cost per Item	10			
2					
3	Number of Items	10	20	30	
4	Total Cost	100	200	300	
5					
6					
7					

=$B$1*B3   =$B$1*C3   =$B$1*D3

This cell contains
the formula
=$B$1*B3

If you copy the formula to other cells in
the worksheet, the cell reference B1 does
not change in the new formulas.

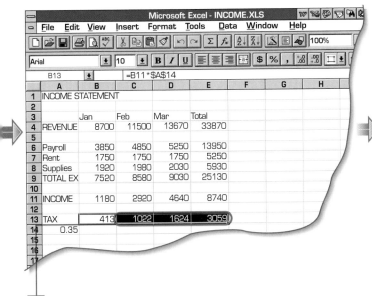

6 Release the button and
the results of the formulas
appear.

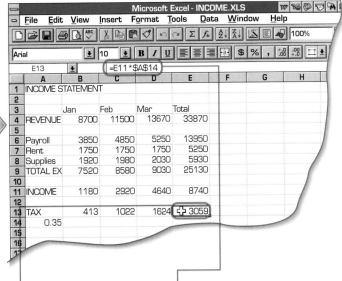

7 To see how the cell
references changed,
move the mouse ⬚
over a cell that received
a copy of the formula
(example: **E13**) and then
press the left button.

◆ The absolute reference in
the formula did not change
(example: **A14**). The relative
reference in the formula did
change (example: **E11**).

INSERT A ROW OR COLUMN

You can add a row or column to your worksheet if you want to insert new data.

INSERT A ROW

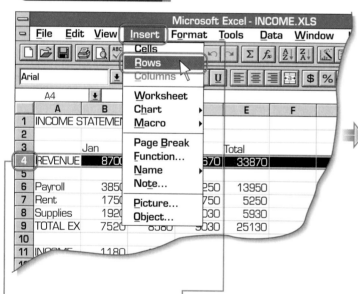

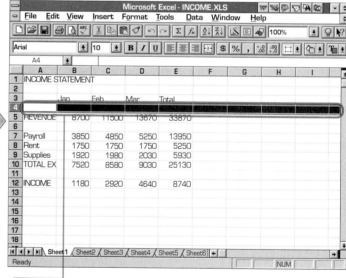

Excel inserts a row above the row you select.

1 To select a row, move the mouse ⊹ over the row heading (example: **row 4**) and then press the left button.

2 Move the mouse ⫣ over **Insert** and then press the left button.

3 Move the mouse ⫣ over **Rows** and then press the left button.

◆ The new row appears and all the rows that follow shift downward.

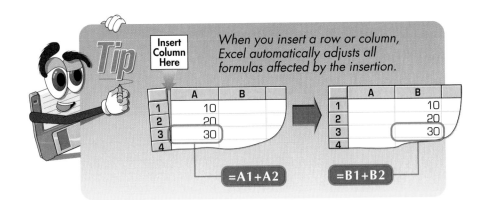

Tip

Insert Column Here

When you insert a row or column, Excel automatically adjusts all formulas affected by the insertion.

=A1+A2   =B1+B2

INSERT A COLUMN

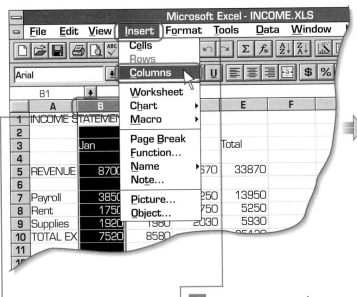

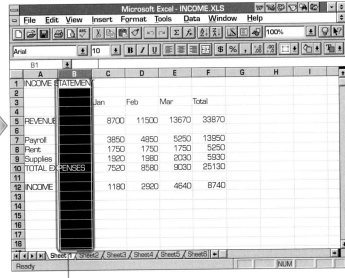

Excel inserts a column to the left of the column you select.

1 To select a column, move the mouse ⊕ over the column heading (example: **column B**) and then press the left button.

2 Move the mouse ⟋ over **Insert** and then press the left button.

3 Move the mouse ⟋ over **Columns** and then press the left button.

◆ The new column appears and all the columns that follow shift to the right.

DELETE A ROW OR COLUMN

You can delete a row or column from your worksheet. This lets you remove cells you no longer need.

DELETE A ROW

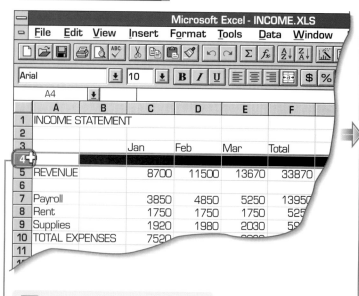

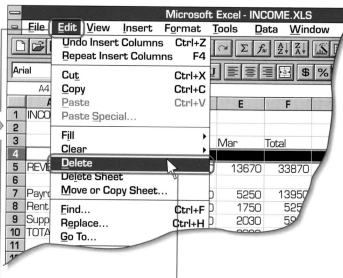

1 To select the row you want to delete, move the mouse ⊕ over the row heading (example: **row 4**) and then press the left button.

2 Move the mouse ⩘ over **Edit** and then press the left button.

3 Move the mouse ⩘ over **Delete** and then press the left button.

188

• Insert a Row or Column   • Change Column Width
• **Delete a Row or Column**   • Change Row Height

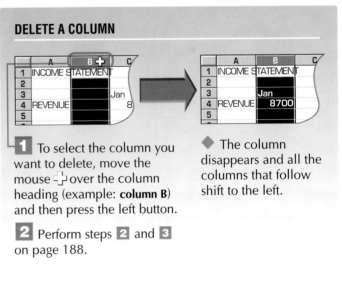

Tip

#REF!

If #REF! appears in a cell in your worksheet, you have deleted data needed to calculate a formula.

1 *To immediately cancel the deletion, move the mouse ⬚ over ▣ and then press the left button.*

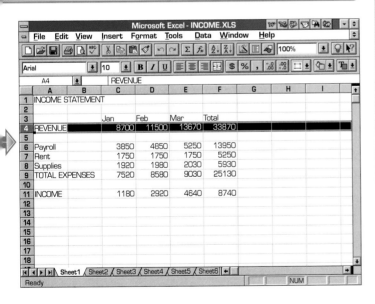

◆ The row disappears and all the rows that follow shift upward.

DELETE A COLUMN

1 To select the column you want to delete, move the mouse ⬚ over the column heading (example: **column B**) and then press the left button.

2 Perform steps **2** and **3** on page 188.

◆ The column disappears and all the columns that follow shift to the left.

CHANGE COLUMN WIDTH

You can improve the appearance of your worksheet and display hidden data by changing the width of columns.

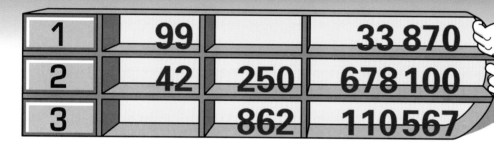

CHANGE COLUMN WIDTH

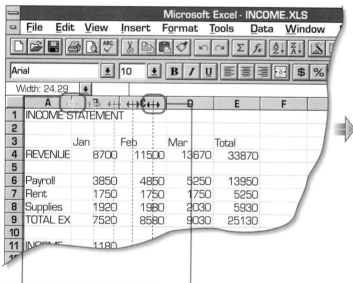

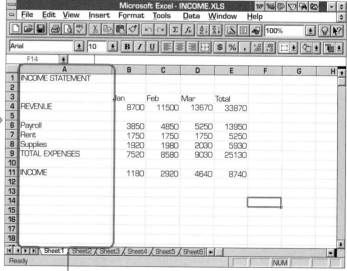

1 Move the mouse ⊕ over the right edge of the column heading you want to change (example: **column A**) and ⊕ changes to ↔.

2 Press and hold down the left button as you drag the edge of the column to a new position.

◆ A dotted line indicates the new column width.

3 Release the button and the new column width appears.

WORKING WITH ROWS AND COLUMNS

- Insert a Row or Column
- Delete a Row or Column
- **Change Column Width**
- Change Row Height

EXCEL

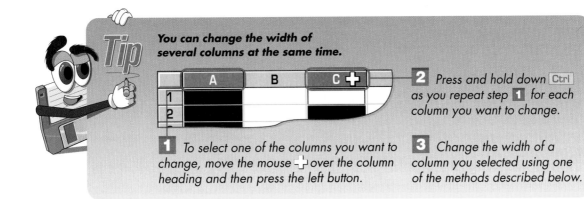

Tip

You can change the width of several columns at the same time.

1 To select one of the columns you want to change, move the mouse ⊹ over the column heading and then press the left button.

2 Press and hold down Ctrl as you repeat step **1** for each column you want to change.

3 Change the width of a column you selected using one of the methods described below.

CHANGE COLUMN WIDTH AUTOMATICALLY

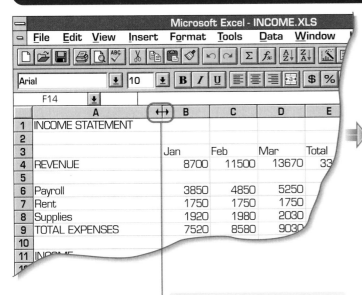

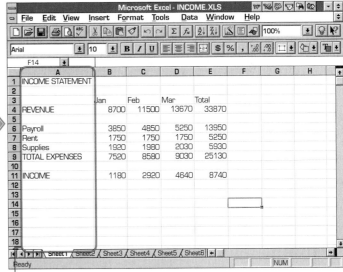

You can have Excel adjust the column width to fit the longest item in the column.

1 Move the mouse ⊹ over the right edge of the column heading you want to change (example: **column A**) and ⊹ changes to ↔ .

2 Quickly press the left button twice.

◆ The column width changes to fit the longest item in the column.

CHANGE ROW HEIGHT

You can change the height of a row. This is useful if you want to add space between the rows of data in your worksheet.

CHANGE ROW HEIGHT

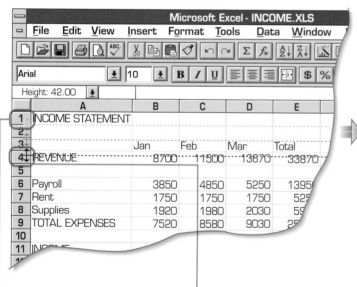

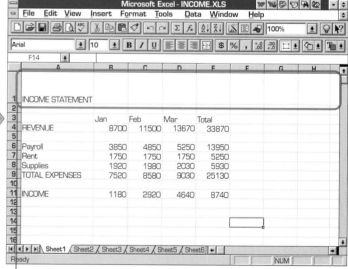

1 Move the mouse ⊹ over the bottom edge of the row heading you want to change (example: **row 1**) and ⊹ changes to ‡.

2 Press and hold down the left button as you drag the edge of the row to a new position.

◆ A dotted line indicates the new row height.

3 Release the button and the new row height appears.

- Insert a Row or Column
- Delete a Row or Column
- Change Column Width
- **Change Row Height**

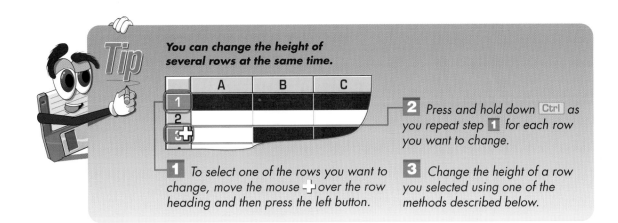

You can change the height of several rows at the same time.

2 Press and hold down Ctrl as you repeat step **1** for each row you want to change.

1 To select one of the rows you want to change, move the mouse ✛ over the row heading and then press the left button.

3 Change the height of a row you selected using one of the methods described below.

CHANGE ROW HEIGHT AUTOMATICALLY

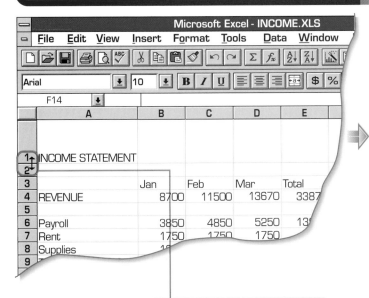

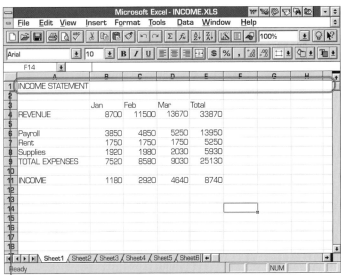

You can have Excel adjust the row height to fit the tallest item in the row.

1 Move the mouse ✛ over the bottom edge of the row heading you want to change (example: **row 1**) and ✛ changes to ✚.

2 Quickly press the left button twice.

◆ The row height changes to fit the tallest item in the row.

CHANGE APPEARANCE OF NUMBERS

You can change the appearance of numbers in your worksheet without retyping them. This can make the numbers easier to understand.

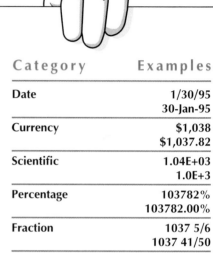

Category	Examples
Date	1/30/95
	30-Jan-95
Currency	$1,038
	$1,037.82
Scientific	1.04E+03
	1.0E+3
Percentage	103782%
	103782.00%
Fraction	1037 5/6
	1037 41/50

CHANGE APPEARANCE OF NUMBERS

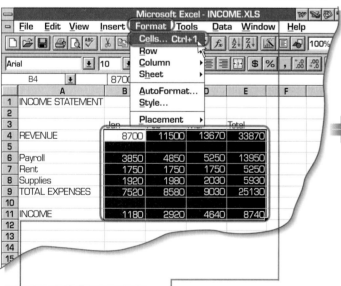

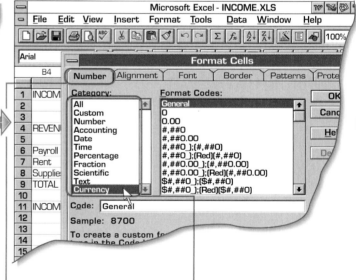

1 Select the cells containing the numbers you want to change.

Note: To select cells, refer to page 140.

2 Move the mouse ⩗ over **Format** and then press the left button.

3 Move the mouse ⩗ over **Cells** and then press the left button.

◆ The **Format Cells** dialog box appears.

4 Move the mouse ⩗ over the **Number** tab and then press the left button.

5 Move the mouse ⩗ over the category that contains the number style you want to use (example: **Currency**) and then press the left button.

*Note: If you do not know which category contains the style you want to use, select **All**. This will display a list of all the styles.*

• **Change Appearance of Numbers**
• Align Data
• Center Data Across Columns
• Bold, Italic and Underline

• Clear Formats
• Change Fonts
• Add Borders
• Format a Worksheet Automatically

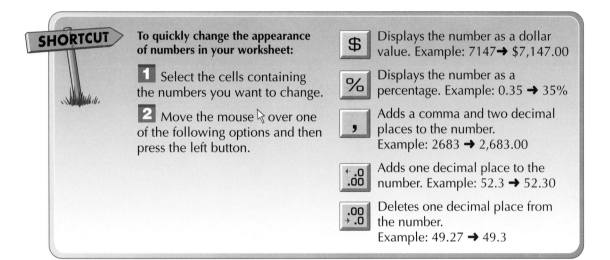

SHORTCUT

To quickly change the appearance of numbers in your worksheet:

1 Select the cells containing the numbers you want to change.

2 Move the mouse ⌖ over one of the following options and then press the left button.

$ Displays the number as a dollar value. Example: 7147➜ $7,147.00

% Displays the number as a percentage. Example: 0.35 ➜ 35%

, Adds a comma and two decimal places to the number. Example: 2683 ➜ 2,683.00

.0 .00 Adds one decimal place to the number. Example: 52.3 ➜ 52.30

.00 .0 Deletes one decimal place from the number. Example: 49.27 ➜ 49.3

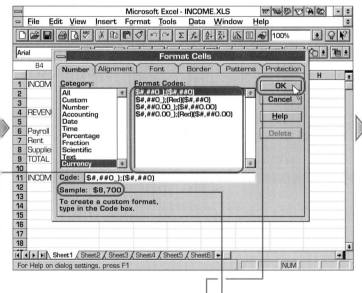

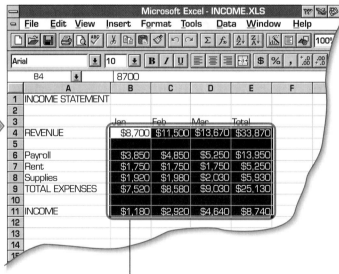

◆ This area displays the styles in the category you selected.

6 Move the mouse ⌖ over the style you want to use and then press the left button.

◆ This area displays a sample of the style you selected.

7 Move the mouse ⌖ over **OK** and then press the left button.

◆ The numbers in the cells you selected display the new style.

Note: If number signs (#) appear in a cell, the column is not wide enough to display the entire number. To change the column width, refer to page 190.

You can change the position of data in each cell of your worksheet. Excel offers several alignment options.

Data — Left Align

Data — Center

Data — Right Align

ALIGN DATA

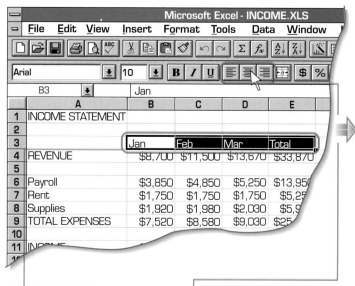

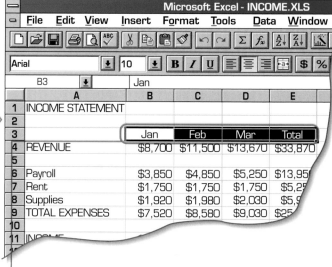

1 Select the cells containing the data you want to align.

Note: To select cells, refer to page 140.

2 Move the mouse over one of the options listed below and then press the left button.

▤ Left align data

▤ Center data

▤ Right align data

◆ The data in the cells you selected displays the new alignment.

Note: In this example, the data appears centered in the cells.

- Change Appearance of Numbers
- **Align Data**
- **Center Data Across Columns**
- Bold, Italic and Underline
- Clear Formats
- Change Fonts
- Add Borders
- Format a Worksheet Automatically

You can center data across columns in your worksheet. This is useful for displaying titles.

CENTER DATA ACROSS COLUMNS

1 Select the cells you want to center the data between.

2 Move the mouse ⊳ over ⊞ and then press the left button.

◆ Excel displays the data centered between the cells you selected.

Note: For best results, the first cell you select should contain the data you want to center.

You can use the Bold, Italic and Underline features to emphasize important data.

bold *italic* <u>underline</u>

BOLD, ITALIC AND UNDERLINE

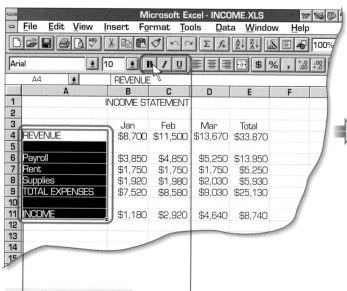

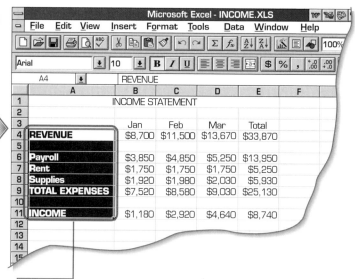

1 Select the cells containing the data you want to change.

Note: To select cells, refer to page 140.

2 Move the mouse ⟲ over one of the following options and then press the left button.

B Bold data

I Italicize data

<u>U</u> Underline data

◆ The data in the cells you selected appears in the new style.

Note: In this example, the data appears in the bold style.

Remove Bold, Italic or Underline

Repeat steps **1** and **2**.

198

- Change Appearance of Numbers
- Align Data
- Center Data Across Columns
- **Bold, Italic and Underline**
- **Clear Formats**
- Change Fonts
- Add Borders
- Format a Worksheet Automatically

If you have applied several formats to cells in your worksheet, you can quickly remove all the formatting at once.

CLEAR FORMATS

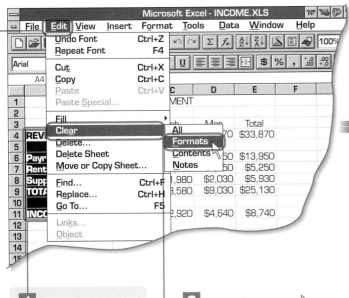

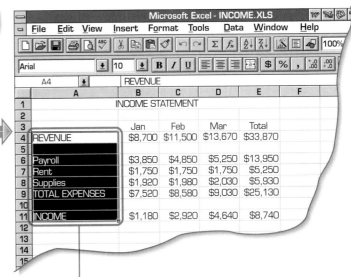

1 Select the cells displaying the formats you want to remove.

Note: To select cells, refer to page 140.

2 Move the mouse ⌖ over **Edit** and then press the left button.

3 Move the mouse ⌖ over **Clear** and then press the left button.

4 Move the mouse ⌖ over **Formats** and then press the left button.

◆ All formats disappear from the cells you selected. The data remains unchanged.

You can change the design and size of data in your worksheet to emphasize headings and make data easier to read.

CHANGE FONTS

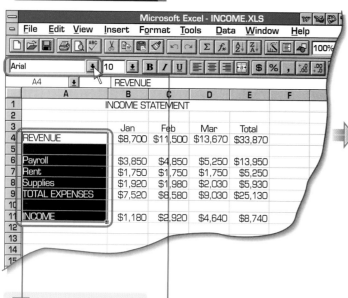

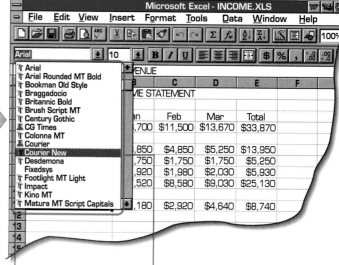

1 Select the cells containing the data you want to change to a new font.

Note: To select cells, refer to page 140.

◆ The **Font** box displays the font of the active cell (example: **Arial**).

2 To display a list of the available fonts, move the mouse ⟍ over ⬇ beside the **Font** box and then press the left button.

◆ A list of the available fonts for your computer appears.

3 Press ⬇ or ⬆ on your keyboard until you highlight the font you want to use (example: **Courier New**).

4 To select the highlighted font, press **Enter**.

• Change Appearance of Numbers
• Align Data
• Center Data Across Columns
• Bold, Italic and Underline
• Clear Formats
• **Change Fonts**
• Add Borders
• Format a Worksheet Automatically

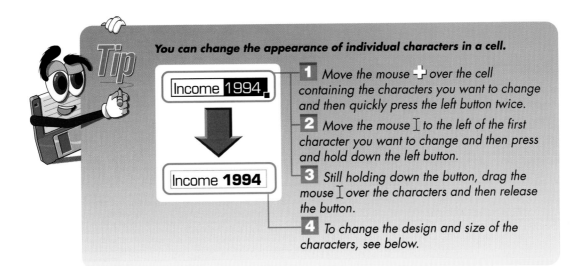

You can change the appearance of individual characters in a cell.

Income 1994

↓

Income **1994**

1 Move the mouse ✛ over the cell containing the characters you want to change and then quickly press the left button twice.

2 Move the mouse I to the left of the first character you want to change and then press and hold down the left button.

3 Still holding down the button, drag the mouse I over the characters and then release the button.

4 To change the design and size of the characters, see below.

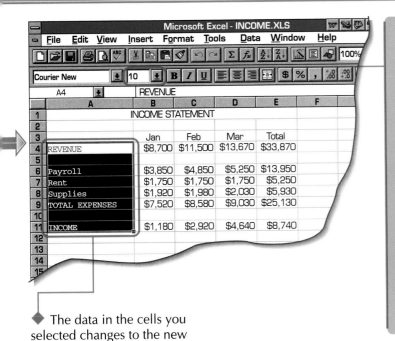

◆ The data in the cells you selected changes to the new font.

CHANGE FONT SIZE

You can increase or decrease the size of data in your worksheet.

1 Select the cells containing the data you want to change to a new font size.

Note: To select cells, refer to page 140.

2 Move the mouse ↕ over ⬇ beside the **Font Size** box and then press the left button. A list of the available font sizes appears.

3 Move the mouse ↕ over the font size you want to use (example: **16**) and then press the left button.

Note: Excel measures the size of data in points. There are approximately 72 points per inch.

CHANGE FONTS

You can change the design and size of data at the same time by using the Format Cells dialog box.

CHANGE FONTS

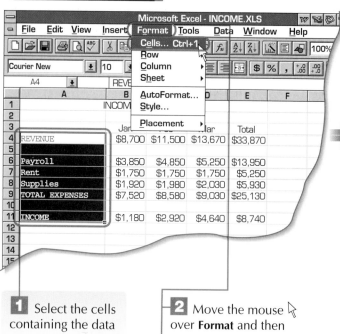

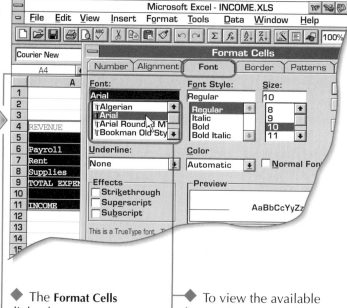

1 Select the cells containing the data you want to change.

Note: To select cells, refer to page 140.

2 Move the mouse over **Format** and then press the left button.

3 Move the mouse over **Cells** and then press the left button.

◆ The **Format Cells** dialog box appears.

4 Move the mouse over the **Font** tab and then press the left button.

◆ To view the available font options, move the mouse over ⬆ or ⬇ and then press the left button.

5 Move the mouse over the font you want to use (example: **Arial**) and then press the left button.

- Change Appearance of Numbers
- Align Data
- Center Data Across Columns
- Bold, Italic and Underline

- Clear Formats
- **Change Fonts**
- Add Borders
- Format a Worksheet Automatically

Tip

You can select an underline style in the Format Cells dialog box.

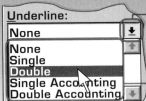

Underline:
None ⬇
None ⬆
Single
Double
Single Accounting
Double Accounting ⬇

1 To select an underline style, move the mouse ⬉ over ⬇ in the **Underline:** box and then press the left button.

2 Move the mouse ⬉ over the underline style you want to use and then press the left button.

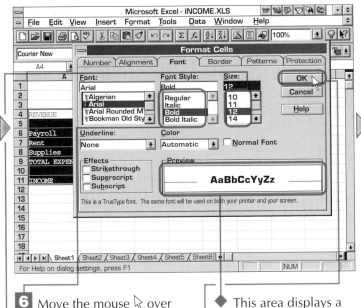

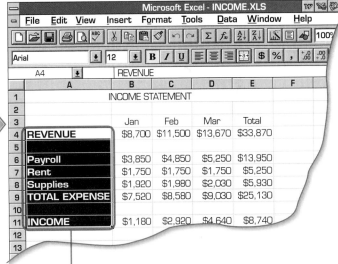

6 Move the mouse ⬉ over the font style you want to use (example: **Bold**) and then press the left button.

7 Move the mouse ⬉ over the font size you want to use (example: **12**) and then press the left button.

*Note: To select an underline style, see the **Tip** above.*

◆ This area displays a sample of the font you selected.

8 Move the mouse ⬉ over **OK** and then press the left button.

◆ The data in the cells you selected displays the font changes.

ADD BORDERS

You can add borders to draw attention to important data in your worksheet.

ADD BORDERS

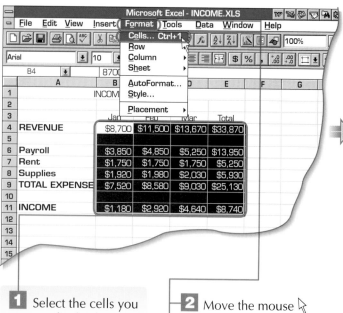

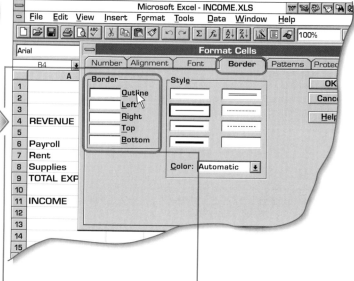

1 Select the cells you want to display borders.

Note: To select cells, refer to page 140.

2 Move the mouse over **Format** and then press the left button.

3 Move the mouse over **Cells** and then press the left button.

◆ The **Format Cells** dialog box appears.

4 Move the mouse over the **Border** tab and then press the left button.

5 Move the mouse over the border you want to add (example: **Outline**) and then press the left button.

- Change Appearance of Numbers
- Align Data
- Center Data Across Columns
- Bold, Italic and Underline
- Clear Formats
- Change Fonts
- Add Borders
- Format a Worksheet Automatically

EXCEL

SHORTCUT

To quickly add borders to cells in your worksheet:

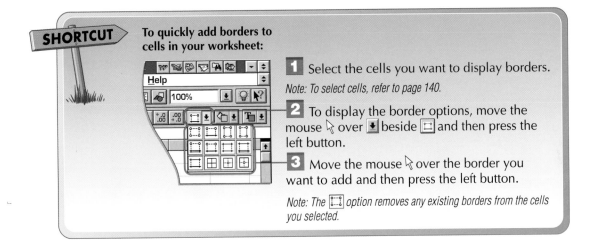

1 Select the cells you want to display borders.

Note: To select cells, refer to page 140.

2 To display the border options, move the mouse over ▼ beside ▦ and then press the left button.

3 Move the mouse over the border you want to add and then press the left button.

Note: The ▦ option removes any existing borders from the cells you selected.

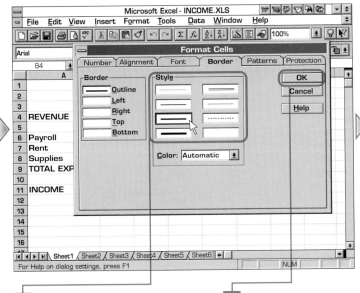

6 To select a line style for the border, move the mouse over the style and then press the left button.

7 Repeat steps **5** and **6** for each border you want to add.

8 Move the mouse over **OK** and then press the left button.

9 To view the borders, move the mouse outside the selected area and then press the left button.

◆ The cells display the borders.

205

Excel provides a selection of designs that you can choose from to quickly format your worksheet.

FORMAT A WORKSHEET AUTOMATICALLY

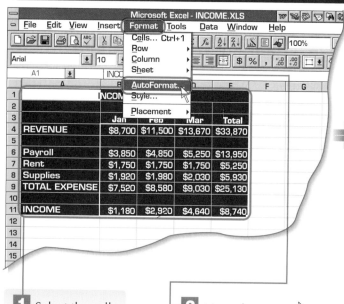

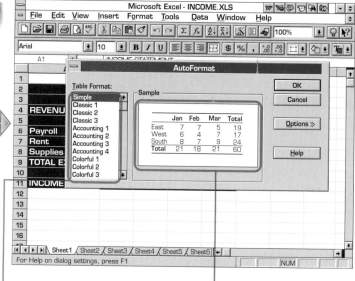

1 Select the cells you want to format.

Note: To select cells, refer to page 140.

2 Move the mouse over **Format** and then press the left button.

3 Move the mouse over **AutoFormat** and then press the left button.

◆ The **AutoFormat** dialog box appears.

◆ This area displays a list of the available designs.

◆ This area displays a sample of the highlighted design.

206

- Change Appearance of Numbers
- Align Data
- Center Data Across Columns
- Bold, Italic and Underline
- Clear Formats
- Change Fonts
- Add Borders
- **Format a Worksheet Automatically**

To remove an AutoFormat design from your worksheet:

1 Select the cells displaying the design you want to remove.

Note: To select cells, refer to page 140.

2 Perform steps **2** to **5** below, selecting **None** in step **4**.

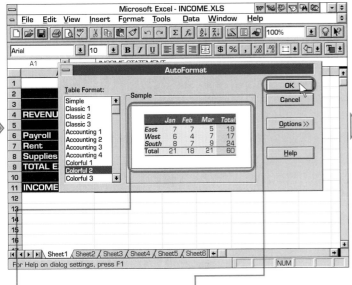

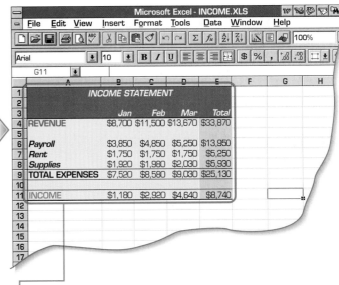

4 Press ⬇ or ⬆ on your keyboard until the **Sample** box displays the design you want to use (example: **Colorful 2**).

5 To select the design, move the mouse ⬀ over **OK** and then press the left button.

◆ Excel applies the design to the cells you selected.

Note: To deselect cells, move the mouse ⬐ over any cell in your worksheet and then press the left button.

The Print Preview feature lets you see on screen what your worksheet will look like when printed.

PREVIEW A WORKSHEET

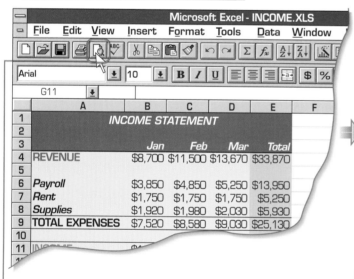

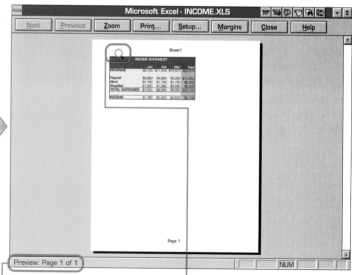

1 To display your worksheet in the Print Preview window, move the mouse over and then press the left button.

◆ The first page of your worksheet appears.

◆ The status bar at the bottom of your screen tells you which page you are viewing.

2 To magnify an area of the page, move the mouse over the area (changes to) and then press the left button.

• **Preview a Worksheet**   • Print a Worksheet
• **Change Margins**   • Add a Header or Footer

If your worksheet consists of more than one page,
you can use these buttons to switch between the
pages in the Print Preview window.

Next	Previous

◆ *To view the next*
page, move the mouse
over **Next** *and then press*
the left button.

◆ *To view the previous*
page, move the mouse
over **Previous** *and then*
press the left button.

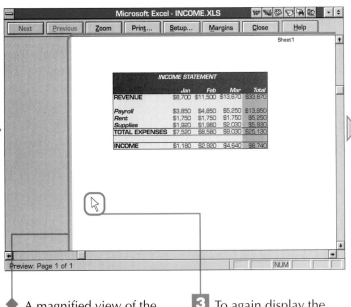

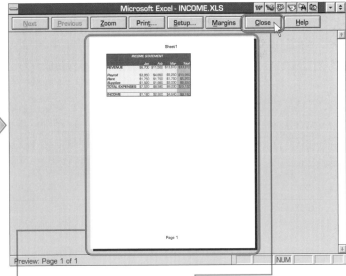

◆ A magnified view of the
area appears.

◆ To browse through the
page, press ↓, ↑, → or ←
on your keyboard.

3 To again display the
entire page, move the
mouse ⇖ anywhere over
the page and then press
the left button.

◆ The entire page
appears on your screen.

4 To close the Print
Preview window and return
to your worksheet, move the
mouse ⇖ over **Close** and then
press the left button.

CHANGE MARGINS

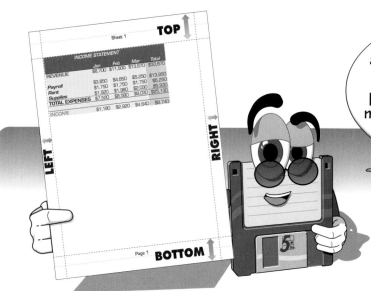

A margin is the amount of space between data and an edge of your paper. You can change the margins for your worksheet in the Print Preview window.

When you begin a worksheet, the top and bottom margins are set at 1 inch. The left and right margins are set at 0.75 inches.

CHANGE MARGINS

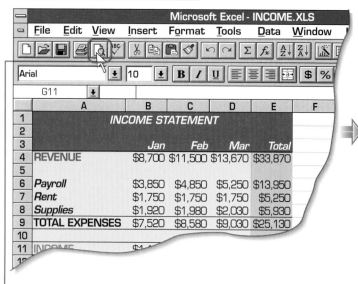

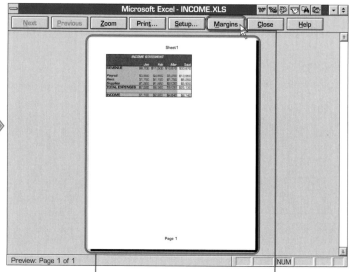

1 To display your worksheet in the Print Preview window, move the mouse ⌕ over 🔍 and then press the left button.

◆ The first page of your worksheet appears.

Note: For more information on using the Print Preview feature, refer to page 208.

2 To display the margins, move the mouse ⌕ over **Margins** and then press the left button.

Note: To hide the margins, repeat step **2**.

CHANGE COLUMN WIDTH

You can easily change the width of columns in the Print Preview window.

1 Perform steps **1** and **2** on page 210.

2 To change the width of a column, move the mouse ⟍ over the column handle and ⟍ changes to ↔.

3 Press and hold down the left button as you drag the column to a new width. Then release the button.

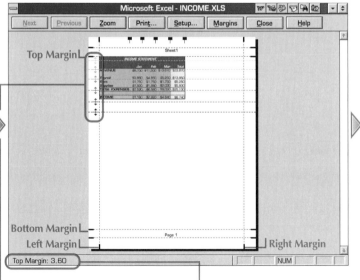

Top Margin
Bottom Margin
Left Margin
Right Margin
Top Margin: 3.60
Preview: Page 1 of 1

3 To change the position of a margin, move the mouse ⟍ over the margin handle and ⟍ changes to ↕ or ↔.

4 Press and hold down the left button as you drag the margin to a new location.

◆ A dotted line indicates the location of the new margin.

◆ The bottom of your screen displays the new measurement as you drag the margin.

5 Release the button to display the new margin.

6 To close the Print Preview window and return to your worksheet, move the mouse ⟍ over **Close** and then press the left button.

Note: Margins are only visible when you display your worksheet in the Print Preview window.

PRINT A WORKSHEET

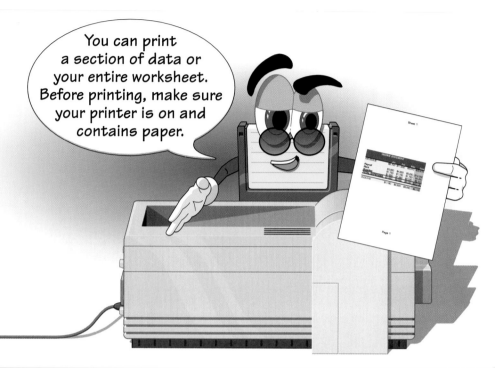

> You can print a section of data or your entire worksheet. Before printing, make sure your printer is on and contains paper.

PRINT A WORKSHEET

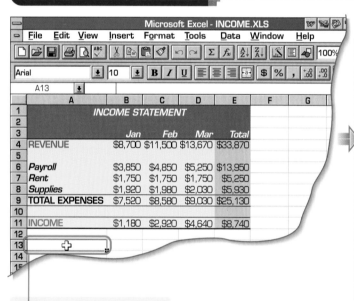

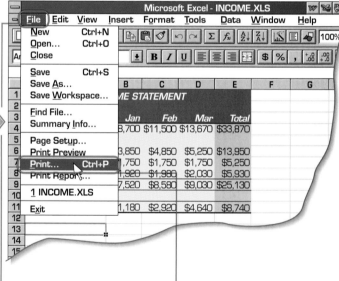

1 To print your entire worksheet, move the mouse ⊹ over any cell in the worksheet and then press the left button.

◆ To print a section of your worksheet, select the cells you want to print.

Note: To select cells, refer to page 140.

2 Move the mouse ⍉ over **File** and then press the left button.

3 Move the mouse ⍉ over **Print** and then press the left button.

◆ The **Print** dialog box appears.

- Preview a Worksheet
- Change Margins
- **Print a Worksheet**
- Add a Header or Footer

SHORTCUT

To quickly print your entire worksheet, move the mouse ⌕ over 🖨 and then press the left button.

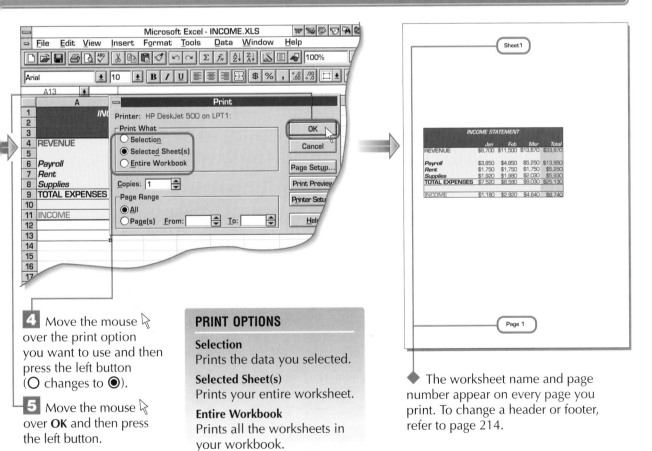

4 Move the mouse ⌕ over the print option you want to use and then press the left button (○ changes to ◉).

5 Move the mouse ⌕ over **OK** and then press the left button.

PRINT OPTIONS

Selection
Prints the data you selected.

Selected Sheet(s)
Prints your entire worksheet.

Entire Workbook
Prints all the worksheets in your workbook.

◆ The worksheet name and page number appear on every page you print. To change a header or footer, refer to page 214.

ADD A HEADER OR FOOTER

Headers and footers display information at the top and bottom of each page.

Sheet1

INCOME STATEMENT

Page 1

◆ Header

Excel automatically prints the name of the worksheet at the top of each page. You can change this header at any time.

◆ Footer

Excel automatically prints the page number at the bottom of each page. You can change this footer at any time.

ADD A HEADER OR FOOTER

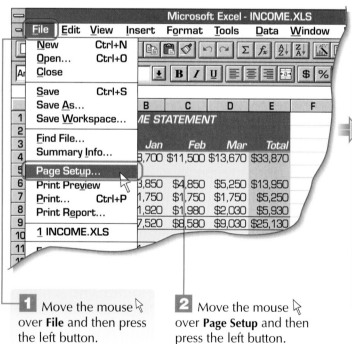

1 Move the mouse ⬚ over **File** and then press the left button.

2 Move the mouse ⬚ over **Page Setup** and then press the left button.

◆ The **Page Setup** dialog box appears.

3 Move the mouse ⬚ over the **Header/Footer** tab and then press the left button.

4 To create a header, move the mouse ⬚ over **Custom Header** and then press the left button.

◆ To create a footer, move the mouse ⬚ over **Custom Footer** and then press the left button.

214

• Preview a Worksheet   • Print a Worksheet
• Change Margins   • **Add a Header or Footer**

You can use these buttons to change the appearance of a header or footer or to add additional information. These buttons appear in both the Header and Footer dialog boxes.

 Inserts the page number.

 Inserts the total number of pages in your worksheet.

Inserts the current date.

A Displays the **Font** dialog box so you can format text you have selected.

Inserts the current time.

Inserts the name of the workbook.

Inserts the name of the worksheet.

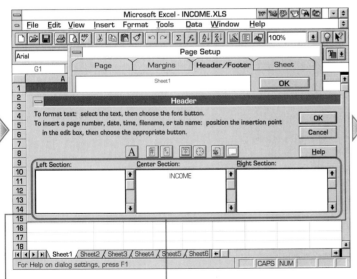

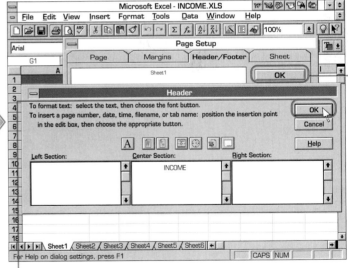

5 Move the mouse ☝ over the box under **Center Section:** and then press the left button.

6 To remove the existing text, press `Delete` or `◆Backspace` on your keyboard until the text disappears.

7 Move the mouse ☝ over the box for the area of the page where you want to display the header or footer (example: **Center Section:**) and then press the left button.

8 Type the text (example: **INCOME**).

9 Move the mouse ☝ over **OK** and then press the left button.

10 Move the mouse ☝ over **OK** in the **Page Setup** dialog box and then press the left button.

Note: Headers and footers are only visible when you display your worksheet in the ***Print Preview*** *window. For more information, refer to page 208.*

The worksheet displayed on your screen is part of a workbook. Like a three-ring binder, a workbook contains several sheets that you can easily flip through. This lets you view the contents of each worksheet.

SWITCH BETWEEN WORKSHEETS

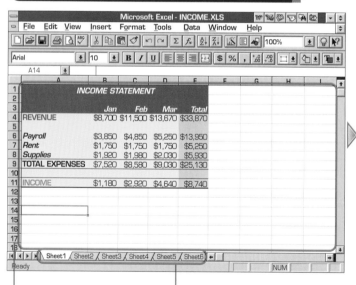

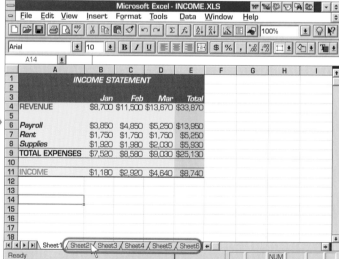

◆ The worksheet displayed on your screen is one of 16 worksheets in the current workbook.

◆ The current worksheet displays a white tab.

◆ The other worksheets display gray tabs.

◆ The contents of the current worksheet are displayed on your screen. The contents of the other worksheets are hidden behind this worksheet.

1 To display the contents of another worksheet, move the mouse ⌖ over the worksheet tab (example: **Sheet2**) and then press the left button.

- **Switch Between Worksheets**
- Copy or Move Data Between Worksheets
- Enter a Formula Across Worksheets

You can use the worksheets in a workbook to store related information. For example, you can store information for each division of a company on separate worksheets.

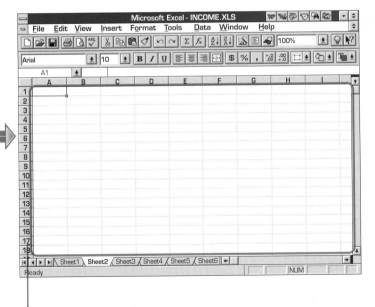

◆ The contents of the worksheet appear.

Excel cannot fit the names of all the worksheets at the bottom of your screen. You can use these buttons to display the other worksheet tabs.

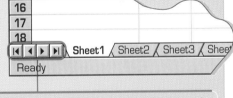

To display the first worksheet tab, move the mouse ⬚ over ◄ and then press the left button.

To scroll left through the worksheet tabs, move the mouse ⬚ over ◄ and then press the left button.

To scroll right through the worksheet tabs, move the mouse ⬚ over ► and then press the left button.

To display the last worksheet tab, move the mouse ⬚ over ►I and then press the left button.

217

COPY OR MOVE DATA BETWEEN WORKSHEETS

Copying or moving data between worksheets saves you time when you are working in one worksheet and want to use data from another.

COPY OR MOVE DATA BETWEEN WORKSHEETS

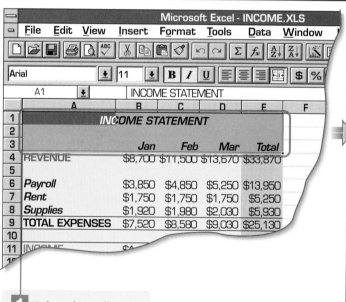

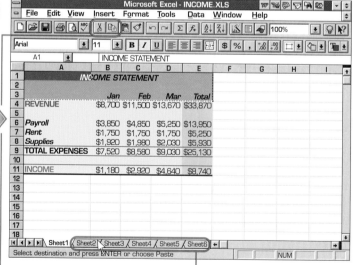

1 Select the cells containing the data you want to copy or move to another worksheet.

Note: To select cells, refer to page 140.

2 To copy the data, move the mouse ⌕ over 🖹 and then press the left button.

◆ To move the data, move the mouse ⌕ over ✂ and then press the left button.

3 Move the mouse ⌕ over the tab of the worksheet where you want to place the data and then press the left button.

The Copy and Move features both place data in a
new location, but they have one distinct difference.

COPY DATA

When you copy
data, the original data
remains in its place.

MOVE DATA

When you move
data, the original
data disappears.

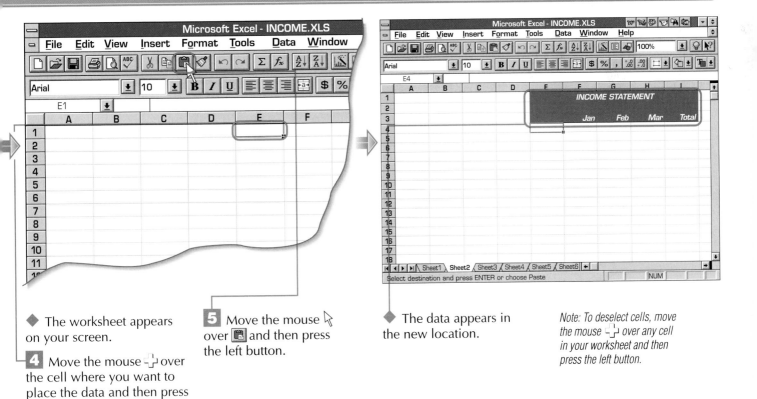

◆ The worksheet appears
on your screen.

4 Move the mouse ⊹ over
the cell where you want to
place the data and then press
the left button. This cell will
become the top left cell of
the new location.

5 Move the mouse ↖
over 🖺 and then press
the left button.

◆ The data appears in
the new location.

*Note: To deselect cells, move
the mouse ⊹ over any cell
in your worksheet and then
press the left button.*

219

ENTER A FORMULA ACROSS WORKSHEETS

You can enter a formula in one worksheet that uses data from other worksheets.

Sheet1

Sheet2

Sheet3

ENTER A FORMULA ACROSS WORKSHEETS

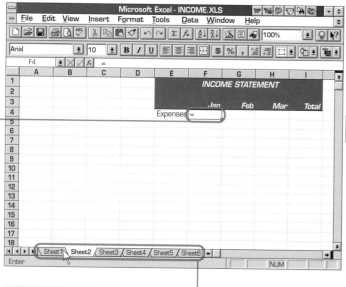

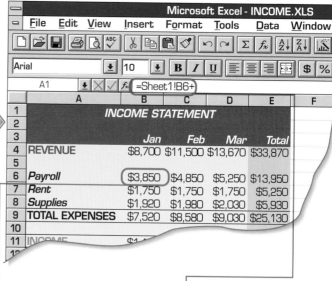

1 Move the mouse ⊕ over the cell where you want to display the result of the formula and then press the left button.

2 To begin the formula, type an equal sign (=).

3 Move the mouse � over the tab of the worksheet containing the data you want to use in the formula and then press the left button.

◆ The worksheet appears on your screen.

4 Move the mouse ⊕ over a cell containing the data you want to use in the formula (example: **B6**) and then press the left button.

5 Type an operator for the formula (example: +).

220

- Switch Between Worksheets
- Copy or Move Data Between Worksheets
- **Enter a Formula Across Worksheets**

The formula bar displays the worksheets and cells used to calculate a formula.

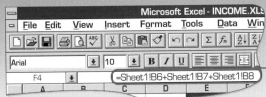

1 Move the mouse ✛ over the cell containing the formula and then press the left button.

◆ The formula bar displays the worksheet name and cell reference for each cell used in the formula.

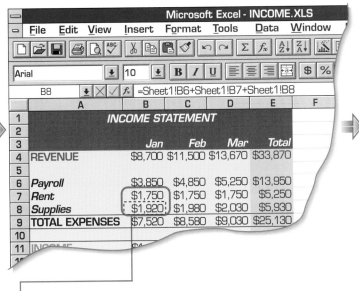

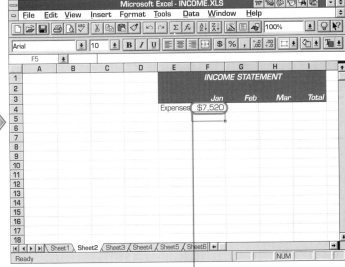

6 Repeat steps **3** to **5** until you have selected all the cells containing the data you want to use in the formula.

*Note: In this example, **Payroll**, **Rent** and **Supplies** for the month of January are added together.*

7 Press **Enter** on your keyboard to complete the formula.

◆ The result of the calculation appears.

221

CREATE A CHART

You can create a chart directly from your worksheet data. Excel provides a ChartWizard to lead you through each step.

CREATE A CHART

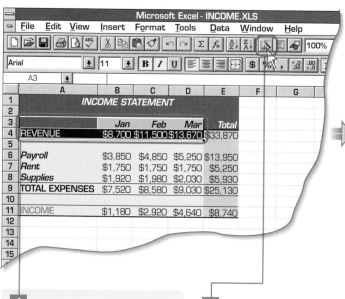

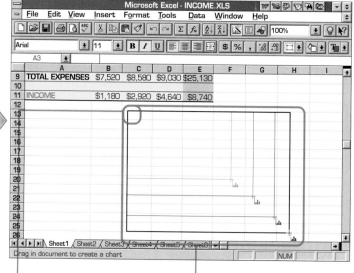

1 Select the cells containing the data you want to chart, including the row and column headings.

Note: To select cells, refer to page 140.

2 Move the mouse ⬚ over ⬚ and then press the left button (⬚ changes to ⁺ₗₗ).

3 Move the mouse ⁺ₗₗ over the location where you want the top left corner of the chart to appear.

4 Press and hold down the left button as you drag the mouse ⁺ₗₗ until the rectangle displays the size of the chart you want. Then release the button.

- **Create a Chart**
- Move a Chart
- Size a Chart
- Add a Data Series to a Chart

- Print a Chart
- Change Chart Type
- Format a Chart Automatically

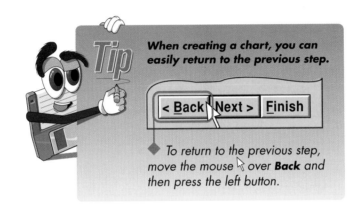

When creating a chart, you can easily return to the previous step.

◆ To return to the previous step, move the mouse ⬚ over **Back** and then press the left button.

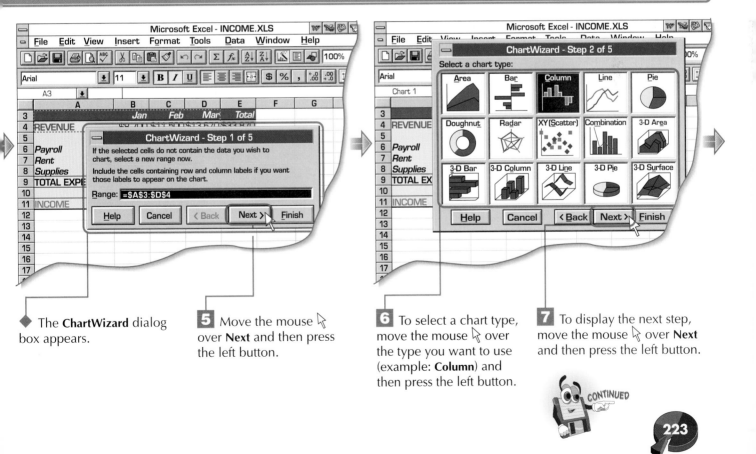

◆ The **ChartWizard** dialog box appears.

5 Move the mouse ⬚ over **Next** and then press the left button.

6 To select a chart type, move the mouse ⬚ over the type you want to use (example: **Column**) and then press the left button.

7 To display the next step, move the mouse ⬚ over **Next** and then press the left button.

CONTINUED

A chart lets you visually display your worksheet data.

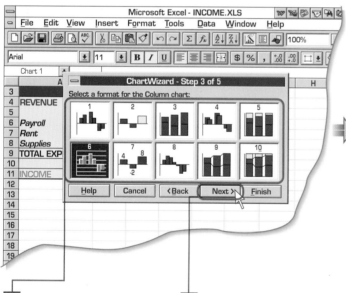

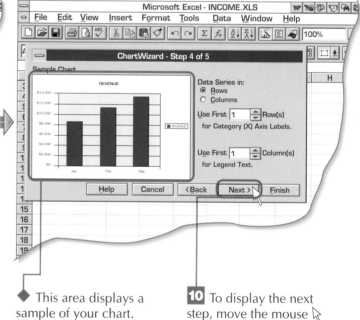

8 To select a format for the chart type you selected, move the mouse ⌖ over the format you want to use (example: **6**) and then press the left button.

9 To display the next step, move the mouse ⌖ over **Next** and then press the left button.

◆ This area displays a sample of your chart.

10 To display the next step, move the mouse ⌖ over **Next** and then press the left button.

- **Create a Chart**
- Move a Chart
- Size a Chart
- Add a Data Series to a Chart

- Print a Chart
- Change Chart Type
- Format a Chart Automatically

If you make changes to the data in your worksheet, Excel will automatically update the chart to reflect the changes.

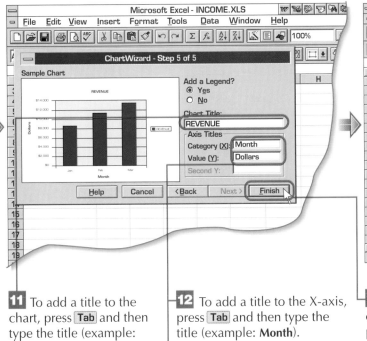

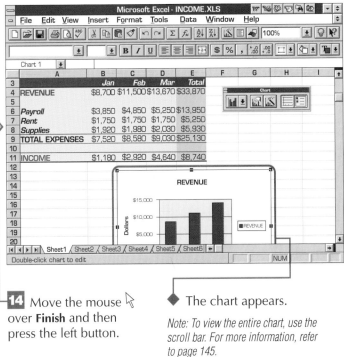

11 To add a title to the chart, press **Tab** and then type the title (example: **REVENUE**).

12 To add a title to the X-axis, press **Tab** and then type the title (example: **Month**).

13 To add a title to the Y-axis, press **Tab** and then type the title (example: **Dollars**).

14 Move the mouse over **Finish** and then press the left button.

◆ The chart appears.

Note: To view the entire chart, use the scroll bar. For more information, refer to page 145.

After you create a chart, you can move it to a more suitable location in your worksheet. You can also change the overall size of the chart.

MOVE A CHART

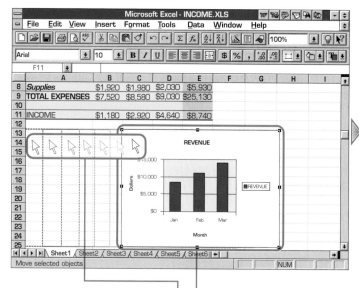

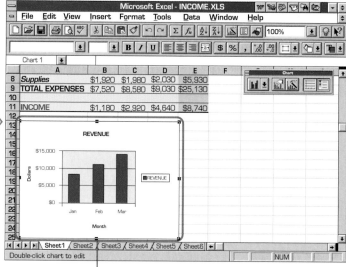

1 To deselect a chart, move the mouse ⊹ over any cell outside the chart and then press the left button.

2 To move a chart, move the mouse ↖ anywhere over the chart.

3 Press and hold down the left button as you drag the chart to a new location.

◆ A dotted box shows the new location.

4 Release the button and the chart moves to the new location.

- Create a Chart
- **Move a Chart**
- **Size a Chart**
- Add a Data Series to a Chart

- Print a Chart
- Change Chart Type
- Format a Chart Automatically

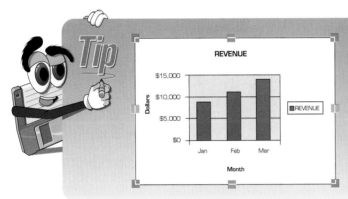

You can change the size of a chart using any handle around the chart.

█ You can use these handles to change the height of a chart.

█ You can use these handles to change the width of a chart.

█ You can use these handles to change the height and width of a chart at the same time.

SIZE A CHART

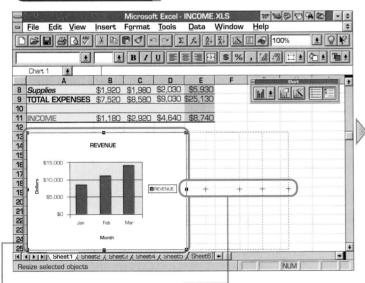

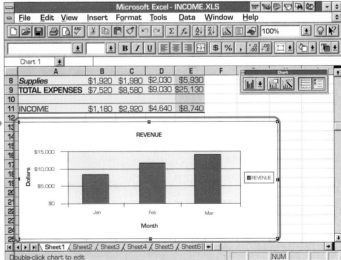

1 To deselect a chart, move the mouse ⌖ over any cell outside the chart and then press the left button.

2 Move the mouse ↳ anywhere over the chart and then press the left button. Handles (■) appear around the chart.

3 Move the mouse ↳ over one of the handles (■) and ↳ changes to ↔.

4 Press and hold down the left button as you drag the chart to the new size.

◆ A dotted box shows the new size.

5 Release the button and the chart displays the new size.

After you create a chart, you can easily add another data series.

A data series is a group of related data representing a row or column from your worksheet.

ADD A DATA SERIES TO A CHART

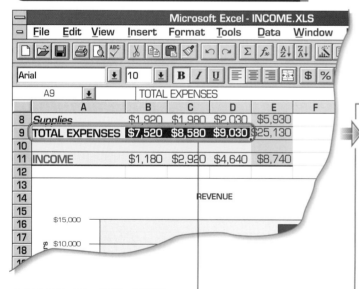

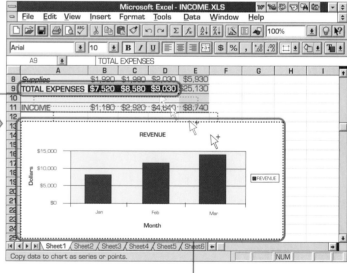

1 To deselect a chart, move the mouse over any cell outside the chart and then press the left button.

2 Select the cells containing the data you want to add to the chart.

Note: To select cells, refer to page 140.

3 Move the mouse over a border of the cells you selected (changes to) and then press and hold down the left button.

4 Still holding down the button, drag the mouse anywhere over the chart. Then release the button.

- Create a Chart
- Move a Chart
- Size a Chart
- **Add a Data Series to a Chart**

- Print a Chart
- Change Chart Type
- Format a Chart Automatically

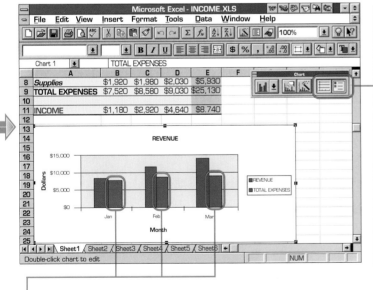

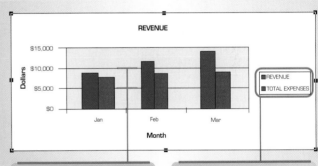

◆ The chart displays the new data series.

*Note: To display the **Chart** toolbar, refer to the **Tip** on page 233.*

GRIDLINES

You can quickly remove or add horizontal gridlines in your chart.

1 Move the mouse ↳ anywhere over the chart and then press the left button.

2 Move the mouse ↳ over 🟰 on the **Chart** toolbar and then press the left button.

LEGEND

You can quickly remove or add a legend in your chart.

1 Move the mouse ↳ anywhere over the chart and then press the left button.

2 Move the mouse ↳ over 🟰 on the **Chart** toolbar and then press the left button.

You can print your chart with the worksheet data or on its own page.

PRINT A CHART WITH WORKSHEET DATA

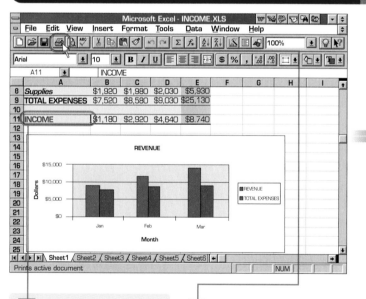

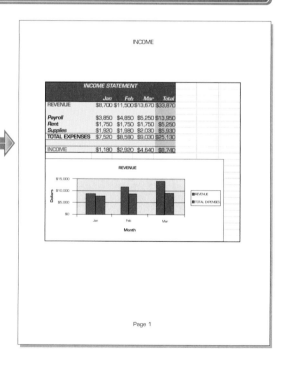

1 Move the mouse ✛ over any cell outside the chart and then press the left button.

2 Move the mouse ▷ over 🖨 and then press the left button.

- Create a Chart
- Move a Chart
- Size a Chart
- Add a Data Series to a Chart
- **Print a Chart**
- Change Chart Type
- Format a Chart Automatically

Tip

For more information on printing your worksheet data, refer to page 212.

PRINT A CHART ON ITS OWN PAGE

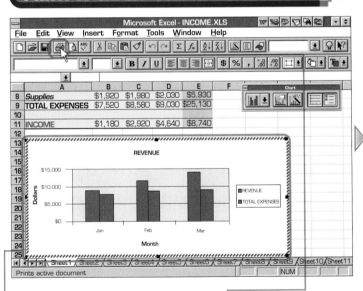

◆ To print a chart on its own page, you must first select the chart. A selected chart displays a colored border.

1 To select a chart, move the mouse anywhere over the chart and then quickly press the left button twice.

2 Move the mouse over and then press the left button.

After creating
a chart, you can
select a new type that
will better suit your
data.

CHANGE CHART TYPE

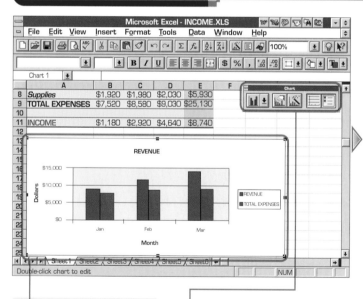

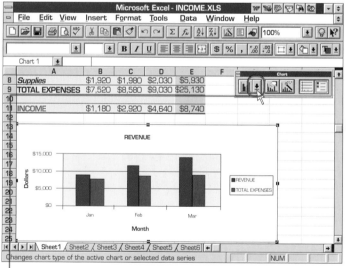

1 Move the mouse ⍟
anywhere over the chart
and then press the left
button.

◆ The **Chart** toolbar appears.

*Note: If the **Chart** toolbar does not
appear on your screen, refer to the **Tip**
on page 233.*

2 Move the mouse ⍟ over ⬇
on the **Chart** toolbar and then
press the left button.

- Create a Chart
- Move a Chart
- Size a Chart
- Add a Data Series to a Chart

- Print a Chart
- **Change Chart Type**
- Format a Chart Automatically

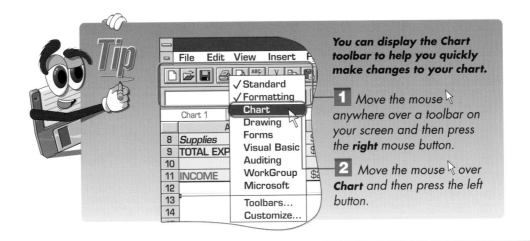

You can display the Chart toolbar to help you quickly make changes to your chart.

1 Move the mouse ↖ anywhere over a toolbar on your screen and then press the **right** mouse button.

2 Move the mouse ↖ over **Chart** and then press the left button.

(Menu shown: ✓Standard, ✓Formatting, Chart, Drawing, Forms, Visual Basic, Auditing, WorkGroup, Microsoft, Toolbars…, Customize…)

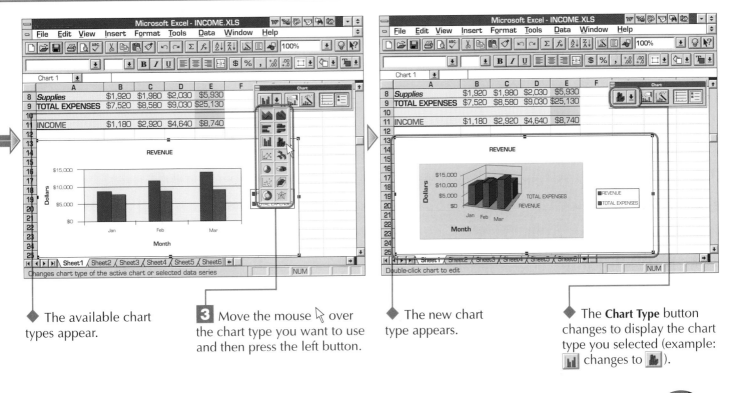

◆ The available chart types appear.

3 Move the mouse ↖ over the chart type you want to use and then press the left button.

◆ The new chart type appears.

◆ The **Chart Type** button changes to display the chart type you selected (example: 📊 changes to 📊).

233

The AutoFormat feature provides a selection of formats that you can choose from to enhance the appearance of your chart.

FORMAT A CHART AUTOMATICALLY

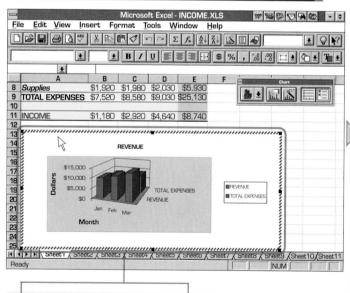

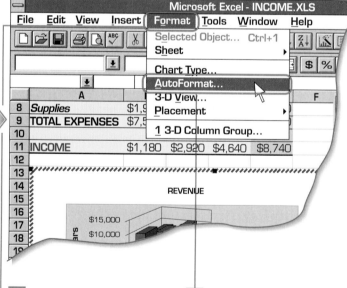

◆ You must first select the chart you want to format. A selected chart displays a colored border.

1 To select a chart, move the mouse ⬚ anywhere over the chart and then quickly press the left button twice.

2 Move the mouse ⬚ over **Format** and then press the left button.

3 Move the mouse ⬚ over **AutoFormat** and then press the left button.

- Create a Chart
- Move a Chart
- Size a Chart
- Add a Data Series to a Chart

- Print a Chart
- Change Chart Type
- **Format a Chart Automatically**

If you are not satisfied with the results of the AutoFormat feature, you can undo the changes.

1 To undo the AutoFormat immediately after applying the format, move the mouse ⊕ over 🔄 and then press the left button.

Note: For more information on the Undo feature, refer to page 161.

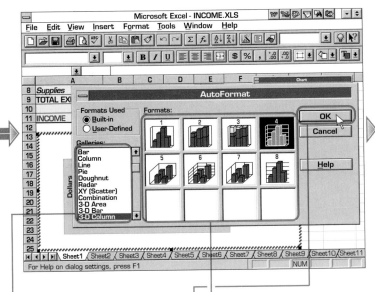

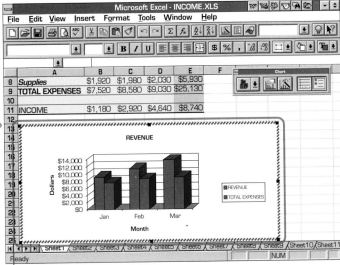

◆ The **AutoFormat** dialog box appears.

4 Move the mouse ⊕ over the chart type you want to use (example: **3-D Column**) and then press the left button.

5 Move the mouse ⊕ over the format you want to use (example: **4**) and then press the left button.

6 Move the mouse ⊕ over **OK** and then press the left button.

◆ Your chart displays the new formats.

POWERPOINT

Lorem Ipsum

- Dolot et ipsum no numi sit luxor ver ipsum no
  - luxor ver batim
    - no numi sit
    - ver batim
  - t ipsum no numi

- Etc cetra nobis pachem pronos no sib non compus mentus locus.

The Perfect Presentation

Mary Kurys

ABC Corporation

Microsoft® PowerPoint® helps you create, organize and design effective presentations.

1 ■ Selling Real Estate
   Mary Kurys
2 ❑ Objective
   ♦ State the desired objective
   ♦ Use multiple points if necessary
3 ❑ Customer Requirements
   ♦ State the needs of the audience
   ♦ Confirm the audience's needs if you are not sure
4 ❑ Meeting the Needs
   ♦ List the products and features, and how each addresses a specific need or solves a specific problem
   ♦ This section may require multiple slides
5 ■ Cost Analysis
   ♦ Point out financial benefits to the customer
   ♦ Compare cost-benefits between you and your competitors
6 ■ Our Strengths
7 ❑ Key Benefits
   ♦ Summarize the key benefits provided by the product, service, or idea being promoted
8 ❑ Next Steps
   ♦ Specify the actions required of your audience

OUTLINE

You can print an outline that contains just the text from your presentation. This lets you view the overall content of your presentation.

HANDOUTS

You can create handouts to help your audience follow your presentation. Handouts contain copies of your slides.

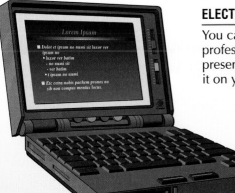

ELECTRONIC PRESENTATIONS

You can create a colorful, professional-looking presentation and then display it on your computer screen.

OVERHEADS

You can create overhead transparencies for your presentation.

SPEAKER'S NOTES

You can create speaker's notes to help you deliver your presentation. These notes contain copies of your slides with all the ideas you want to discuss.

35MM SLIDES

You can create 35mm slides for your presentation.

You can start PowerPoint to create a presentation.

START POWERPOINT

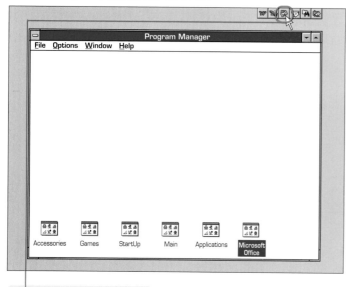

1 Move the mouse ⤢ over 🖳 and then press the left button.

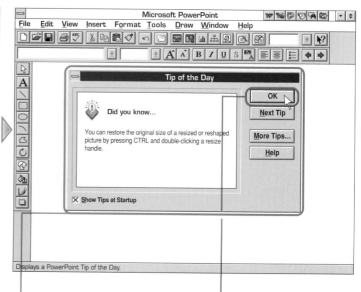

◆ When you start PowerPoint, the **Tip of the Day** dialog box appears. It displays a tip about using PowerPoint.

2 To close this dialog box, move the mouse ⤢ over **OK** and then press the left button.

- Introduction
- **Start PowerPoint**
- Getting Help

*To learn how to use the mouse or select commands, refer to the first section of this book, called **Introduction to Microsoft Office**, starting on page 4.*

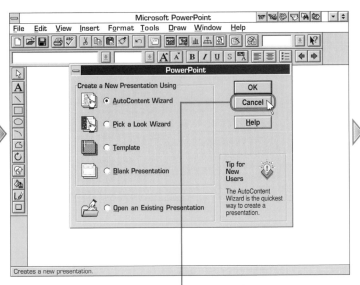

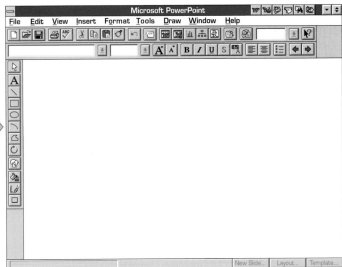

◆ The **PowerPoint** dialog box appears.

3 To close this dialog box, move the mouse ⬚ over **Cancel** and then press the left button.

◆ You can now use PowerPoint to create a presentation.

> If you forget how to perform a task, you can use the Help feature to obtain information. This can save you time by eliminating the need to refer to other sources.

GETTING HELP

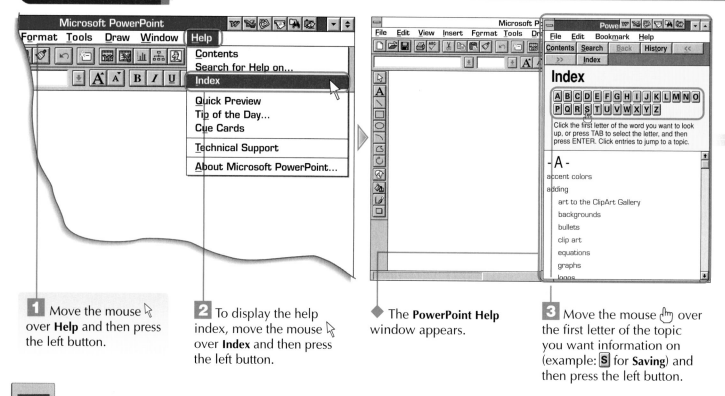

1 Move the mouse ⬚ over **Help** and then press the left button.

2 To display the help index, move the mouse ⬚ over **Index** and then press the left button.

◆ The **PowerPoint Help** window appears.

3 Move the mouse ⬚ over the first letter of the topic you want information on (example: **S** for **Saving**) and then press the left button.

EXIT HELP

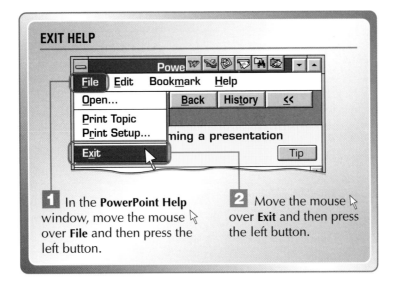

1 In the **PowerPoint Help** window, move the mouse ⌖ over **File** and then press the left button.

2 Move the mouse ⌖ over **Exit** and then press the left button.

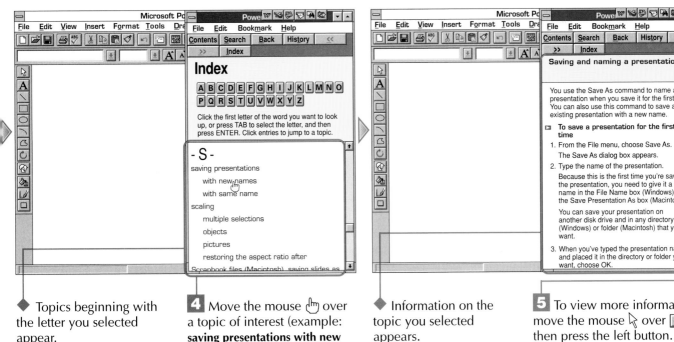
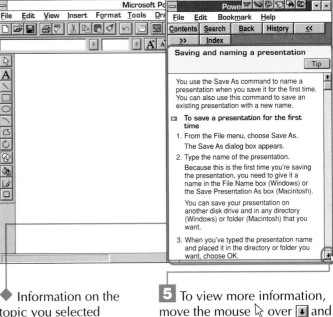

◆ Topics beginning with the letter you selected appear.

◆ To view more topics beginning with that letter, press **PageDown** on your keyboard.

4 Move the mouse 🖑 over a topic of interest (example: **saving presentations with new names**) and then press the left button.

◆ Information on the topic you selected appears.

5 To view more information, move the mouse ⌖ over ⬇ and then press the left button.

The AutoContent Wizard is the quickest way to create a new presentation. This Wizard provides a basic outline that you can personalize to suit your needs.

USING THE AUTOCONTENT WIZARD

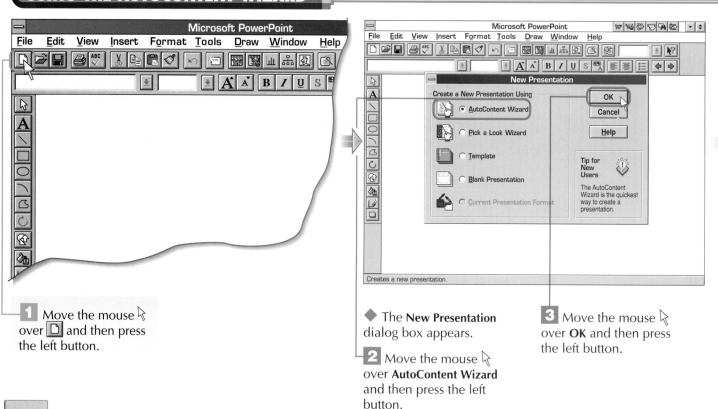

1 Move the mouse over the icon and then press the left button.

◆ The **New Presentation** dialog box appears.

2 Move the mouse over **AutoContent Wizard** and then press the left button.

3 Move the mouse over **OK** and then press the left button.

• **Using the AutoContent Wizard**
• Change Views
• Move Between Slides

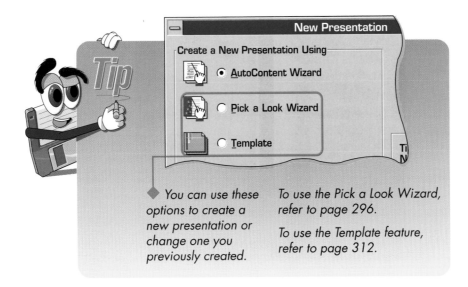

You can use these options to create a new presentation or change one you previously created.

To use the Pick a Look Wizard, refer to page 296.

To use the Template feature, refer to page 312.

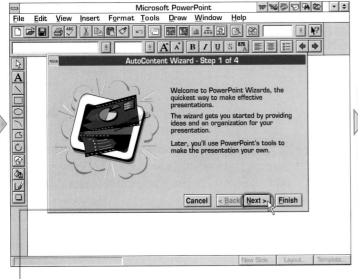

4 Move the mouse ⤢ over **Next** and then press the left button.

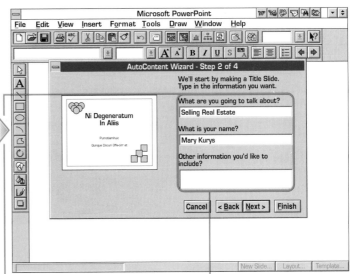

◆ The information you enter in this area will appear on the first slide in your presentation.

5 Type a title for your presentation. Then press **Tab** to move to the next box.

6 Type your name. Then press **Tab** to move to the next box.

CONTINUED

> The AutoContent Wizard provides a basic outline for six types of presentations.

Strategy
Sales
Training
Progress Report
Communicating Bad News
General

USING THE AUTOCONTENT WIZARD (CONTINUED)

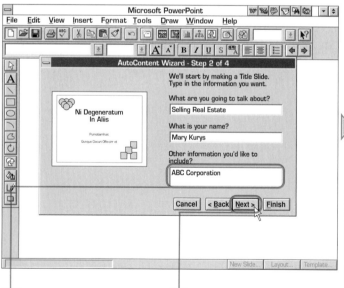

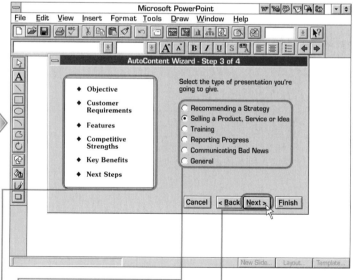

7 Type any other information you want to appear on the first slide.

8 Move the mouse ⬚ over **Next** and then press the left button.

9 Move the mouse ⬚ over the type of presentation you want to create and then press the left button (○ changes to ◉).

◆ This area displays the main topics for the presentation you selected.

10 Move the mouse ⬚ over **Next** and then press the left button.

- **Using the AutoContent Wizard**
- Change Views
- Move Between Slides

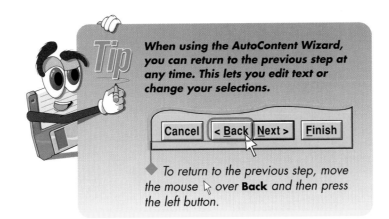

Tip

When using the AutoContent Wizard, you can return to the previous step at any time. This lets you edit text or change your selections.

| Cancel | < Back | Next > | Finish |

◆ *To return to the previous step, move the mouse over **Back** and then press the left button.*

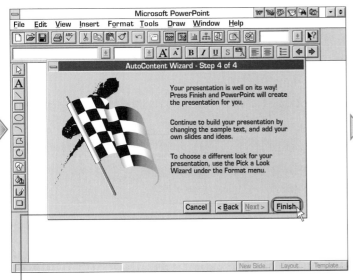

11 Move the mouse over **Finish** and then press the left button.

◆ A sample presentation appears.

◆ Cue Cards also appear, providing step-by-step instructions on how to perform tasks.

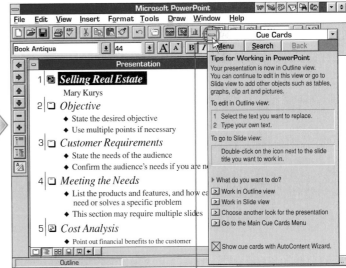

12 To remove the Cue Cards from your screen, move the mouse over ▭ and then quickly press the left button twice.

247

SLIDE VIEW

The Slide view displays one slide at a time, complete with text and graphics. You can use this view when changing the layout or design of your slides.

1 To change to the Slide view, move the mouse ⍾ over ▣ and then press the left button.

OUTLINE VIEW

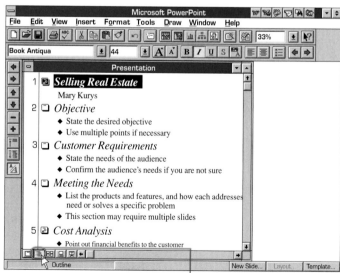

The Outline view displays the text for each slide. You can use this view to see the content of your entire presentation.

1 To change to the Outline view, move the mouse ⍾ over ▤ and then press the left button.

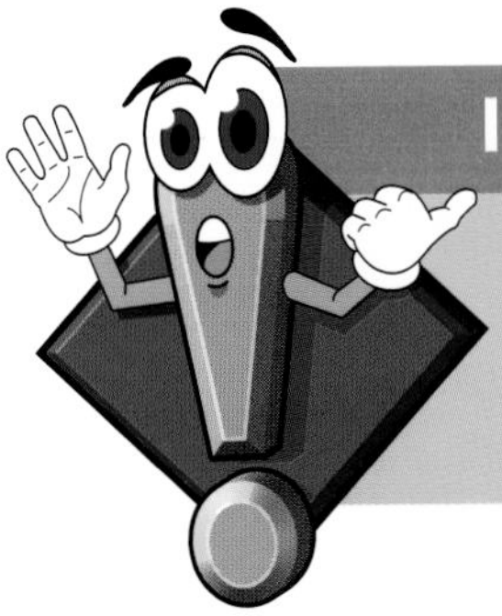

IMPORTANT!

All views display the same slides. If you change a slide in one view, the other views will also display the change.

SLIDE SORTER VIEW

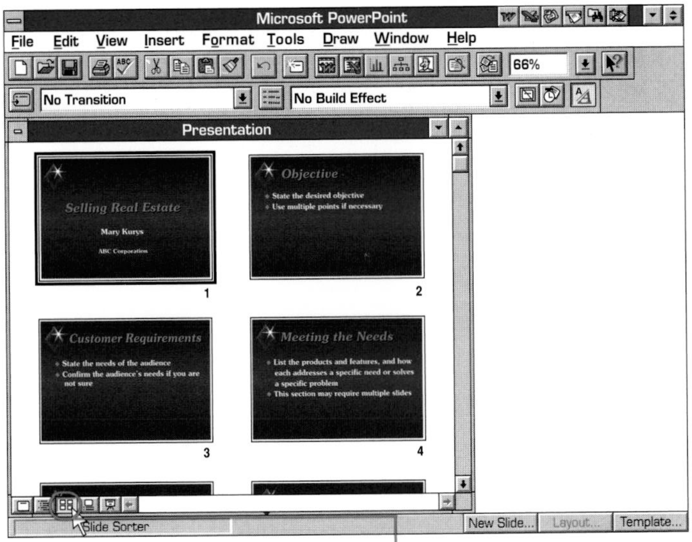

The Slide Sorter view displays a miniature version of each slide. You can use this view to see the order of your slides.

1 To change to the Slide Sorter view, move the mouse over and then press the left button.

NOTES PAGES VIEW

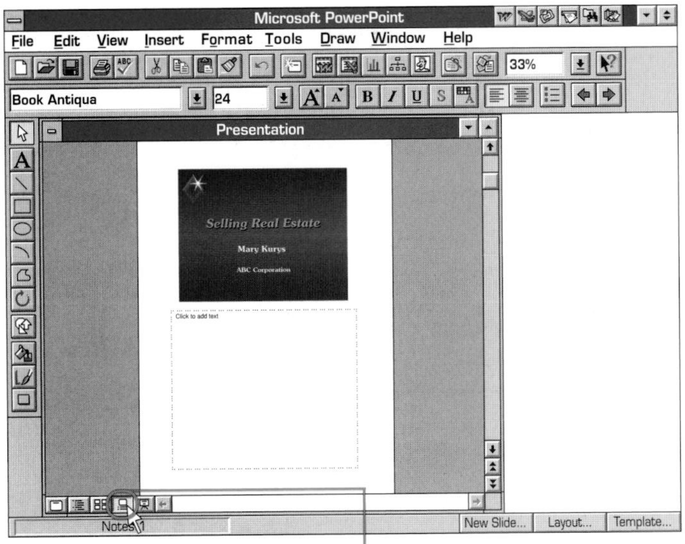

The Notes Pages view lets you add comments about each slide. You can use these comments as a guide when delivering your presentation.

1 To change to the Notes Pages view, move the mouse over and then press the left button.

MOVE BETWEEN SLIDES

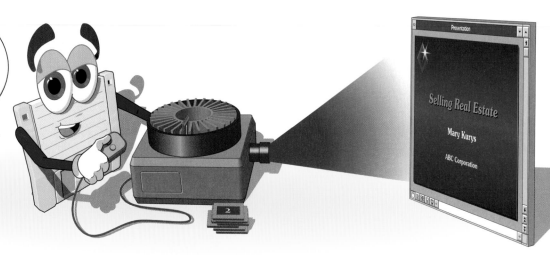

The Slide view displays one slide at a time. You can easily move between the slides.

SLIDE VIEW

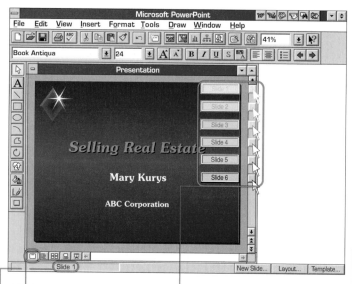

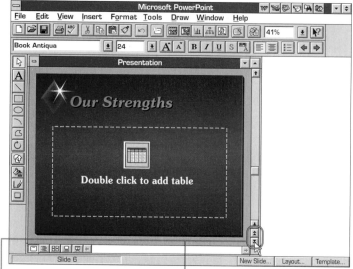

1 To change to the Slide view, move the mouse ⌖ over ▢ and then press the left button.

◆ This area displays the number of the slide displayed on your screen.

QUICKLY SCROLL DOWN

1 Move the mouse ⌖ over ▢ and then press and hold down the left button.

2 Still holding down the left button, drag the mouse ⌖ down the scroll bar until the number of the slide you want to display appears. Then release the button.

MOVE TO PREVIOUS SLIDE

◆ Move the mouse ⌖ over ▲ and then press the left button.

MOVE TO NEXT SLIDE

◆ Move the mouse ⌖ over ▼ and then press the left button.

• Using the AutoContent Wizard
• Change Views
• **Move Between Slides**

The Outline view displays the text for all of your slides. If the text extends beyond one screen, you can scroll up or down to view the hidden text.

OUTLINE VIEW

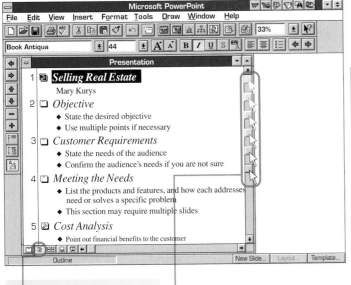

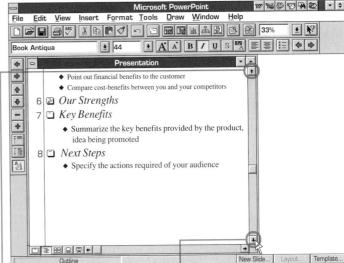

1 To change to the Outline view, move the mouse ⌖ over 🗐 and then press the left button.

QUICKLY SCROLL DOWN

1 Move the mouse ⌖ over ▯ and then press and hold down the left button.

2 Still holding down the left button, drag the mouse ⌖ down the scroll bar. Then release the button.

SCROLL UP ONE LINE

◆ Move the mouse ⌖ over ▲ and then press the left button.

SCROLL DOWN ONE LINE

◆ Move the mouse ⌖ over ▼ and then press the left button.

The Slide Sorter view displays many slides on your screen. If all the slides do not fit on your screen, you can scroll up or down to view the hidden slides.

SLIDE SORTER VIEW

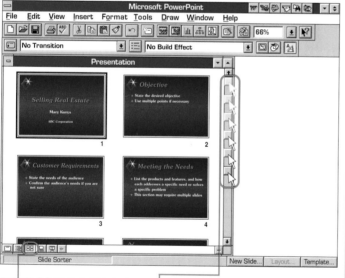

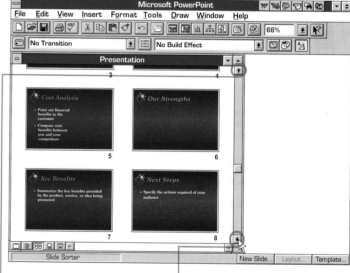

1 To change to the Slide Sorter view, move the mouse ⬚ over 🔲 and then press the left button.

QUICKLY SCROLL DOWN

1 Move the mouse ⬚ over ⬚ and then press and hold down the left button.

2 Still holding down the left button, drag the mouse ⬚ down the scroll bar. Then release the button.

SCROLL UP ONE LINE

◆ Move the mouse ⬚ over ⬆ and then press the left button.

SCROLL DOWN ONE LINE

◆ Move the mouse ⬚ over ⬇ and then press the left button.

The Notes Pages view displays one slide at a time. You can easily move between the slides.

NOTES PAGES VIEW

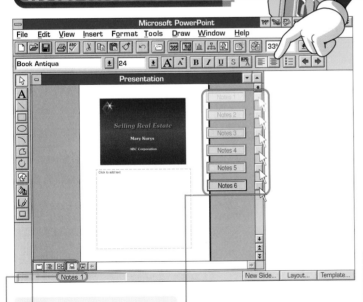

1 To change to the Notes Pages view, move the mouse over and then press the left button.

◆ This area displays the number of the slide displayed on your screen.

QUICKLY SCROLL DOWN

1 Move the mouse over and then press and hold down the left button.

2 Still holding down the left button, drag the mouse down the scroll bar until the number of the slide you want to display appears. Then release the button.

MOVE TO PREVIOUS SLIDE

◆ Move the mouse over and then press the left button.

MOVE TO NEXT SLIDE

◆ Move the mouse over and then press the left button.

253

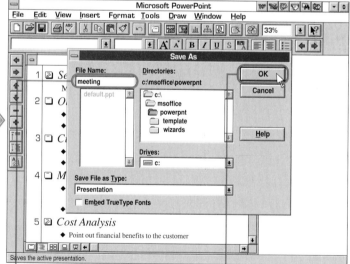

You should save your presentation to store it for future use. This lets you later retrieve the presentation for reviewing or editing purposes.

SAVE A PRESENTATION

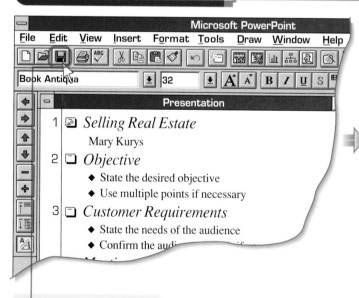

1 Move the mouse ⌀ over 🖫 and then press the left button.

◆ The **Save As** dialog box appears.

*Note: If you previously saved your presentation, the **Save As** dialog box will not appear since you have already named the presentation.*

2 Type a name for the presentation (example: **meeting**). The name can have up to eight characters.

*Note: To make it easier to find your presentation later on, do not type an extension. PowerPoint will automatically add the **ppt** extension to the name (example: **meeting.ppt**).*

3 Move the mouse ⌀ over **OK** and then press the left button.

◆ The **Summary Info** dialog box appears.

- **Save a Presentation**
- Close a Presentation
- Exit PowerPoint
- Open a Presentation

IMPORTANT!

You should save your presentation every 5 to 10 minutes to store any changes made since the last time you saved the presentation.

◆ To save changes, move the mouse ▷ over 🔲 and then press the left button.

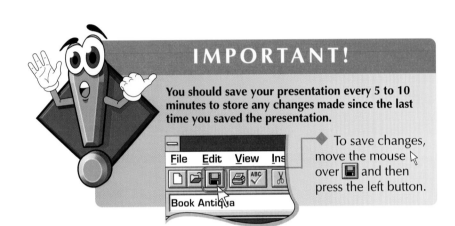

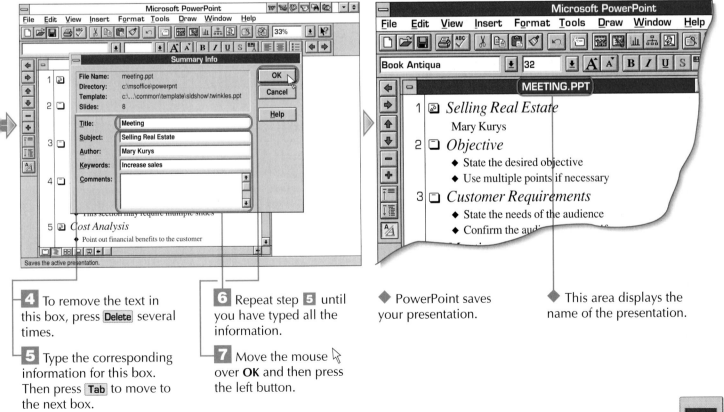

4 To remove the text in this box, press **Delete** several times.

5 Type the corresponding information for this box. Then press **Tab** to move to the next box.

6 Repeat step **5** until you have typed all the information.

7 Move the mouse ▷ over **OK** and then press the left button.

◆ PowerPoint saves your presentation.

◆ This area displays the name of the presentation.

> When you finish working with a presentation, you can close the presentation to remove it from your screen.

CLOSE A PRESENTATION

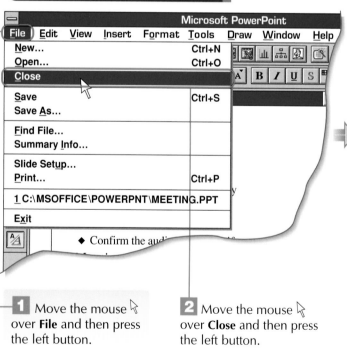

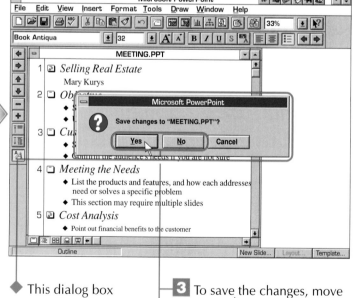

1 Move the mouse ⌖ over **File** and then press the left button.

2 Move the mouse ⌖ over **Close** and then press the left button.

◆ This dialog box appears if you have not saved changes made to your presentation.

3 To save the changes, move the mouse ⌖ over **Yes** and then press the left button.

◆ To close the presentation without saving the changes, move the mouse ⌖ over **No** and then press the left button.

256

• Save a Presentation   • **Exit PowerPoint**
• **Close a Presentation** • Open a Presentation

When you finish using PowerPoint, you can easily exit the program.

EXIT POWERPOINT

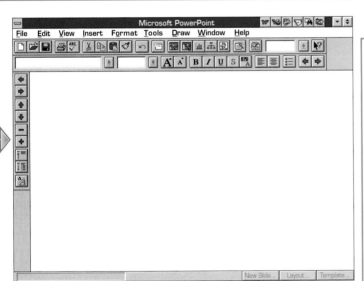

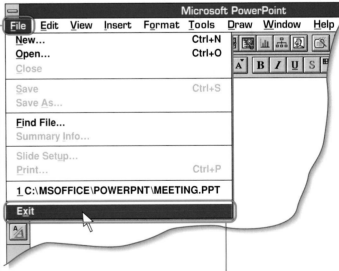

◆ The presentation disappears from your screen.

1 To save your presentation before exiting, refer to page 254.

2 Move the mouse ⟶ over **File** and then press the left button.

3 Move the mouse ⟶ over **Exit** and then press the left button.

Note: To restart PowerPoint, refer to page 240.

You can open a saved presentation and display it on your screen. This lets you review and edit the presentation.

OPEN A PRESENTATION

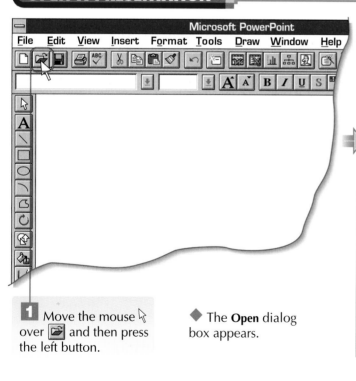

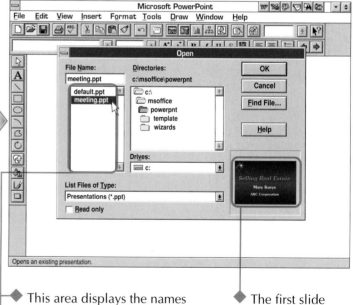

1 Move the mouse ⬐ over 🗁 and then press the left button.

◆ The **Open** dialog box appears.

◆ This area displays the names of the presentations you can open.

2 To view the first slide of a presentation in this list, move the mouse ⬐ over the name (example: **meeting.ppt**) and then press the left button.

◆ The first slide in the presentation appears.

- Save a Presentation
- Close a Presentation
- Exit PowerPoint
- **Open a Presentation**

POWERPOINT

SHORTCUT

The File menu displays the names of the last four presentations you opened.

Note: In this example, only one presentation has been opened.

File

New...	Ctrl+N
Open...	Ctrl+O
Close	
Save	Ctrl+S
Save As...	
Find File...	
Summary Info...	
Slide Setup...	
Print...	Ctrl+P
1 **C:\MSOFFICE\POWERPNT\MEETING.PPT**	
Exit	

To open one of the presentations listed:

1 Move the mouse ⌖ over **File** and then press the left button.

2 Move the mouse ⌖ over the name of the presentation you want to open and then press the left button.

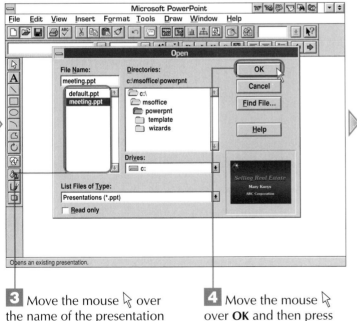

3 Move the mouse ⌖ over the name of the presentation you want to open and then press the left button.

4 Move the mouse ⌖ over **OK** and then press the left button.

◆ PowerPoint opens the presentation and displays it on your screen. You can now make changes to the presentation.

◆ This area displays the name of the presentation.

259

You can enlarge the presentation window to fill your screen. This lets you view more of your presentation.

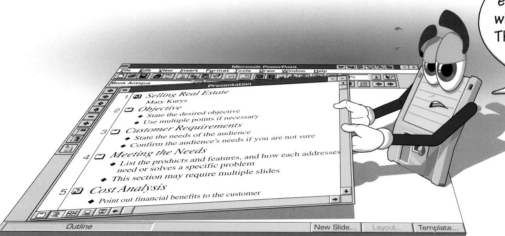

MAXIMIZE A WINDOW

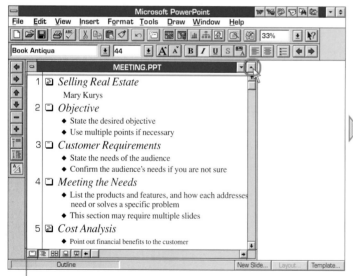

1 To enlarge the presentation window, move the mouse ⌖ over ▲ and then press the left button.

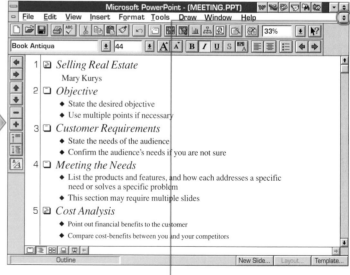

◆ The window enlarges to fill your screen.

RESTORE A WINDOW

1 To restore the window to its original size, move the mouse ⌖ over ⬍ and then press the left button.

260

- **Maximize a Window**
- **Show Titles**
- Select Text
- Delete Text
- Replace Text
- Undo Last Change
- Insert Text
- Move Text
- Check Spelling

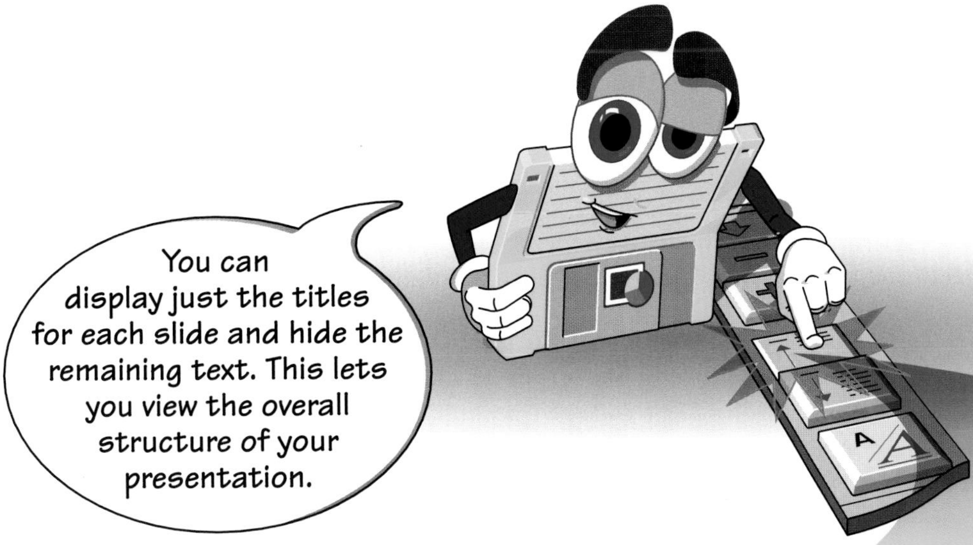
You can display just the titles for each slide and hide the remaining text. This lets you view the overall structure of your presentation.

SHOW TITLES

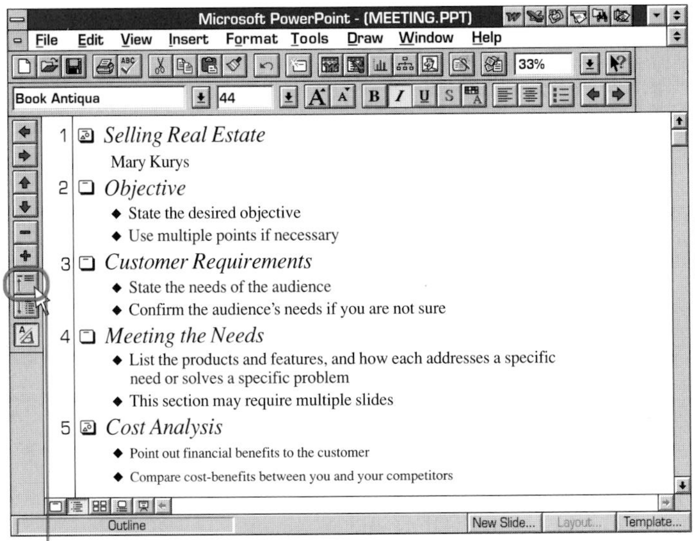
Microsoft PowerPoint - [MEETING.PPT]
File Edit View Insert Format Tools Draw Window Help
Book Antiqua
44
33%
1 Selling Real Estate
Mary Kurys
2 Objective
State the desired objective
Use multiple points if necessary
3 Customer Requirements
State the needs of the audience
Confirm the audience's needs if you are not sure
4 Meeting the Needs
List the products and features, and how each addresses a specific need or solves a specific problem
This section may require multiple slides
5 Cost Analysis
Point out financial benefits to the customer
Compare cost-benefits between you and your competitors
Outline
New Slide...
Layout...
Template...

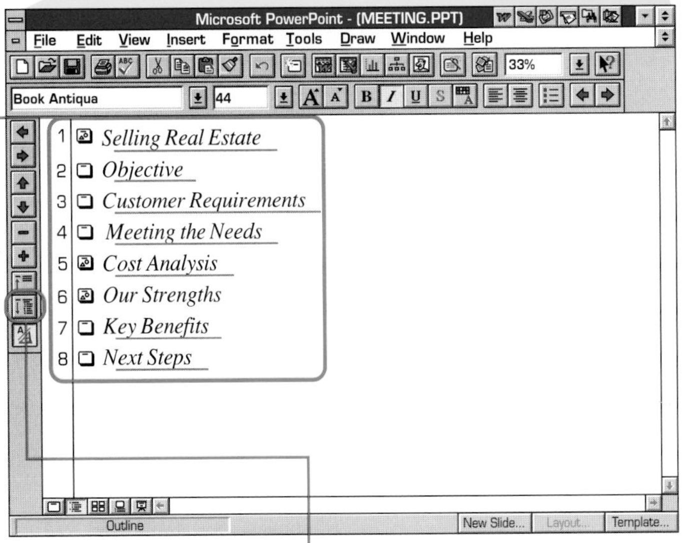
Microsoft PowerPoint - [MEETING.PPT]
File Edit View Insert Format Tools Draw Window Help
Book Antiqua
44
33%
1 Selling Real Estate
2 Objective
3 Customer Requirements
4 Meeting the Needs
5 Cost Analysis
6 Our Strengths
7 Key Benefits
8 Next Steps
Outline
New Slide...
Layout...
Template...

1 To show just the titles for the slides in your presentation, move the mouse over and then press the left button.

◆ PowerPoint shows only the titles for the slides.

◆ A gray line below a title indicates the text for the slide is hidden.

SHOW ALL

1 To again show the titles and the text for the slides, move the mouse over and then press the left button.

Before editing or changing the look of text in your presentation, you must select the text you want to work with. Selected text appears highlighted on your screen.

SELECT A WORD

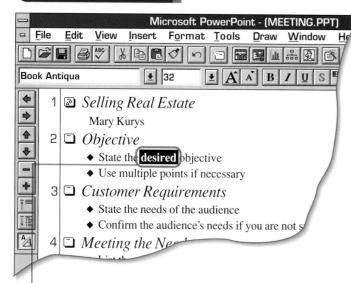

1 Move the mouse I over the word you want to select and then quickly press the left button twice.

Note: To cancel a text selection, move the mouse I outside the selected area and then press the left button.

SELECT ANY AMOUNT OF TEXT

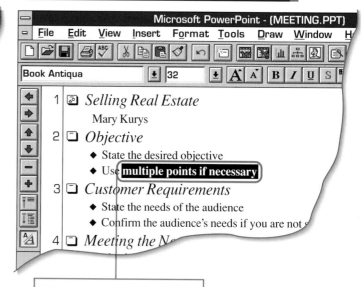

1 Move the mouse I over the first word you want to select.

2 Press and hold down the left button as you drag the mouse I over the text. Then release the button.

- Maximize a Window
- Show Titles
- **Select Text**
- Delete Text
- Replace Text
- Undo Last Change
- Insert Text
- Move Text
- Check Spelling

Tip

To select your entire presentation, press Ctrl + A.

SELECT A POINT

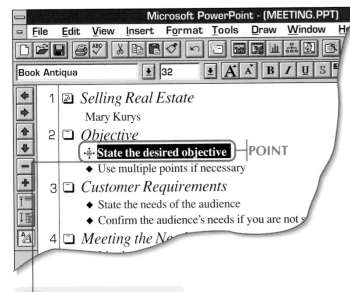

1 Move the mouse I over the symbol (◆) beside the point you want to select and I changes to ✛. Then press the left button.

SELECT AN ENTIRE SLIDE

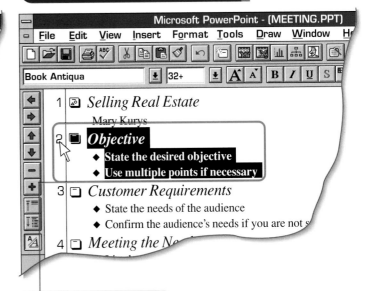

1 Move the mouse ⇖ over the number of the slide you want to select (example: **2**) and then press the left button.

You can delete text you no longer want to appear in your presentation.

DELETE A CHARACTER

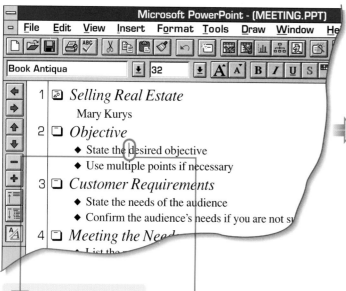

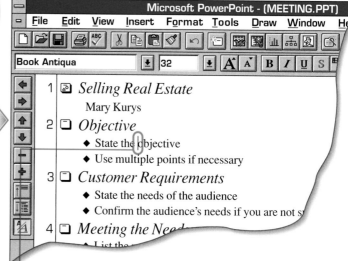

1 Move the mouse I to the left of the first character you want to delete and then press the left button.

◆ The flashing line moves to the location you selected. This line is called the **insertion point**.

2 Press Delete once for each character or space you want to remove (example: press Delete 8 times).

◆ You can also use +Backspace to remove characters. To do so, position the insertion point to the **right** of the first character you want to remove and then press +Backspace.

- Maximize a Window
- Show Titles
- Select Text
- **Delete Text**
- Replace Text
- Undo Last Change
- Insert Text
- Move Text
- Check Spelling

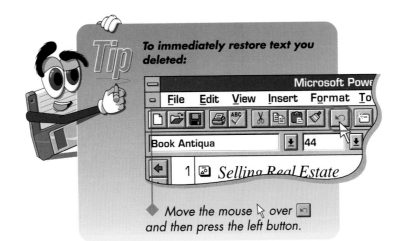

To immediately restore text you deleted:

◆ Move the mouse ⬚ over ↺ and then press the left button.

DELETE SELECTED TEXT

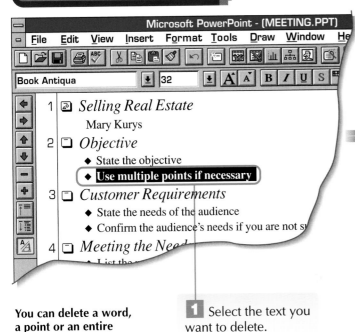

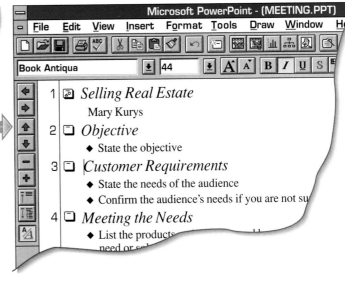

You can delete a word, a point or an entire slide.

1 Select the text you want to delete.

Note: To select text, refer to page 262.

2 Press **Delete** to remove the text.

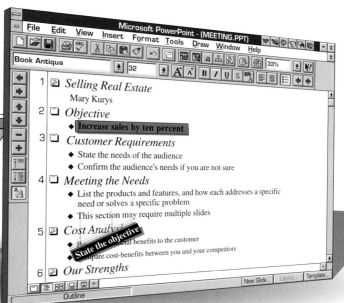

You can replace the text displayed on your screen with your own text.

REPLACE TEXT

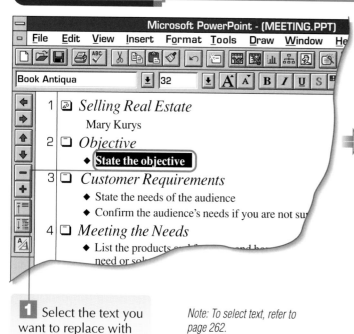

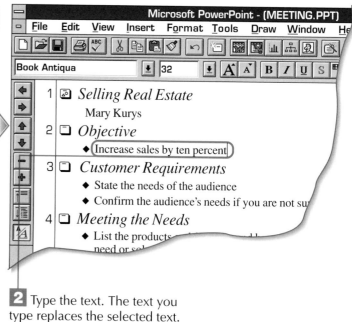

1 Select the text you want to replace with new text.

Note: To select text, refer to page 262.

2 Type the text. The text you type replaces the selected text.

- Maximize a Window
- Show Titles
- Select Text
- Delete Text
- **Replace Text**
- **Undo Last Change**
- Insert Text
- Move Text
- Check Spelling

PowerPoint remembers the last change you made to your presentation. If you regret this change, you can cancel it by using the Undo feature.

UNDO YOUR LAST CHANGE

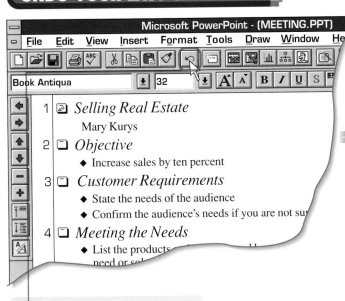

1 To cancel the last change you made to your presentation, move the mouse ⬦ over ↰ and then press the left button.

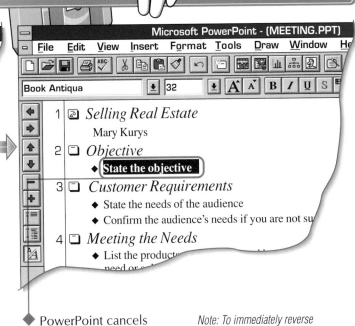

◆ PowerPoint cancels your last change.

Note: To immediately reverse the results of using the Undo feature, repeat step **1**.

267

PowerPoint makes it easy to add text to your presentations.

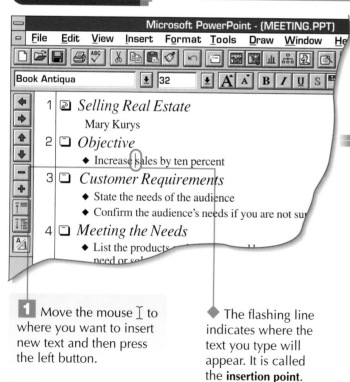

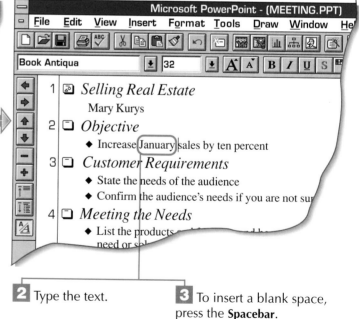

1 Move the mouse I to where you want to insert new text and then press the left button.

◆ The flashing line indicates where the text you type will appear. It is called the **insertion point**.

2 Type the text.

3 To insert a blank space, press the **Spacebar**.

Note: The words to the right of the new text are pushed forward.

- Maximize a Window
- Show Titles
- Select Text
- Delete Text
- Replace Text
- Undo Last Change
- **• Insert Text**
- Move Text
- Check Spelling

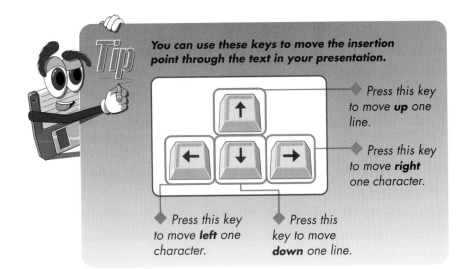

You can use these keys to move the insertion point through the text in your presentation.

◆ Press this key to move **up** one line.

◆ Press this key to move **right** one character.

◆ Press this key to move **left** one character.

◆ Press this key to move **down** one line.

INSERT A NEW POINT

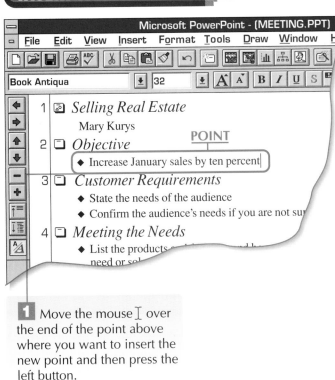

1 Move the mouse ⌶ over the end of the point above where you want to insert the new point and then press the left button.

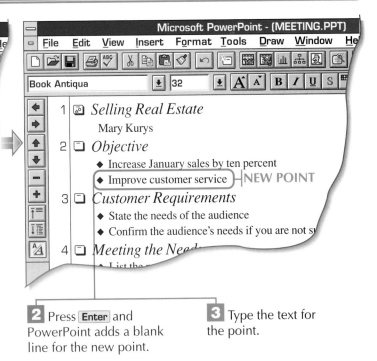

2 Press **Enter** and PowerPoint adds a blank line for the new point.

3 Type the text for the point.

269

You can move text from one location in your presentation to another. This lets you easily reorganize your ideas.

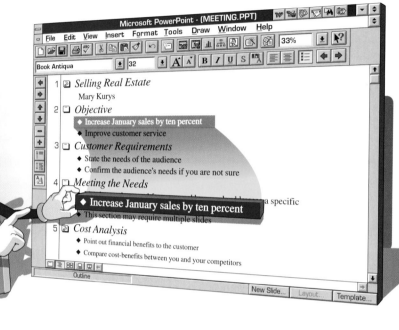

MOVE A POINT

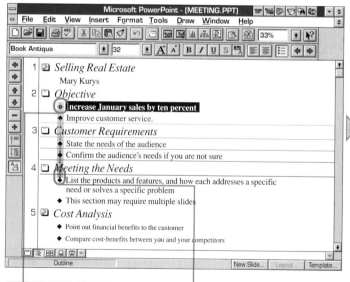

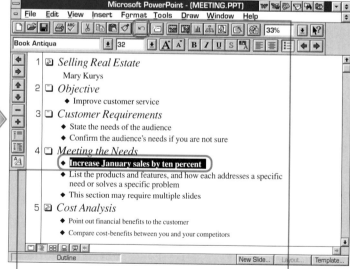

1 Move the mouse ╬ over the symbol (◆) beside the point you want to move.

2 Press and hold down the left button as you drag the mouse I to where you want to place the point.

◆ A black line indicates where the point will appear.

3 Release the left button and the point appears in the new location.

◆ To immediately cancel the move, position the mouse ⇖ over 🔄 and then press the left button.

- Maximize a Window
- Show Titles
- Select Text
- Delete Text
- Replace Text
- Undo Last Change
- Insert Text
- **Move Text**
- Check Spelling

You can also use the Slide Sorter view to change the order of your slides.

For more information, refer to page 317.

MOVE A SLIDE

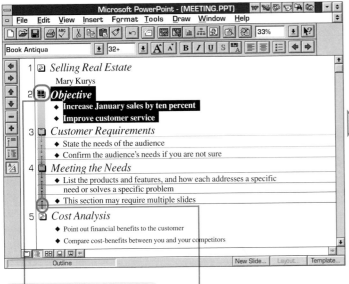

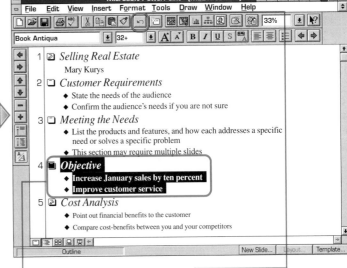

1 Move the mouse ✛ over the symbol (☐) beside the number of the slide you want to move.

2 Press and hold down the left button as you drag the mouse ↕ to where you want to place the slide.

◆ A black line indicates where the slide will appear.

3 Release the left button and the slide appears in the new location.

◆ To immediately cancel the move, position the mouse ↖ over ↶ and then press the left button.

You can use the Spelling feature to find and correct spelling errors in your presentation.

PowerPoint compares every word in your presentation to words in its own dictionary. If a word does not exist in the dictionary, PowerPoint considers it misspelled.

CHECK SPELLING

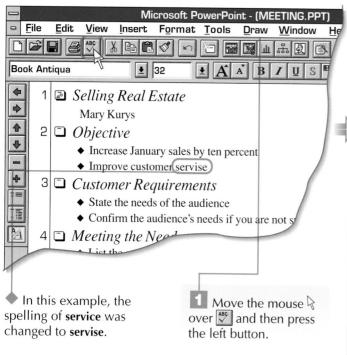

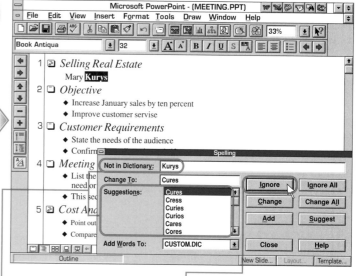

◆ In this example, the spelling of **service** was changed to **servise**.

1 Move the mouse over and then press the left button.

◆ The **Spelling** dialog box appears if PowerPoint finds a spelling error.

◆ PowerPoint displays the first word it does not recognize and suggestions to correct the error.

IGNORE MISSPELLED WORD

2 If you do not want to change the spelling of the word, move the mouse over **Ignore** and then press the left button.

- Maximize a Window
- Show Titles
- Select Text
- Delete Text
- Replace Text
- Undo Last Change
- Insert Text
- Move Text
- **Check Spelling**

The spell check will not find a correctly spelled word used in the wrong context.

Example:

The girl is **sit** years old.

You must review your presentation carefully to find this type of error.

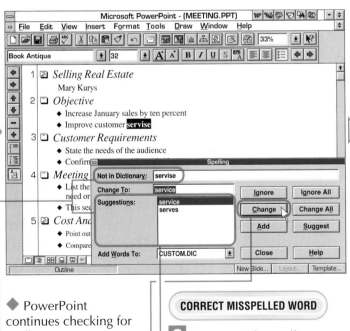

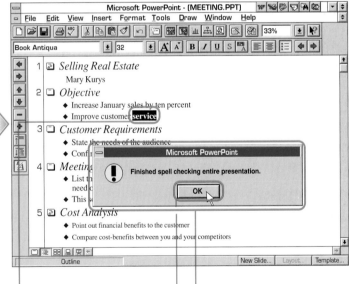

◆ PowerPoint continues checking for spelling errors.

◆ PowerPoint displays the next word it does not recognize and suggestions to correct the error.

CORRECT MISSPELLED WORD

3 To correct the spelling, move the mouse ⟋ over the word you want to use and then press the left button.

4 Move the mouse ⟋ over **Change** and then press the left button.

◆ PowerPoint corrects the word and continues checking for spelling errors.

5 Ignore or correct spelling errors until PowerPoint finishes checking your presentation.

◆ This dialog box appears when the spell check is complete.

6 To close the dialog box, move the mouse ⟋ over **OK** and then press the left button.

273

You can have PowerPoint arrange text and graphics on a slide for you.

Customer Requirements

CHANGE THE SLIDE LAYOUT

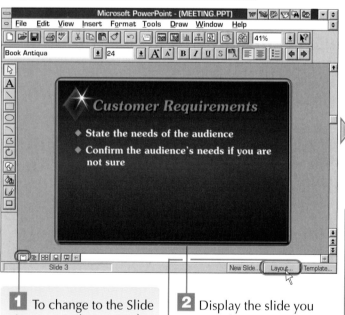

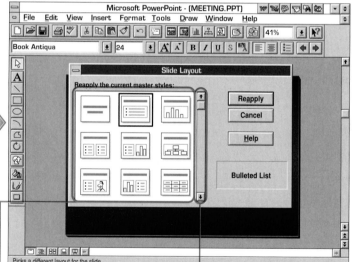

1 To change to the Slide view, move the mouse ⬚ over ⬚ and then press the left button.

2 Display the slide you want to change (example: slide 3).

Note: To move between slides, refer to page 250.

3 Move the mouse ⬚ over **Layout** and then press the left button.

◆ The **Slide Layout** dialog box appears.

◆ This area displays the available layouts.

◆ To browse through the available layouts, move the mouse ⬚ over ⬚ or ⬚ and then press the left button.

**Some layouts let you add objects
such as pictures and graphs to a slide.**

You can use these
layouts to add a clip
art image to a slide.

You can use these layouts
to add a graph to a slide.

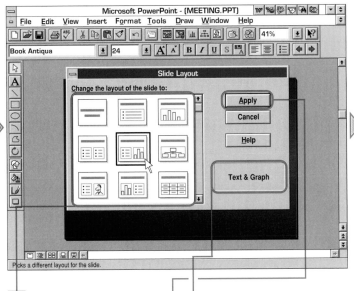

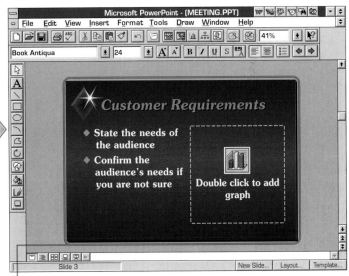

4 Move the mouse ⬚
over the layout you want
to apply to the slide and
then press the left button.

◆ This area displays the
items you can add to the
slide using the layout you
selected.

5 Move the mouse ⬚
over **Apply** and then press
the left button.

◆ The slide displays
the new layout.

You can add a new slide to your presentation at any time. This lets you add a new topic that you want to discuss.

ADD A NEW SLIDE

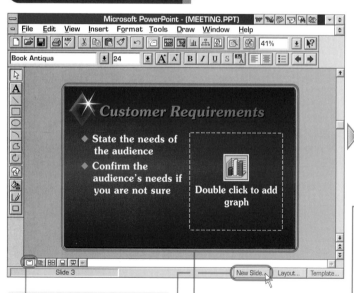

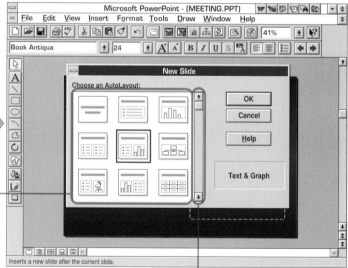

1 To change to the Slide view, move the mouse ⌖ over ▭ and then press the left button.

2 Display the slide you want to appear before the new slide (example: slide 3).

Note: To move between slides, refer to page 250.

3 Move the mouse ⌖ over **New Slide** and then press the left button.

◆ The **New Slide** dialog box appears.

◆ This area displays the available layouts for the new slide.

◆ To browse through the available layouts, move the mouse ⌖ over ▼ or ▲ and then press the left button.

- Change the Slide Layout
- Add a New Slide
- Add Clip Art
- Add an Organization Chart
- Add a Graph
- Change Graph Type

You can select a different layout for a slide at any time.

Note: For more information, refer to page 274.

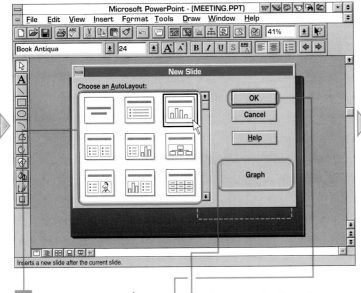

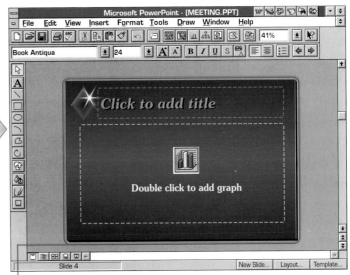

4 Move the mouse ⬚ over the layout you want to apply to the new slide and then press the left button.

◆ This area displays the items you can add to the slide using the layout you selected.

5 Move the mouse ⬚ over **OK** and then press the left button.

◆ The new slide appears, displaying the layout you selected.

277

ADD CLIP ART

PowerPoint provides hundreds of clip art images that you can add to your slides. These images will enhance your presentation.

Clip Art Image

ADD CLIP ART

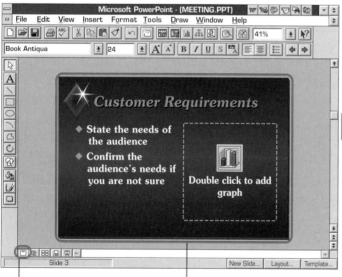

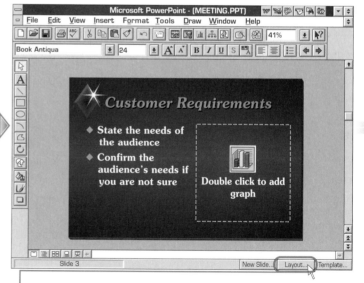

1 To change to the Slide view, move the mouse over ▭ and then press the left button.

2 Display the slide you want to add a clip art image to (example: slide 3).

Note: To move between slides, refer to page 250.

3 To change the layout of the slide, move the mouse over **Layout** and then press the left button.

- Change the Slide Layout
- Add a New Slide
- **Add Clip Art**
- Add an Organization Chart
- Add a Graph
- Change Graph Type

Tip

A clip art image is a professionally designed drawing that you can add to your slides. Clip art images can include such items as maps, cartoons or buildings.

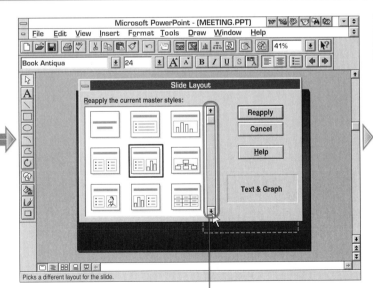

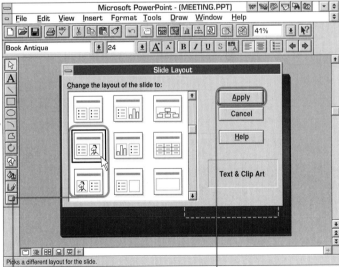

◆ The **Slide Layout** dialog box appears.

4 To browse through the available layouts, move the mouse ⬓ over ⬇ or ⬆ and then press the left button.

5 To add a clip art image to the slide, move the mouse ⬓ over one of these layouts and then press the left button.

6 Move the mouse ⬓ over **Apply** and then press the left button.

CONTINUED

Clip art images can make your presentation more interesting and entertaining.

ADD CLIP ART (CONTINUED)

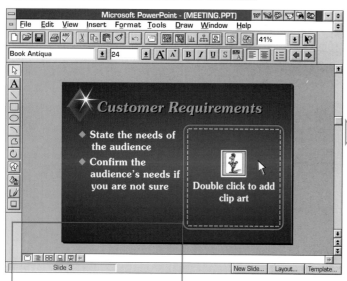

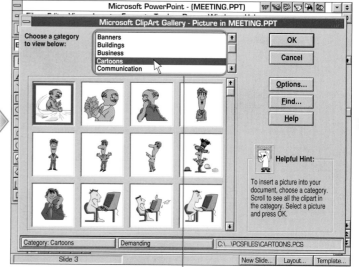

◆ The slide now displays an area for the clip art image.

7 To add a clip art image, move the mouse ⬚ over this area and then quickly press the left button twice.

Note: If this is the first time you are adding a clip art image to a presentation, refer to the **Tip** on page 281.

◆ The **Microsoft ClipArt Gallery** dialog box appears.

8 Move the mouse ⬚ over the clip art images you want to view and then press the left button.

Note: To view all of the clip art images, select **All Categories**.

• Change the Slide Layout
• Add a New Slide
• **Add Clip Art**
• Add an Organization Chart
• Add a Graph
• Change Graph Type

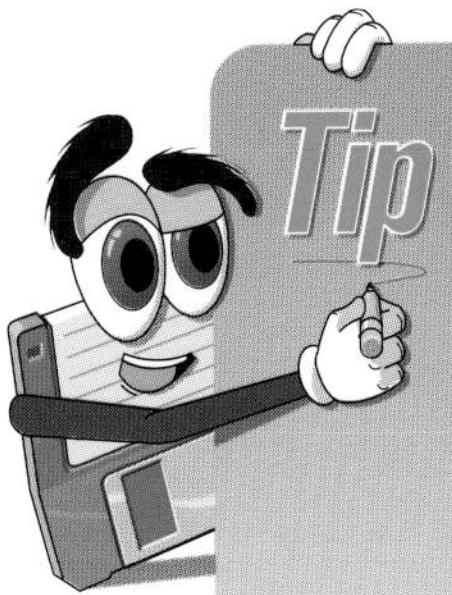

This dialog box appears the first time you add clip art to a presentation.

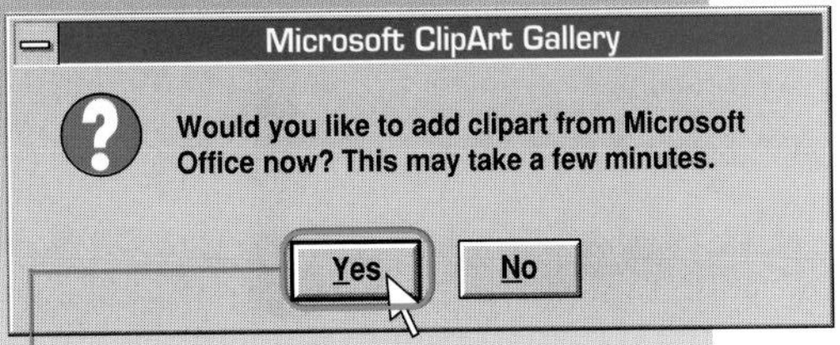

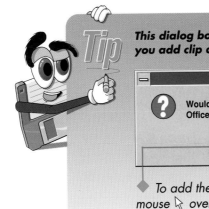

◆ *To add the clip art, move the mouse over **Yes** and then press the left button.*

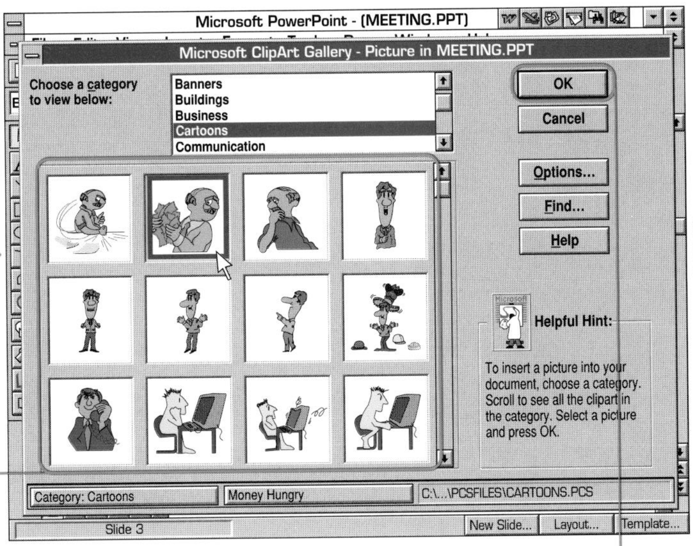

◆ The clip art images appear.

9 Move the mouse over the clip art image you want to use and then press the left button.

10 Move the mouse over **OK** and then press the left button.

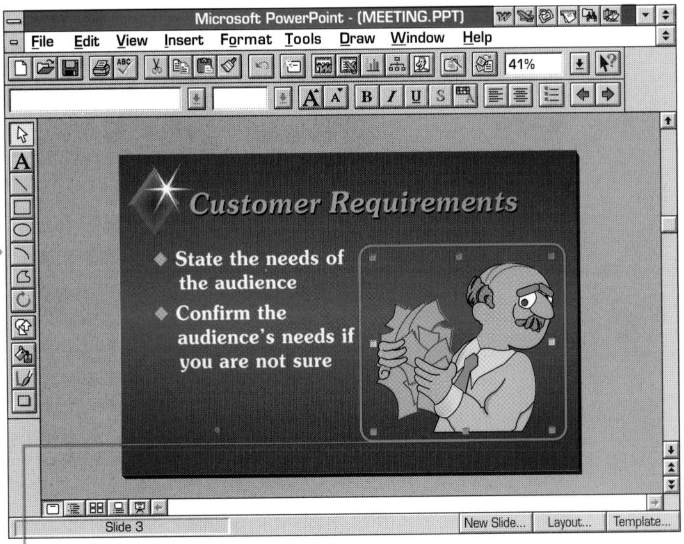

◆ The clip art image you selected appears on the slide.

11 The squares around the image let you size the image. To remove these squares, move the mouse outside the image area and then press the left button.

Note: To move or size a clip art image, refer to page 306.

You can add an organization chart to a slide. This is useful if you want to show the structure of a company.

ADD AN ORGANIZATION CHART

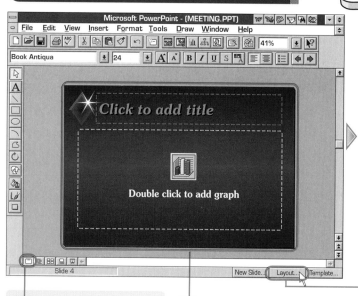

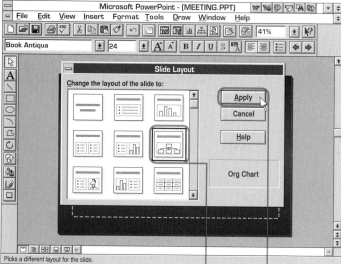

1 To change to the Slide view, move the mouse ▷ over ▢ and then press the left button.

2 Display the slide you want to add an organization chart to (example: slide 4).

Note: To move between slides, refer to page 250.

3 To change the layout of the slide, move the mouse ▷ over **Layout** and then press the left button.

◆ The **Slide Layout** dialog box appears.

4 Move the mouse ▷ over the layout displaying the organization chart and then press the left button.

5 Move the mouse ▷ over **Apply** and then press the left button.

- Change the Slide Layout
- Add a New Slide
- Add Clip Art
- **Add an Organization Chart**
- Add a Graph
- Change Graph Type

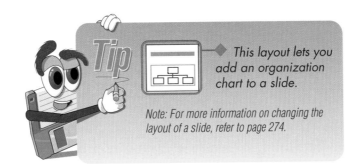

Tip

This layout lets you add an organization chart to a slide.

Note: For more information on changing the layout of a slide, refer to page 274.

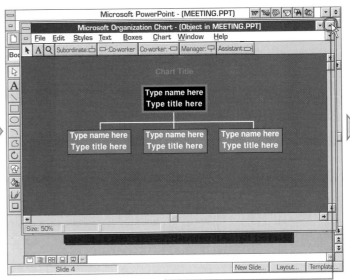

◆ The slide now displays an area for the organization chart.

6 To create an organization chart, move the mouse ⬚ over this area and then quickly press the left button twice.

◆ **The Microsoft Organization Chart** window appears.

7 To enlarge this window to fill your screen, move the mouse ⬚ over ▲ and then press the left button.

CONTINUED

283

PowerPoint creates a simple organization chart that you can customize.

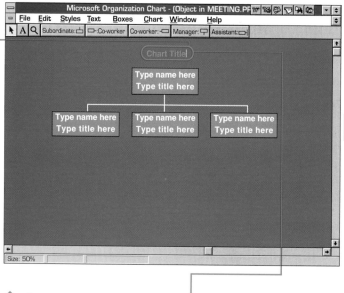

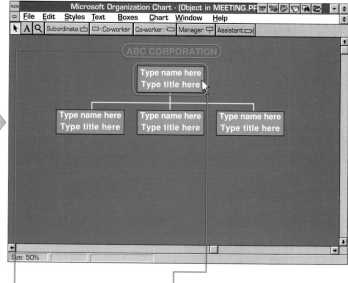

◆ The organization chart fills your screen.

8 To change the title of the chart, move the mouse I to the right of the title and then press the left button.

◆ A flashing line appears after the last character in the title.

9 Press **←Backspace** until the existing title disappears.

10 Type a title for your chart.

11 To select a box you want to replace with new text, move the mouse ⍈ over the box and then press the left button.

- Change the Slide Layout
- Add a New Slide
- Add Clip Art
- **Add an Organization Chart**
- Add a Graph
- Change Graph Type

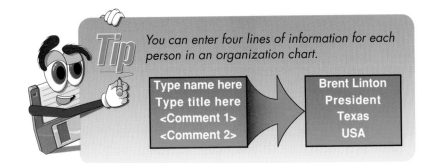

Tip

You can enter four lines of information for each person in an organization chart.

| Type name here |
| Type title here |
| <Comment 1> |
| <Comment 2> |

→

| **Brent Linton** |
| **President** |
| **Texas** |
| **USA** |

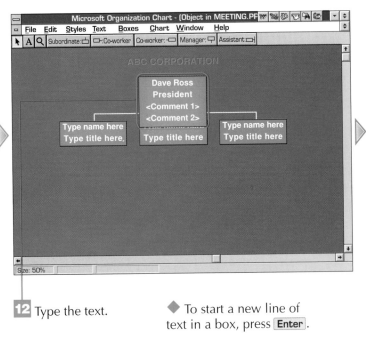

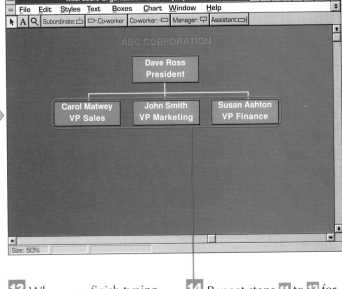

12 Type the text.

◆ To start a new line of text in a box, press **Enter**.

13 When you finish typing the information for the person, move the mouse ⌖ outside the box and then press the left button.

14 Repeat steps **11** to **13** for each person you want to include in the chart.

ADD AN ORGANIZATION CHART

You can add another person to your organization chart, such as a co-worker or manager.

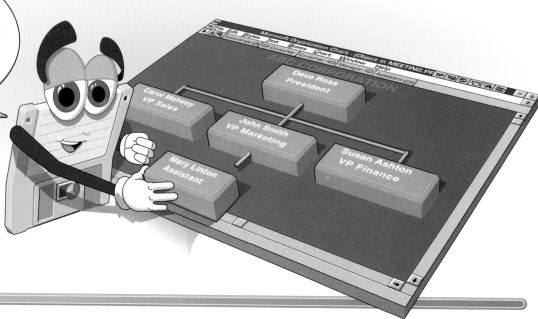

ADD A BOX

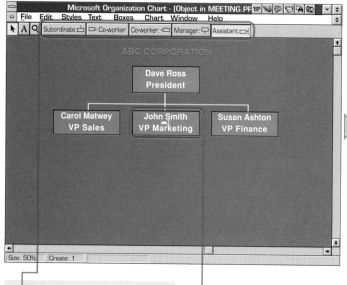

Size: 50%   Create: 1

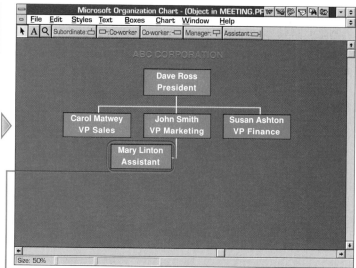

Size: 50%

1 Move the mouse ▹ over the type of box you want to add (example: **Assistant**) and then press the left button.

2 Move the mouse ▭ over the box you want to connect the new box to and then press the left button.

◆ The new box appears.

3 Type the text you want to appear in the new box.

◆ To start a new line of text, press **Enter**.

4 When you finish typing the text, move the mouse ▹ outside the box and then press the left button.

- Change the Slide Layout
- Add a New Slide
- Add Clip Art
- **Add an Organization Chart**
- Add a Graph
- Change Graph Type

You can easily remove a person from your organization chart.

DELETE A BOX

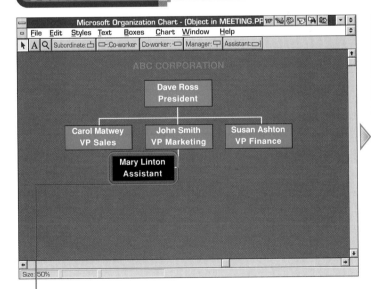

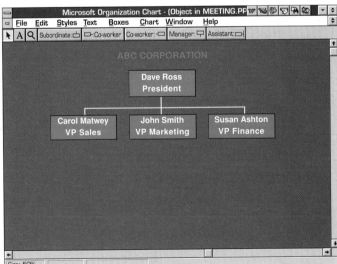

1 Move the mouse ⌖ over the box you want to delete and then press the left button.

2 Press **Delete** on your keyboard.

◆ The box disappears.

ADD AN ORGANIZATION CHART

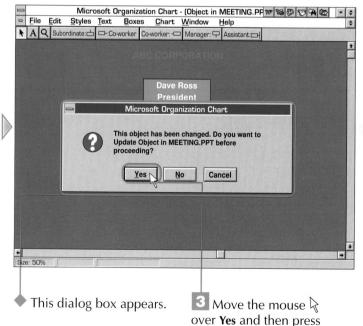

When your organization chart is complete, you must exit the charting program. This lets you see how the chart looks on the slide.

EXIT AND RETURN TO THE SLIDE

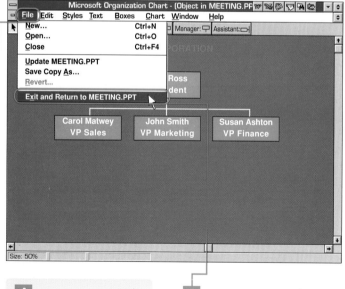

1 Move the mouse ⬚ over **File** and then press the left button.

2 Move the mouse ⬚ over **Exit and Return to** and then press the left button.

◆ This dialog box appears.

3 Move the mouse ⬚ over **Yes** and then press the left button.

- Change the Slide Layout
- Add a New Slide
- Add Clip Art
- **Add an Organization Chart**
- Add a Graph
- Change Graph Type

IMPORTANT!

You cannot make changes to an organization chart directly on a slide. To make changes, move the mouse ⌖ over the chart and then quickly press the left button twice. This starts the **Microsoft Organization Chart** program and lets you modify the chart.

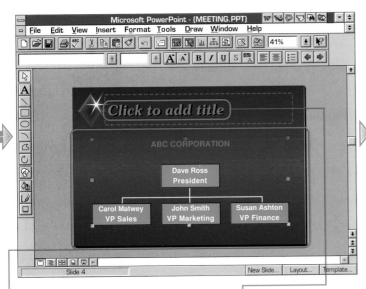

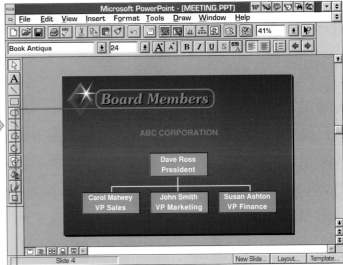

◆ The organization chart appears on the slide.

◆ The squares around the chart let you size the chart. To remove these squares, move the mouse ⌖ outside the chart area and then press the left button.

4 To add a title to the slide, move the mouse I over this area and then press the left button.

5 Type a title.

6 To deselect the title, move the mouse ⌖ outside the title area and then press the left button.

Note: To move or size a chart, refer to page 306.

289

You can show trends and compare data by adding a graph to a slide. A graph has a greater impact than a simple list of numbers.

ADD A GRAPH

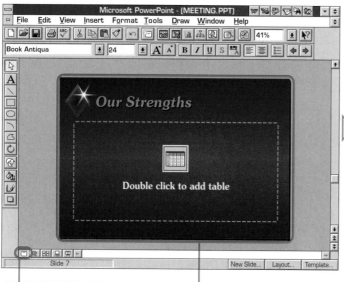

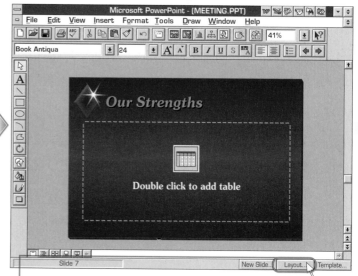

1 To change to the Slide view, move the mouse ↖ over 🔲 and then press the left button.

2 Display the slide you want to add a graph to (example: slide 7).

Note: To move between slides, refer to page 250.

3 To change the layout of the slide, move the mouse ↖ over **Layout** and then press the left button.

• Change the Slide Layout
• Add a New Slide
• Add Clip Art
• Add an Organization Chart
• **Add a Graph**
• Change Graph Type

These layouts let you add a graph to a slide.

Note: For more information on changing the layout of a slide, refer to page 274.

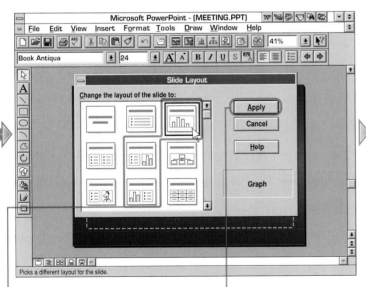

◆ The **Slide Layout** dialog box appears.

4 To add a graph to the slide, move the mouse ⬚ over one of these layouts and then press the left button.

5 Move the mouse ⬚ over **Apply** and then press the left button.

◆ The slide now displays an area for the graph.

6 To add a graph, move the mouse ⬚ over this area and then quickly press the left button twice.

CONTINUED

291

When you create a graph, PowerPoint provides a Datasheet where you enter data. PowerPoint uses this data to create the graph.

ADD A GRAPH (CONTINUED)

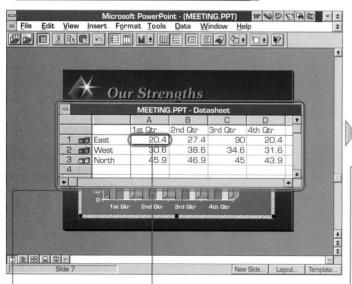

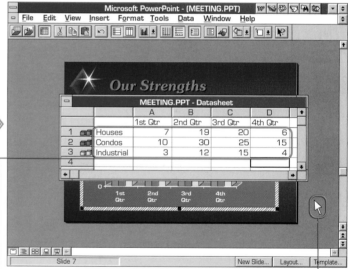

◆ A Datasheet appears, displaying sample data. This shows you where you can enter your own information.

7 To change the data in a cell, move the mouse over the cell and then press the left button.

◆ A thick border appears around the cell.

8 Type the data and then press **Enter**.

9 Repeat steps **7** and **8** until you finish entering all of your data.

Note: You can also press ↓, ↑, ← or → on your keyboard to quickly move between cells.

10 To hide the Datasheet and view the graph, move the mouse outside the Datasheet area and then press the left button.

- Change the Slide Layout
- Add a New Slide
- Add Clip Art
- Add an Organization Chart
- **Add a Graph**
- Change Graph Type

Tip

After creating a graph, you can move or size the graph on the slide.

Note: For more information, refer to page 306.

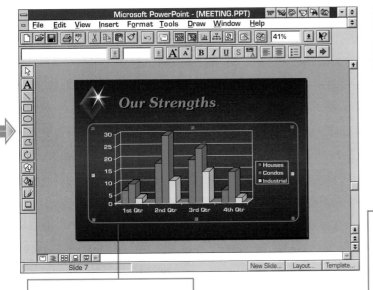

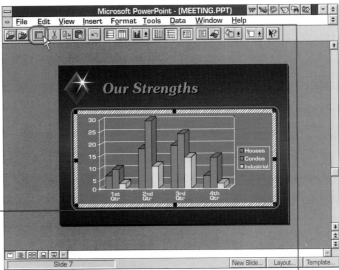

◆ The graph appears on the slide.

◆ The squares around the graph let you size the graph. To remove these squares, move the mouse � outside the graph area and then press the left button.

DISPLAY THE DATASHEET

1 To view or make changes to the data used in your graph, move the mouse ⍟⍟ over the graph and then quickly press the left button twice.

2 To display the Datasheet, move the mouse ⍟ over ▦ and then press the left button.

◆ The graph will reflect any changes you make to the Datasheet.

293

CHANGE GRAPH TYPE

> After creating a graph, you can select a new graph type that will better suit your data.

CHANGE GRAPH TYPE

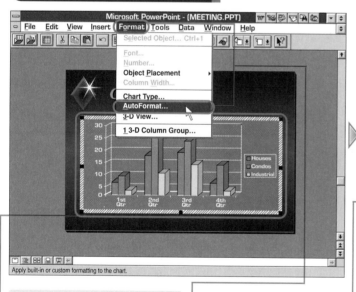

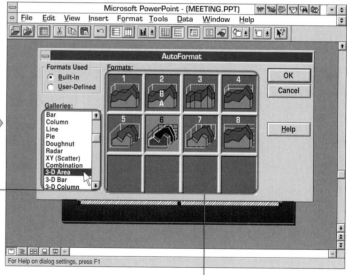

1 To select the graph, move the mouse ⌖ over the graph and then quickly press the left button twice.

◆ A thick border appears around the graph.

2 Move the mouse ⌖ over **Format** and then press the left button.

3 Move the mouse ⌖ over **AutoFormat** and then press the left button.

◆ The **AutoFormat** dialog box appears.

4 Move the mouse ⌖ over the type of graph you want to use and then press the left button.

◆ This area displays the available styles for the type of graph you selected.

- Change the Slide Layout
- Add a New Slide
- Add Clip Art
- Add an Organization Chart
- Add a Graph
- **Change Graph Type**

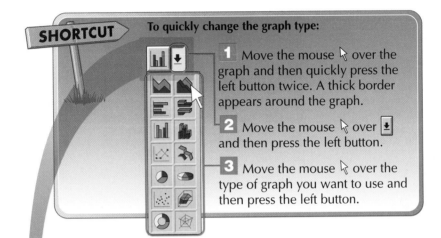

SHORTCUT

To quickly change the graph type:

1 Move the mouse ⟋ over the graph and then quickly press the left button twice. A thick border appears around the graph.

2 Move the mouse ⟋ over ⊞ and then press the left button.

3 Move the mouse ⟋ over the type of graph you want to use and then press the left button.

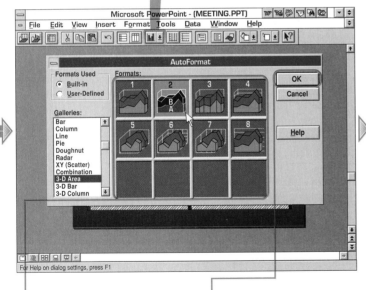

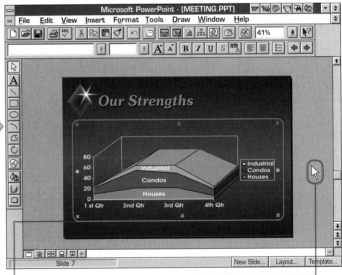

5 Move the mouse ⟋ over the style you want to use (example: **2**) and then press the left button.

6 Move the mouse ⟋ over **OK** and then press the left button.

◆ Your graph displays the new style.

7 To deselect the graph, move the mouse ⟋ outside the graph area and then press the left button.

The Pick a Look Wizard helps you enhance your presentation. You can use this feature to change the design and add additional information to your visuals.

USING THE PICK A LOOK WIZARD

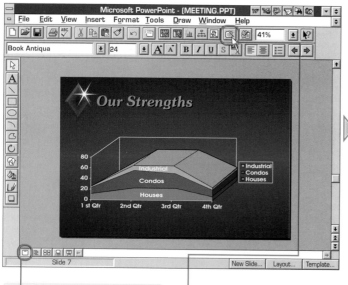

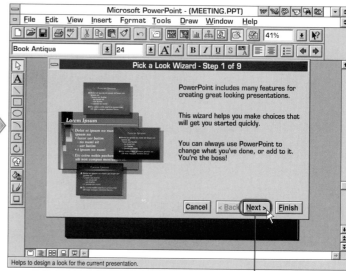

1 To change to the Slide view, move the mouse over 🔲 and then press the left button.

2 Move the mouse over 🖼 and then press the left button.

◆ The **Pick a Look Wizard** dialog box appears.

3 Move the mouse over **Next** and then press the left button.

- **Using the Pick a Look Wizard**
- Edit Text in Slide View
- Move and Size a Text Box
- Add an AutoShape
- Move and Size an Object
- Emphasize Text
- Change Text Size
- Change Font of Text
- Using Templates

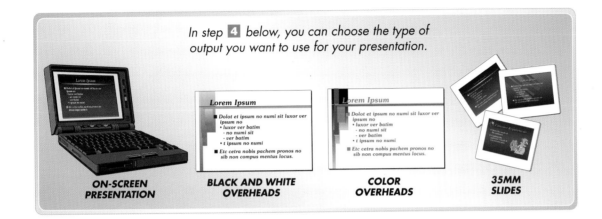

In step **4** *below, you can choose the type of output you want to use for your presentation.*

ON-SCREEN PRESENTATION   **BLACK AND WHITE OVERHEADS**   **COLOR OVERHEADS**   **35MM SLIDES**

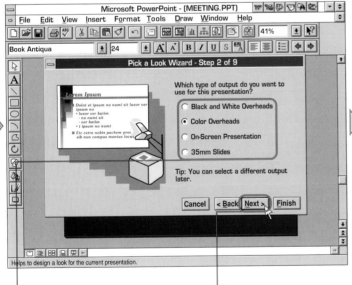

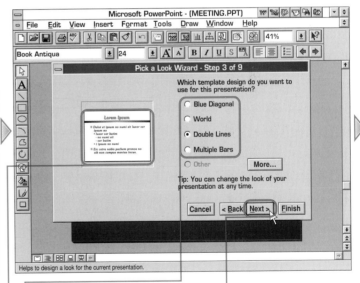

4 Move the mouse ⍟ over the type of output you want to use for your presentation and then press the left button (○ changes to ●).

5 Move the mouse ⍟ over **Next** and then press the left button.

6 Move the mouse ⍟ over the design you want to use and then press the left button.

Note: Only four designs are available in this dialog box. For other designs, refer to page 312.

◆ This area displays a sample of the design you selected.

7 Move the mouse ⍟ over **Next** and then press the left button.

CONTINUED

The Pick a Look Wizard lets you add additional information, such as the date, to your slides, notes, handouts and outline.

USING THE PICK A LOOK WIZARD (CONTINUED)

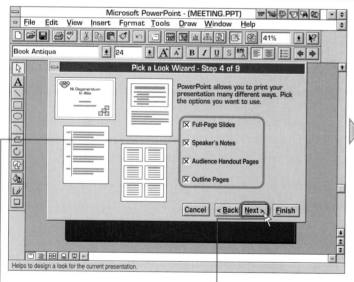

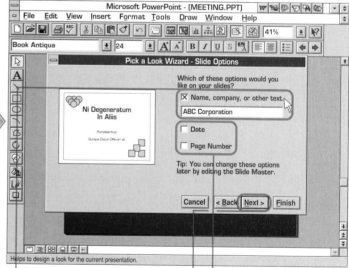

8 All of these items are part of your presentation. If you do not want to include an item, move the mouse ⟷ over the item and then press the left button (⊠ changes to ☐).

9 Move the mouse ⟷ over **Next** and then press the left button.

*Note: A dialog box will appear for each item that displays an ⊠ in step **8**.*

10 To add text to an item in your presentation, move the mouse ⟷ over this option and then press the left button (☐ changes to ⊠). Press **Tab** and then type the text.

Note: ⊠ means an option will appear on the item. ☐ means an option will not appear.

11 To add the date or page number, move the mouse ⟷ over the option and then press the left button.

12 Move the mouse ⟷ over **Next** and then press the left button.

- **Using the Pick a Look Wizard**
- Edit Text in Slide View
- Move and Size a Text Box
- Add an AutoShape
- Move and Size an Object
- Emphasize Text
- Change Text Size
- Change Font of Text
- Using Templates

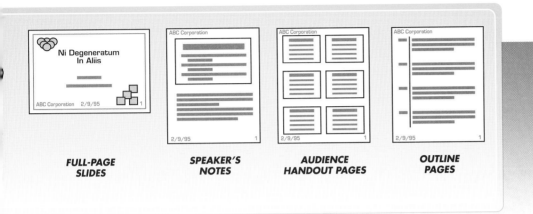

FULL-PAGE SLIDES

SPEAKER'S NOTES

AUDIENCE HANDOUT PAGES

OUTLINE PAGES

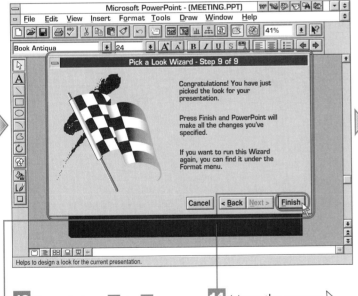

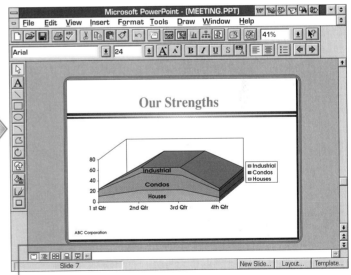

13 Repeat steps **10** to **12** for each item that displays an ⊠ in step **8**.

◆ When you finish using the Pick a Look Wizard, this dialog box appears.

14 Move the mouse ⬧ over **Finish** and then press the left button.

◆ PowerPoint applies the changes to your presentation.

Note: PowerPoint displays symbols on each slide to represent the page number (##) and date (ll). These symbols will be replaced with the proper information when you print your presentation.

You can edit text in the Slide view. This lets you see how the changes will affect the overall appearance of your slide.

EDIT TEXT

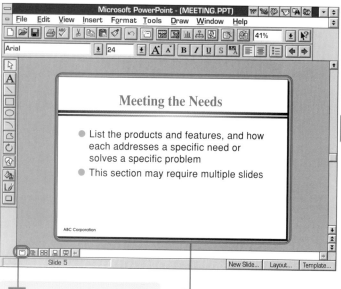

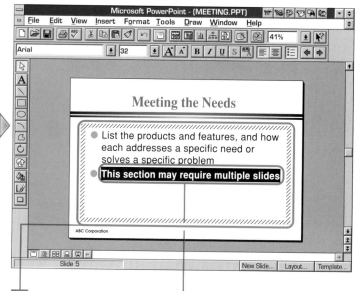

1 To change to the Slide view, move the mouse over □ and then press the left button.

2 Display the slide you want to edit (example: slide 5).

Note: To move between slides, refer to page 250.

3 Move the mouse I anywhere over the text you want to edit and then press the left button. A border appears around the text.

4 To delete text, select the text you want to remove. Then press **Delete**.

Note: To select text, refer to page 262.

For more information on editing text, refer to pages 264 to 270.

- Using the Pick a Look Wizard
- **Edit Text in Slide View**
- Move and Size a Text Box
- Add an AutoShape
- Move and Size an Object
- Emphasize Text
- Change Text Size
- Change Font of Text
- Using Templates

DELETE A LIST OF POINTS

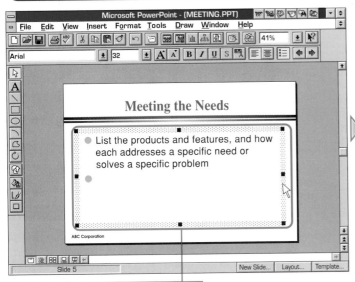

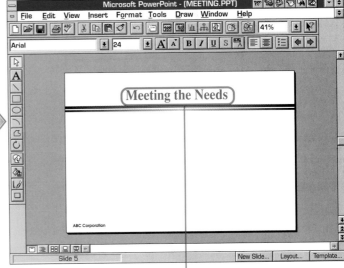

1 Move the mouse I anywhere over the list of points you want to delete and then press the left button. A border appears around the list.

2 Move the mouse ⬚ over the border and then press the left button. Squares appear on the border.

3 Press **Delete** twice and the list disappears.

◆ You can use the same method to remove a title from a slide.

MOVE AND SIZE A TEXT BOX

You can easily change the size or location of a text box on a slide. This is useful if you want to place a picture beside a list of points.

Text Box

SIZE A TEXT BOX

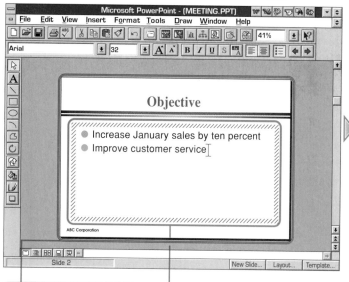

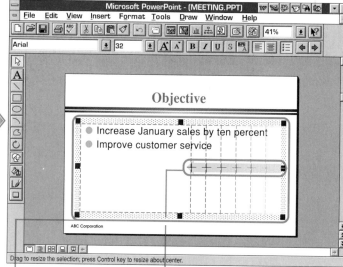

1 Display the slide you want to change (example: slide 2).

Note: To move between slides, refer to page 250.

2 Move the mouse I over the text in the text box you want to size and then press the left button. A border appears around the text.

3 Move the mouse ⟨ over the border and then press the left button. Squares appear on the border.

4 Move the mouse ⟨ over one of the squares and ⟨ changes to ↔.

5 Press and hold down the left button as you drag the mouse + until the text box is the size you want. Then release the button.

- Using the Pick a Look Wizard
- Edit Text in Slide View
- **Move and Size a Text Box**
- Add an AutoShape
- Move and Size an Object
- Emphasize Text
- Change Text Size
- Change Font of Text
- Using Templates

You change the size of a text box using any square around the text.

■ You can use these squares to change the height of a text box.

■ You can use these squares to change the width of a text box.

■ You can use these squares to change the height and width of a text box at the same time.

MOVE A TEXT BOX

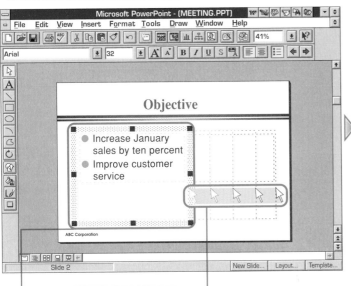

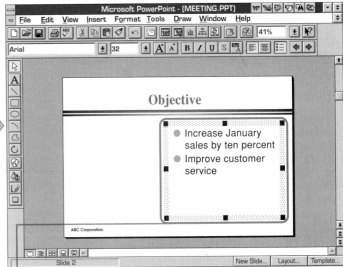

1 Move the mouse I over the text in the text box you want to move and then press the left button. A border appears around the text.

2 Move the mouse ⌖ over the border and then press and hold down the left button as you drag the text box to a new location.

3 Release the button and the text box appears in the new location.

You can add shapes such as arrows and stars to the slides in your presentation. A shape can help emphasize your information.

ADD AN AUTOSHAPE

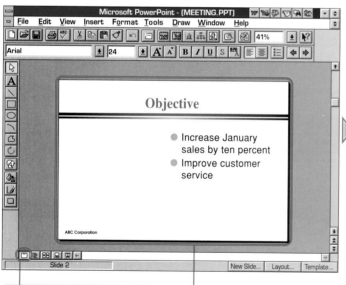

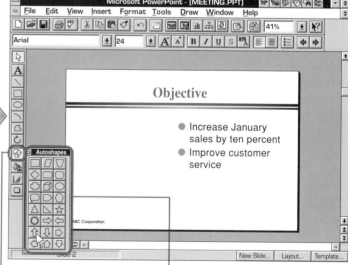

1 To change to the Slide view, move the mouse ⬚ over ☐ and then press the left button.

2 Display the slide you want to add a shape to (example: slide 2).

Note: To move between slides, refer to page 250.

3 Move the mouse ⬚ over ⬚ and then press the left button.

◆ The **Autoshapes** toolbar appears, displaying the shapes you can add to your slide.

4 Move the mouse ⬚ over the shape you want to add and then press the left button.

304

- Using the Pick a Look Wizard
- Edit Text in Slide View
- Move and Size a Text Box
- **Add an AutoShape**
- Move and Size an Object
- Emphasize Text
- Change Text Size
- Change Font of Text
- Using Templates

Tip

You can move or size
a shape after you add
it to a slide.

Note: For more information,
refer to page 306.

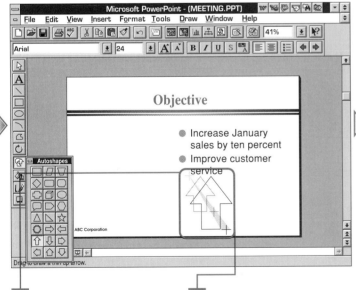

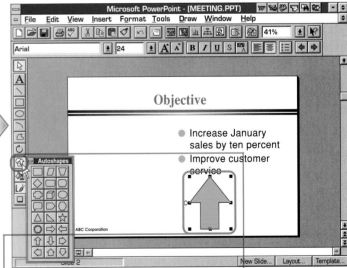

5 Move the mouse + over the location where you want the top left corner of the shape to appear.

6 Press and hold down the left button as you drag the mouse + until the shape is the size you want.

7 Release the button and the shape appears.

8 The squares around the shape let you size the shape. To remove these squares, move the mouse ⬚ outside the shape area and then press the left button.

9 To hide the **Autoshapes** toolbar, move the mouse ⬚ over 🔲 and then press the left button.

You can easily change the location or size of an object on a slide.

MOVE AN OBJECT

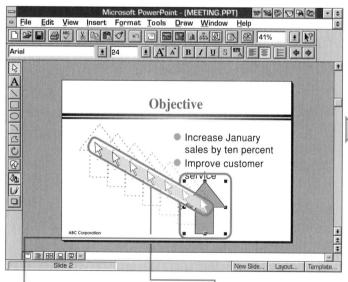

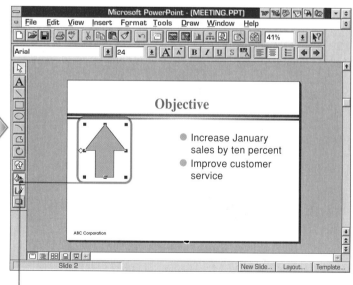

1 Move the mouse ⌖ over the object you want to move and then press and hold down the left button.

2 Still holding down the left button, drag the mouse ⌖ to where you want to place the object.

3 Release the button and the object appears in the new location.

DELETE AN OBJECT

1 To select the object you want to delete, move the mouse ⌖ over the object and then press the left button.

2 Press Delete on your keyboard.

SIZE AN OBJECT

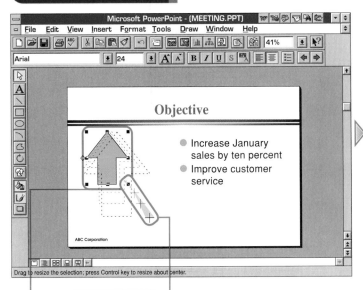

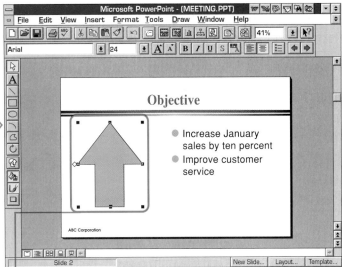

1 To select the object you want to size, move the mouse ⌖ over the object and then press the left button. Squares appear around the object.

2 Move the mouse ⌖ over one of the squares and ⌖ changes to ↖.

3 Press and hold down the left button as you drag the mouse + until the object is the size you want.

4 Release the button and the object changes to the new size.

You can use these styles to emphasize important information in your presentation.

bold *italic* <u>underline</u> shadow

EMPHASIZE TEXT

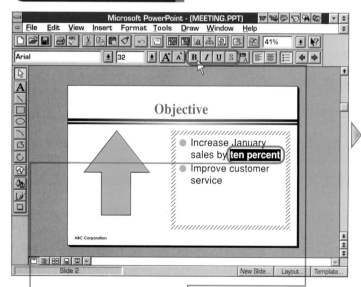

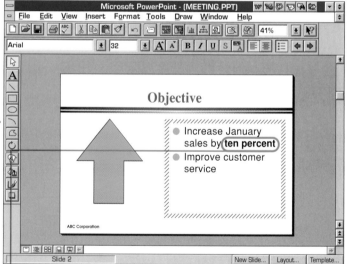

1 Select the text you want to change.

Note: To select text, refer to page 262.

2 Move the mouse ⬭ over one of the following options and then press the left button.

B	Bold text
I	Italicize text
U	Underline text
S	Shadow text

◆ The text you selected appears in the new style.

Note: To deselect text, move the mouse I outside the selected area and then press the left button.

◆ To remove a style, repeat steps **1** and **2**.

308

- Using the Pick a Look Wizard
- Edit Text in Slide View
- Move and Size a Text Box
- Add an AutoShape
- Move and Size an Object
- **Emphasize Text**
- **Change Text Size**
- Change Font of Text
- Using Templates

You can change the size of text in your presentation.

CHANGE TEXT SIZE

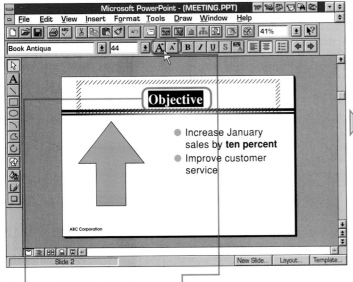

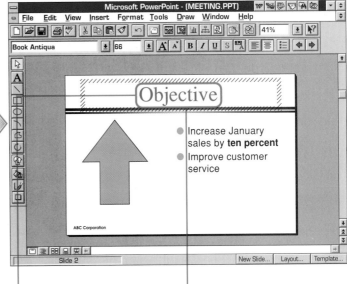

1 Select the text you want to change.

Note: To select text, refer to page 262.

2 Move the mouse ⌖ over one of the following options and then press the left button.

A' Increase text size

A' Decrease text size

◆ The text increases or decreases in size.

3 Repeat step **2** until the text is the size you want.

Note: To deselect text, move the mouse ⌶ outside the selected area and then press the left button.

309

You can enhance the appearance of your presentation by changing the design of text.

CHANGE FONT OF TEXT

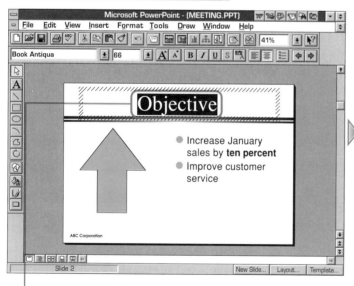

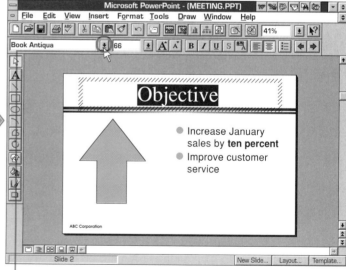

1 Select the text you want to change.

Note: To select text, refer to page 262.

2 To display a list of the available fonts, move the mouse ⓀＬ over ⬇ beside the **Font** box and then press the left button.

310

- Using the Pick a Look Wizard
- Edit Text in Slide View
- Move and Size a Text Box
- Add an AutoShape
- Move and Size an Object
- Emphasize Text
- Change Text Size
- Change Font of Text
- Using Templates

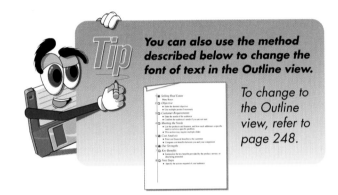

You can also use the method described below to change the font of text in the Outline view.

To change to the Outline view, refer to page 248.

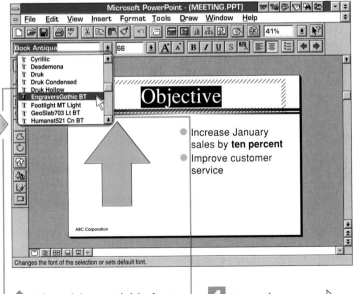

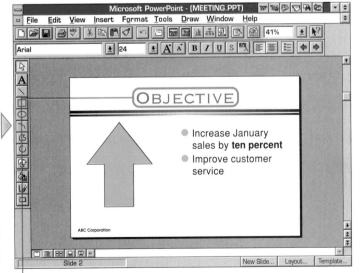

◆ A list of the available fonts for your computer appears.

3 To browse through the available fonts, move the mouse ↳ over ▼ or ▲ and then press the left button.

4 Move the mouse ↳ over the font you want to use and then press the left button.

◆ The text you selected changes to the new font.

Note: To deselect text, move the mouse ↳ outside the slide and then press the left button.

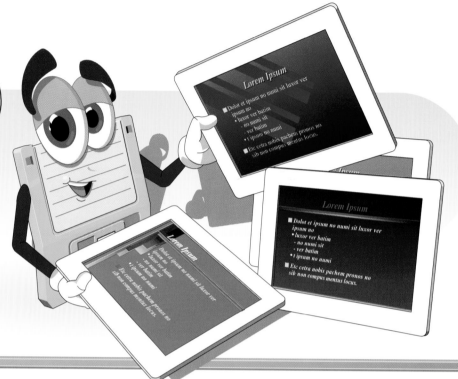

PowerPoint offers over 100 predesigned slides, called templates. You can select a different template to give your slides a new look.

USING TEMPLATES

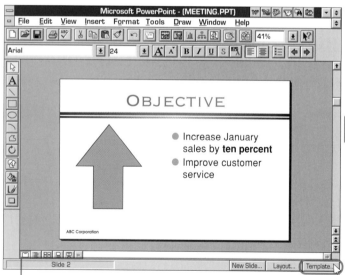

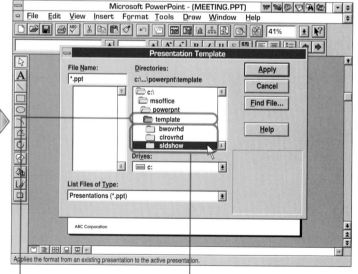

1 Move the mouse � over **Template** and then press the left button.

◆ The **Presentation Template** dialog box appears.

2 Move the mouse � over **template** and then quickly press the left button twice.

3 Move the mouse � over the type of presentation you want to create (example: **sldshow**) and then quickly press the left button twice.

*Note: For more information, refer to the **Tip** on page 313.*

- Using the Pick a Look Wizard
- Edit Text in Slide View
- Move and Size a Text Box

- Add an AutoShape
- Move and Size an Object
- Emphasize Text

- Change Text Size
- Change Font of Text
- **Using Templates**

Tip

The Template feature provides designs for these types of presentations.

bwovrhd	*black-and-white overheads*
clrovrhd	*color overheads*
sldshow	*on-screen slide show or 35mm slides*

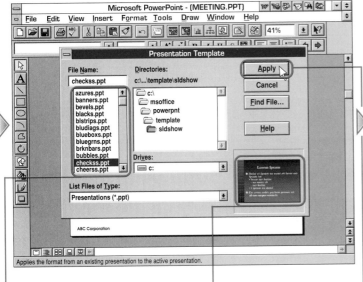

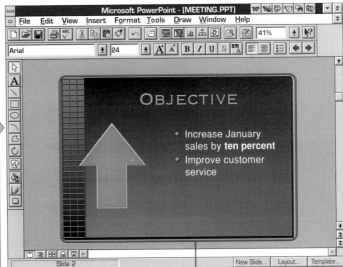

◆ This area displays a list of templates for the type of presentation you selected.

4 Move the mouse ℕ over a template you want to view (example: **checkss.ppt**) and then press the left button.

◆ This area displays a sample of the template you selected.

5 Repeat step **4** until the template you want to use appears.

6 Move the mouse ℕ over **Apply** and then press the left button.

◆ All the slides in your presentation change to the new design.

313

You can create speaker's notes containing copies of your slides with all the ideas you want to discuss. These notes will help guide you through your presentation.

ADD SPEAKER'S NOTES

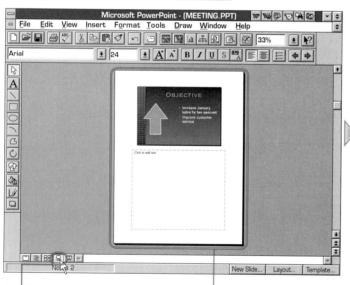

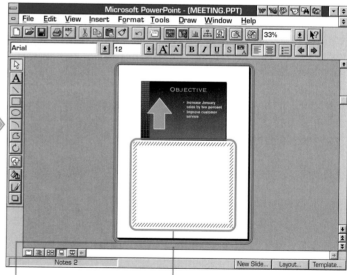

1 To change to the Notes Pages view, move the mouse ▷ over 🖳 and then press the left button.

◆ A page appears, displaying a slide and an area for adding notes.

2 Display the slide you want to add notes to (example: slide 2).

Note: To move between slides, refer to page 253.

3 Move the mouse I over this area and then press the left button.

◆ A border appears around the area.

- **Add Speaker's Notes**
- Delete a Slide
- Reorder Slides
- Set Up Slides
- Print a Presentation
- View a Slide Show
- Rehearse a Slide Show
- Add Builds to Slides
- Add Slide Transitions

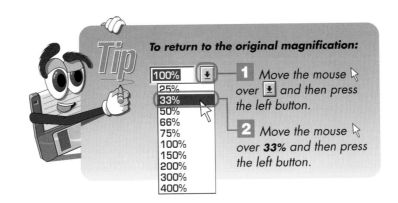

To return to the original magnification:

1 Move the mouse over ⬇ and then press the left button.

2 Move the mouse over **33%** and then press the left button.

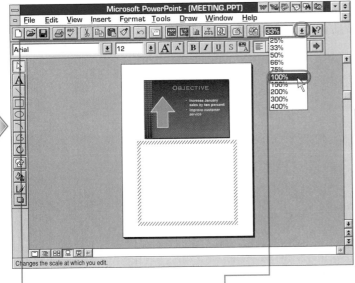

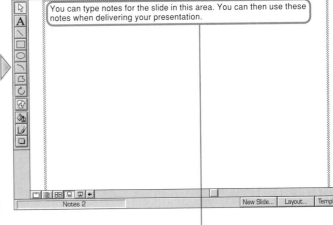

4 To magnify the text area, move the mouse ⬚ over ⬇ at the top right corner of your screen and then press the left button.

5 Move the mouse ⬚ over **100%** and then press the left button.

◆ The text area is magnified.

6 Type the ideas you want to discuss when you display the slide.

DELETE A SLIDE   REORDER SLIDES

> You can permanently remove a slide that you no longer need.

DELETE A SLIDE

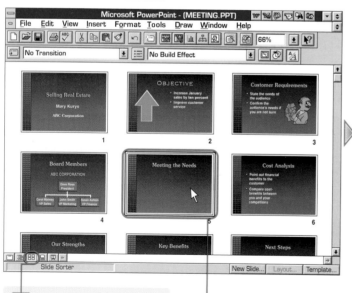 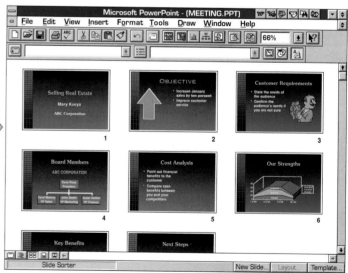

1 To change to the Slide Sorter view, move the mouse ⌖ over ⊞ and then press the left button.

2 Move the mouse ⌖ over the slide you want to delete and then press the left button.

3 Press **Delete** and the slide disappears.

- Add Speaker's Notes
- **Delete a Slide**
- **Reorder Slides**

- Set Up Slides
- Print a Presentation
- View a Slide Show

- Rehearse a Slide Show
- Add Builds to Slides
- Add Slide Transitions

> PowerPoint lets you easily change the order of the slides in your presentation.

REORDER SLIDES

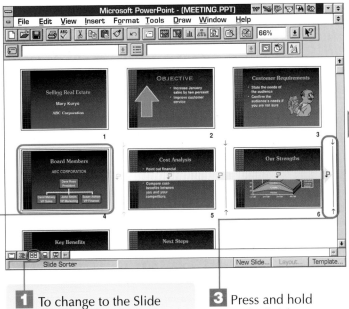

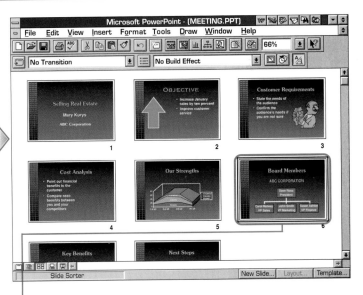

1 To change to the Slide Sorter view, move the mouse over [88] and then press the left button.

2 Move the mouse over the slide you want to move to a new location.

3 Press and hold down the left button as you drag the mouse to where you want to place the slide. A line indicates where the slide will appear.

4 Release the button and the slide appears in the new location.

317

Before printing your presentation, you must specify the size and orientation you want to use for the different parts of your presentation.

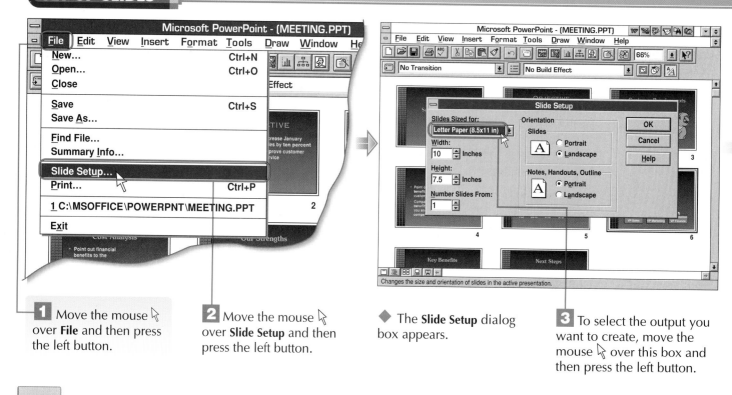

1 Move the mouse ⌖ over **File** and then press the left button.

2 Move the mouse ⌖ over **Slide Setup** and then press the left button.

◆ The **Slide Setup** dialog box appears.

3 To select the output you want to create, move the mouse ⌖ over this box and then press the left button.

- Add Speaker's Notes
- Delete a Slide
- Reorder Slides
- **Set Up Slides**
- Print a Presentation
- View a Slide Show
- Rehearse a Slide Show
- Add Builds to Slides
- Add Slide Transitions

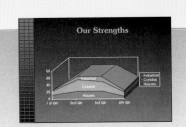

Landscape

This is the usual orientation for slides.

Portrait

This is the usual orientation for your outline, notes and handouts.

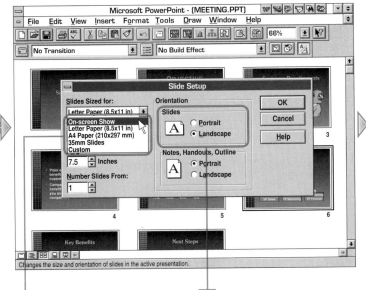

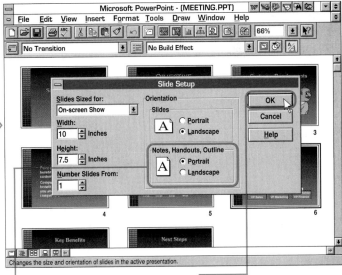

4 Move the mouse ⬚ over the output you want to create and then press the left button.

*Note: To print overhead transparencies, select the **Letter Paper** option.*

5 Move the mouse ⬚ over the orientation you want to use for the slides and then press the left button.

6 Move the mouse ⬚ over the orientation you want to use for the notes, handouts and outline and then press the left button.

7 Move the mouse ⬚ over **OK** and then press the left button.

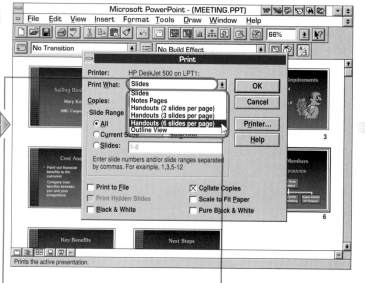

You can print your entire presentation, including your outline, slides, notes and handouts.

PRINT A PRESENTATION

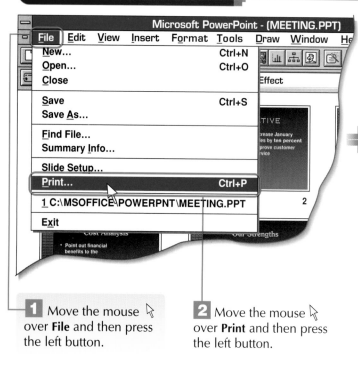

1 Move the mouse ⌖ over **File** and then press the left button.

2 Move the mouse ⌖ over **Print** and then press the left button.

◆ The **Print** dialog box appears.

3 To select the part of the presentation you want to print, move the mouse ⌖ over this box and then press the left button.

4 Move the mouse ⌖ over what you want to print and then press the left button.

- Add Speaker's Notes
- Delete a Slide
- Reorder Slides
- Set Up Slides
- *Print a Presentation*
- View a Slide Show
- Rehearse a Slide Show
- Add Builds to Slides
- Add Slide Transitions

Tip

You can print the following slide ranges:

All	Prints every slide in the presentation
Current Slide	Prints the selected slide or the slide displayed on your screen
Slides:	Prints the slides you specify

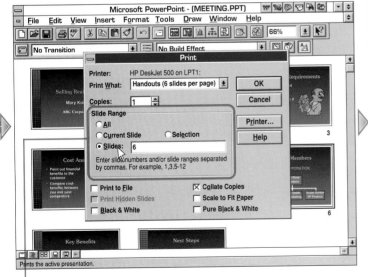

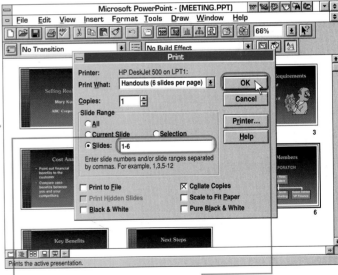

5 Move the mouse ⬚ over the slide range you want to print (example: **Slides:**) and then press the left button. ○ changes to ◉.

*Note: For information on the slide range options, refer to the **Tip** above.*

6 If you selected **Slides:** in step **5**, press Delete until you remove the existing slide numbers. Then type the slides you want to print (example: **1-6**).

7 Move the mouse ⬚ over **OK** and then press the left button.

321

You can view a slide show on your computer screen. During the show, you can use your mouse to draw directly on the slides.

VIEW A SLIDE SHOW

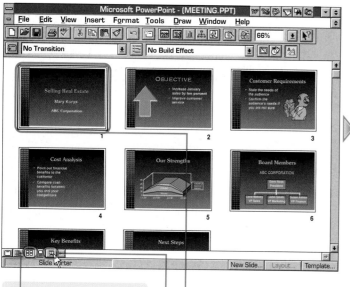

1 To change to the Slide Sorter view, move the mouse ⬚ over 🔲 and then press the left button.

2 To select the slide you want to begin the slide show, move the mouse ⬚ over the slide and then press the left button.

3 To start the slide show, move the mouse ⬚ over 🔲 and then press the left button.

◆ The slide you selected appears on your screen.

Note: You can cancel the slide show at any time by pressing **Esc** on your keyboard.

4 To display the next slide, press the left mouse button or the **Spacebar**.

Note: To display the previous slide, press the **right** mouse button.

- Add Speaker's Notes
- Delete a Slide
- Reorder Slides

- Set Up Slides
- Print a Presentation
- **View a Slide Show**

- Rehearse a Slide Show
- Add Builds to Slides
- Add Slide Transitions

The lines you draw on a slide during a slide show are temporary. They will not appear when the slide show is over.

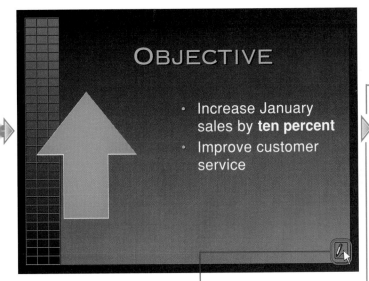

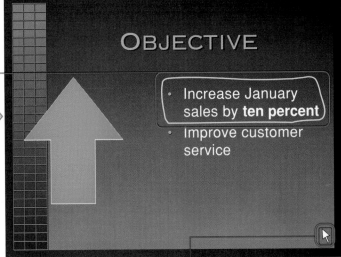

◆ The next slide appears.

5 To draw on the screen, move the mouse ↖ over 🖉 and then press the left button (↖ changes to 🖉).

6 Move the mouse 🖉 over the area where you want to begin drawing.

7 Press and hold down the left button as you drag the mouse 🖉 around the area you want to emphasize. Then release the button.

8 When you finish drawing, move the mouse 🖉 over ↖ and then press the left button.

9 Repeat step **4** until you finish viewing all the slides in your slide show.

323

You can rehearse your slide show and have PowerPoint record the amount of time you spend on each slide.

REHEARSE A SLIDE SHOW

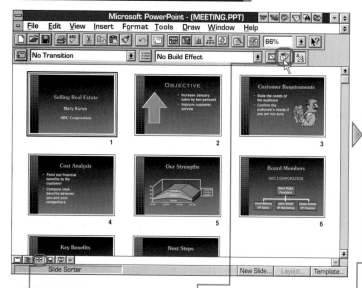

1 To change to the Slide Sorter view, move the mouse ⟨ over 🔳 and then press the left button.

2 To start the slide show, move the mouse ⟨ over 📽 and then press the left button.

◆ The first slide in your slide show appears.

◆ A clock appears at the bottom of your screen, recording the amount of time you spend on each slide.

3 When you finish talking and want to display the next slide, press the left mouse button.

*Note: To display the previous slide, press the **right** mouse button.*

- Add Speaker's Notes
- Delete a Slide
- Reorder Slides

- Set Up Slides
- Print a Presentation
- View a Slide Show

- **Rehearse a Slide Show**
- Add Builds to Slides
- Add Slide Transitions

Tip

You can quit the slide show at any time by pressing Esc on your keyboard.

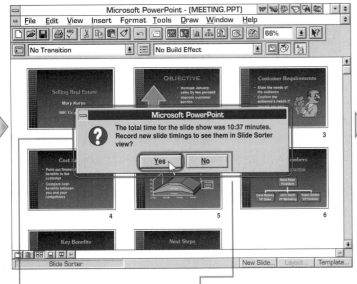

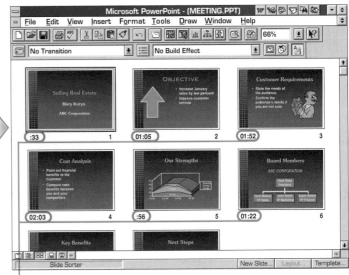

◆ This dialog box appears when you finish your slide show. It displays the total time it took to deliver your presentation.

4 To display the time you spent on each slide, move the mouse ▷ over **Yes** and then press the left button.

*Note: If you do not want to display the time, move the mouse ▷ over **No** and then press the left button.*

◆ PowerPoint displays the time you spent on each slide.

ADD BUILDS TO SLIDES

During a slide show, you can increase interest by revealing the points on a slide one at a time.

ADD BUILDS TO SLIDES

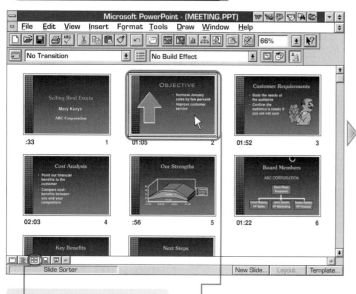

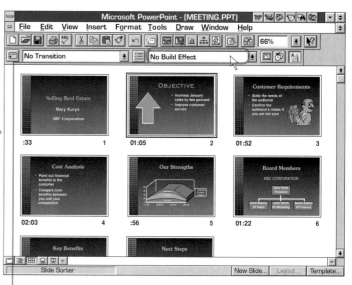

1 To change to the Slide Sorter view, move the mouse ⌖ over ▦ and then press the left button.

2 Move the mouse ⌖ over the slide you want to reveal points one at a time and then press the left button.

3 Move the mouse ⌖ over this box and then press the left button.

• Add Speaker's Notes
• Delete a Slide
• Reorder Slides

• Set Up Slides
• Print a Presentation
• View a Slide Show

• Rehearse a Slide Show
• **Add Builds to Slides**
• Add Slide Transitions

After you add builds to a slide, you can display the points one at a time during a slide show.

◆ *To display the next point on a slide, press the left mouse button or the **Spacebar**.*

Note: *For information on viewing a slide show, refer to page 322.*

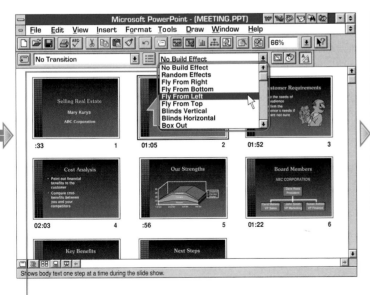

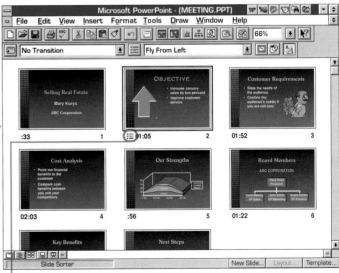

4 Move the mouse ⟲ over the way you want to reveal points on the slide and then press the left button.

Note: *To browse through the available options, move the mouse ⟲ over ⬇ or ⬆ and then press the left button.*

◆ The ⋮⋮⋮ symbol appears below the slide.

327

During a slide show, you can display visual effects as you move from one slide to the next. These effects are called transitions.

FADE THROUGH BLACK

ADD SLIDE TRANSITIONS

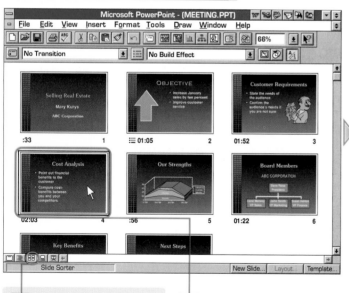

1 To change to the Slide Sorter view, move the mouse ⌖ over ⊞⊞ and then press the left button.

2 Move the mouse ⌖ over the slide you want to display the transition and then press the left button.

3 Move the mouse ⌖ over ⬚ and then press the left button.

◆ The **Transition** dialog box appears.

4 To display a list of the available transitions, move the mouse ⌖ over this box and then press the left button.

5 Move the mouse ⌖ over the transition you want to use and then press the left button.

• Add Speaker's Notes
• Delete a Slide
• Reorder Slides

• Set Up Slides
• Print a Presentation
• View a Slide Show

• Rehearse a Slide Show
• Add Builds to Slides
• **Add Slide Transitions**

To quickly select a transition:

1 Perform steps **1** and **2** on page 328.

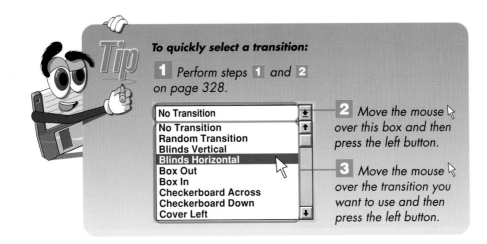

2 Move the mouse over this box and then press the left button.

3 Move the mouse over the transition you want to use and then press the left button.

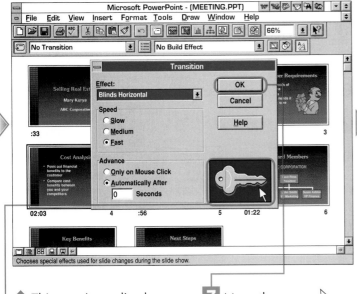

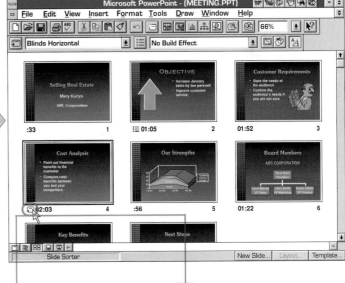

◆ This area immediately demonstrates the transition you selected.

6 To view the transition again, move the mouse over this area and then press the left button.

7 Move the mouse over **OK** and then press the left button.

◆ The symbol appears below the slide.

8 To view the transition, move the mouse over and then press the left button.

329

MAIL

Microsoft Mail lets you exchange messages with other people on a network.

A network is a group of computers connected together to allow people to exchange information.

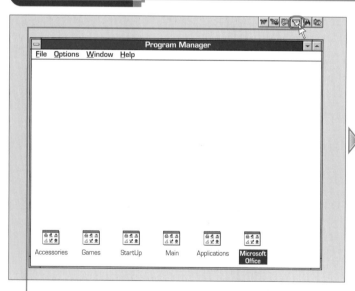

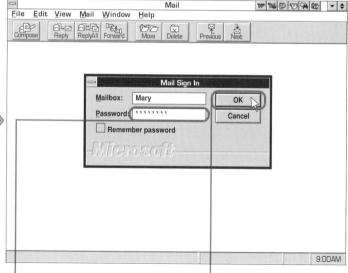

1 Move the mouse ⟋ over 📧 and then press the left button.

*Note: If this is the first time you are using Mail, refer to the **Tip** on page 333.*

◆ The **Mail Sign In** dialog box appears.

2 Type your password. A symbol (x) appears for each character you type.

Note: A password ensures that you are the only one who can read your messages.

3 Move the mouse ⟋ over **OK** and then press the left button.

- **Start Mail**
- Send a Message
- Attach a File to a Message
- Read Messages
- Reply to a Message
- Forward a Message
- Delete a Message
- Exit Mail

This dialog box appears the first time you start Mail. Before using Mail, you must connect to a postoffice to identify where your mail will be stored.

To connect to a postoffice, ask your network or Mail administrator.

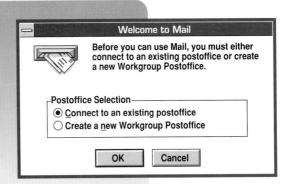

Welcome to Mail

Before you can use Mail, you must either connect to an existing postoffice or create a new Workgroup Postoffice.

Postoffice Selection
- ● **Connect to an existing postoffice**
- ○ **Create a new Workgroup Postoffice**

OK   Cancel

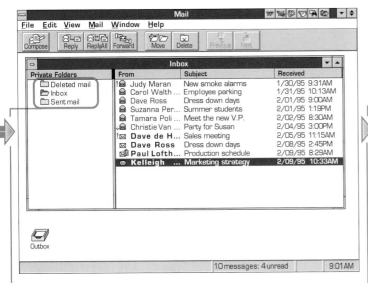

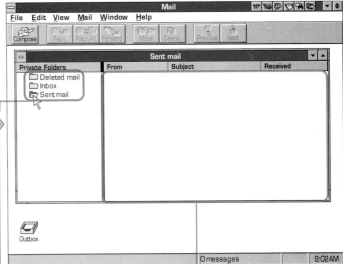

◆ This area displays the folders that store your messages.

Deleted mail or **Wastebasket**
Stores messages you have deleted.

Inbox
Stores messages sent to you.

Sent mail
Stores messages you have sent.

4 To display the contents of a folder, move the mouse over the folder (example: **Sent mail**) and then quickly press the left button twice.

◆ This area displays the contents of the folder you selected. You can only display the contents of one folder at a time.

Note: In this example, no messages have been sent.

You can easily send a message to another person on your network.

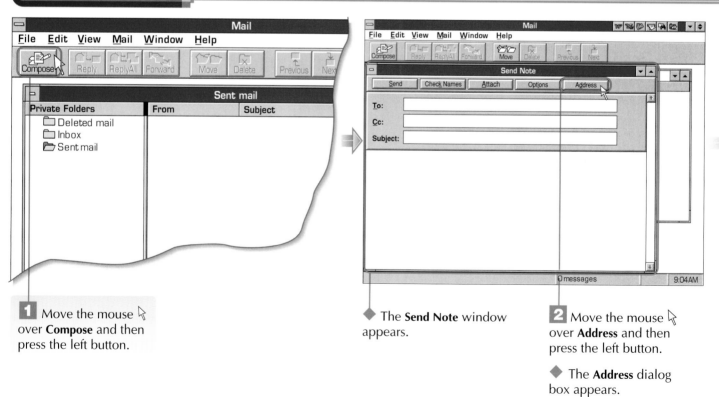

1 Move the mouse ⟍ over **Compose** and then press the left button.

◆ The **Send Note** window appears.

2 Move the mouse ⟍ over **Address** and then press the left button.

◆ The **Address** dialog box appears.

- Start Mail
- **Send a Message**
- Attach a File to a Message
- Read Messages

- Reply to a Message
- Forward a Message
- Delete a Message
- Exit Mail

MAIL

You can send a courtesy copy of your message to a person who is not directly involved but would be interested in your message.

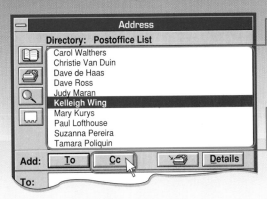

1 In the **Address** dialog box, move the mouse over the name of the person you want to send a courtesy copy to and then press the left button.

2 Move the mouse over **Cc** and then press the left button.

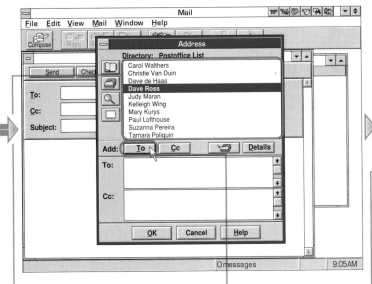

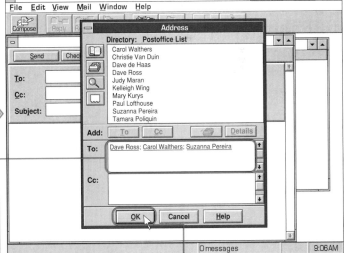

3 To select the person you want to send the message to, move the mouse over the person's name (example: **Dave Ross**) and then press the left button.

4 Move the mouse over **To** and then press the left button.

◆ This area displays the names of the people who will receive the message.

◆ To send the message to more than one person, repeat steps **3** and **4** for each person.

5 Move the mouse over **OK** and then press the left button.

CONTINUED

Sending messages lets you efficiently exchange ideas, request information and organize meetings.

SEND A MESSAGE (CONTINUED)

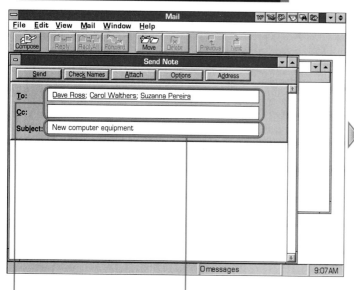

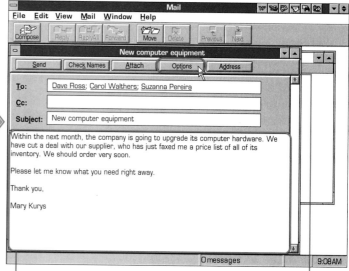

◆ This area displays the name of each person who will receive your message.

6 To enter a subject for the message, move the mouse I over the box beside **Subject:** and then press the left button. Then type the subject of your message.

7 To enter the message, move the mouse I over this area and then press the left button. Then type your message.

Note: If you make a typing error, press **+Backspace** *and then retype.*

8 To set the message options, move the mouse ⬚ over **Options** and then press the left button.

◆ The **Options** dialog box appears.

- Start Mail
- *Send a Message*
- Attach a File to a Message
- Read Messages

- Reply to a Message
- Forward a Message
- Delete a Message
- Exit Mail

MAIL

You can have Mail let you know when a person has read your message by using the Return receipt option.

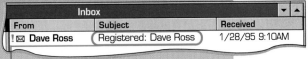

Inbox		
From	Subject	Received
!✉ **Dave Ross**	Registered: Dave Ross	1/28/95 9:10AM

◆ When a person reads your message, Mail will send you a message with the word **Registered:** displayed before the subject.

Note: To select the **Return receipt** option, perform step **9** below.

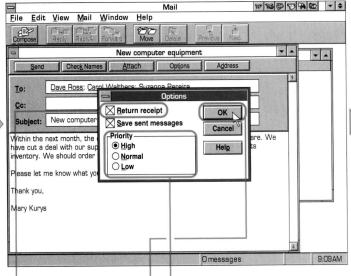

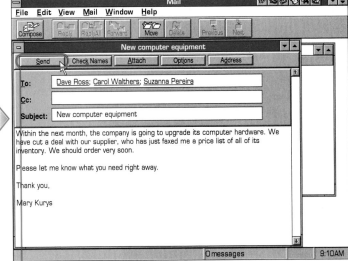

9 If you want to know when each person reads your message, move the mouse ⇗ over **Return receipt** and then press the left button (☐ changes to ☒).

10 To indicate the importance of the message, move the mouse ⇗ over a priority option and then press the left button (○ changes to ⦿).

11 Move the mouse ⇗ over **OK** and then press the left button.

12 To send the message, move the mouse ⇗ over **Send** and then press the left button.

ATTACH A FILE TO A MESSAGE

You can attach a file to a message. This is useful when you want to include additional information with your message.

ATTACH A FILE TO A MESSAGE

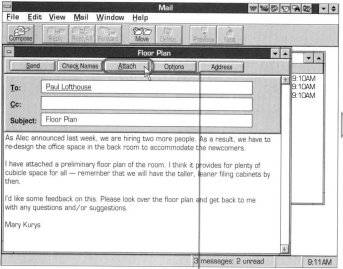

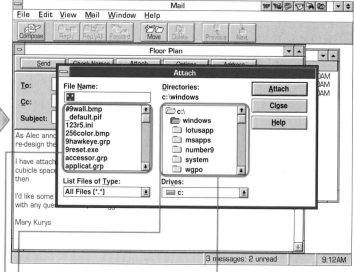

1 Create a message by performing steps **1** to **11**, starting on page 334.

2 Move the mouse ▷ over **Attach** and then press the left button.

◆ The **Attach** dialog box appears.

◆ This area displays the folders stored on your hard drive. The current folder appears darker than the other folders (📁).

◆ This area displays the files stored in the current folder.

3 Move through the folders until you find the file you want to attach.

Note: To move through the folders, refer to your Windows manual.

338

- Start Mail
- Send a Message
- Attach a File to a Message
- Read Messages

- Reply to a Message
- Forward a Message
- Delete a Message
- Exit Mail

MAIL

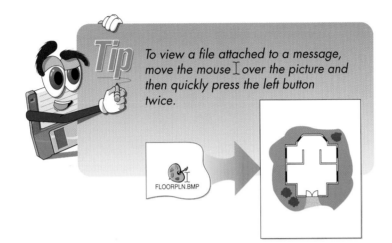

Tip

To view a file attached to a message, move the mouse I over the picture and then quickly press the left button twice.

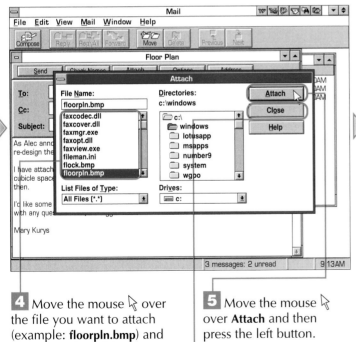

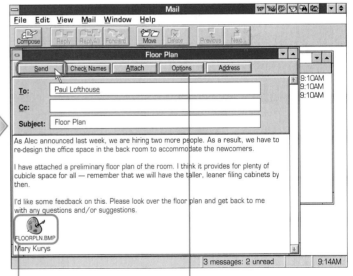

4 Move the mouse ⬦ over the file you want to attach (example: **floorpln.bmp**) and then press the left button.

5 Move the mouse ⬦ over **Attach** and then press the left button.

6 Move the mouse ⬦ over **Close** and then press the left button.

◆ The name of the file appears with a small picture in the message.

7 To send the message, move the mouse ⬦ over **Send** and then press the left button.

You can easily display a message sent to you.

READ MESSAGES

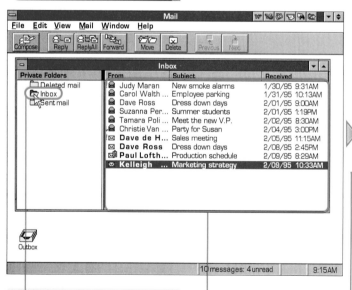

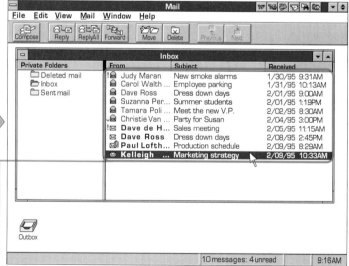

1 To display a list of all the messages sent to you, move the mouse ⇖ over the **Inbox** folder and then quickly press the left button twice.

◆ This area displays a list of all your messages. It includes the subject of each message and the date and time it was received.

2 To read a message, move the mouse ⇖ over the message and then quickly press the left button twice.

- Start Mail
- Send a Message
- Attach a File to a Message
- **Read Messages**
- Reply to a Message
- Forward a Message
- Delete a Message
- Exit Mail

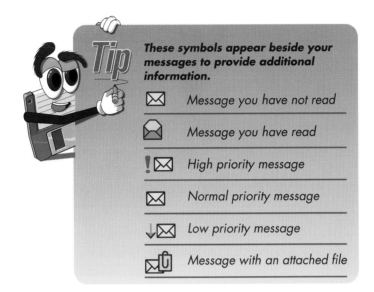

These symbols appear beside your messages to provide additional information.

✉   *Message you have not read*

✉   *Message you have read*

!✉   *High priority message*

✉   *Normal priority message*

↓✉   *Low priority message*

✉↑   *Message with an attached file*

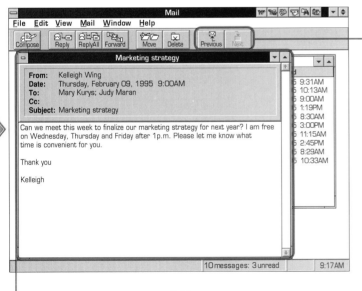

When you finish reading a message, you can use the Previous and Next buttons to quickly move through your messages.

◆ To read the previous message, move the mouse ⍄ over **Previous** and then press the left button.

◆ To read the next message, move the mouse ⍄ over **Next** and then press the left button.

◆ The contents of the message appear.

3 When you finish reading the message, press **Esc** on your keyboard.

REPLY TO A MESSAGE

After reading a message, you can send a reply. This lets you comment on the message or answer questions.

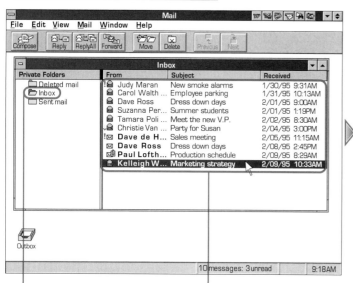

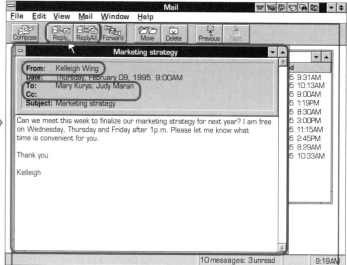

1 To display a list of all the messages sent to you, move the mouse ☇ over the **Inbox** folder and then quickly press the left button twice.

2 To display the message you want to reply to, move the mouse ☇ over the message and then quickly press the left button twice.

◆ The message appears.

3 To send a reply just to the person who sent the message, move the mouse ☇ over **Reply** and then press the left button.

◆ To send a reply to the person who sent the message and to every person listed beside **To:** and **Cc:**, move the mouse ☇ over **ReplyAll** and then press the left button.

- Start Mail
- Send a Message
- Attach a File to a Message
- Read Messages

- **Reply to a Message**
- Forward a Message
- Delete a Message
- Exit Mail

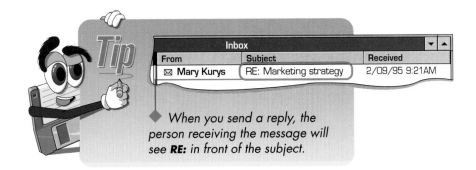

◆ When you send a reply, the person receiving the message will see **RE:** in front of the subject.

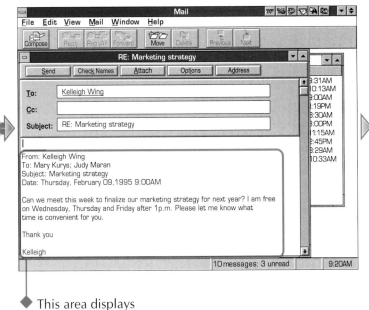

◆ This area displays the original message.

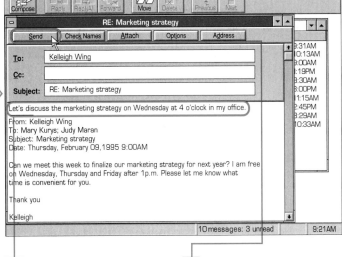

4 To reply to the message, move the mouse I over this area and then press the left button. Then type your reply.

5 To send the reply, move the mouse ☒ over **Send** and then press the left button.

After reading a message, you can add comments and then forward the message to a colleague.

FORWARD A MESSAGE

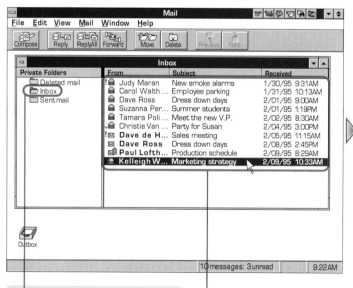

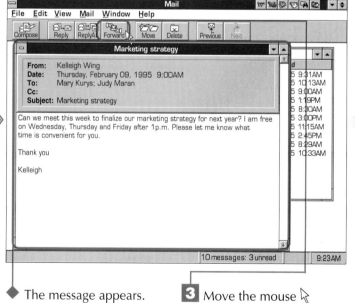

1 To display a list of all the messages sent to you, move the mouse ⌖ over the **Inbox** folder and then quickly press the left button twice.

2 To display the message you want to forward, move the mouse ⌖ over the message and then quickly press the left button twice.

◆ The message appears.

3 Move the mouse ⌖ over **Forward** and then press the left button.

- Start Mail
- Send a Message
- Attach a File to a Message
- Read Messages

- Reply to a Message
- **Forward a Message**
- Delete a Message
- Exit Mail

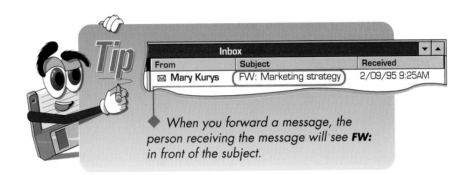

Tip

Inbox		
From	**Subject**	**Received**
✉ **Mary Kurys**	FW: Marketing strategy	2/09/95 9:25AM

◆ When you forward a message, the person receiving the message will see **FW:** in front of the subject.

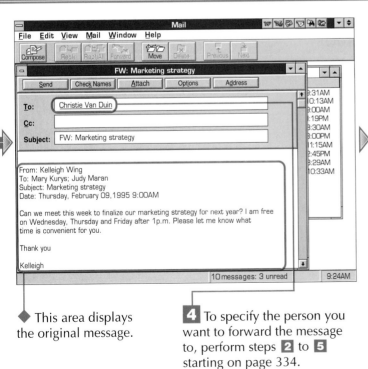

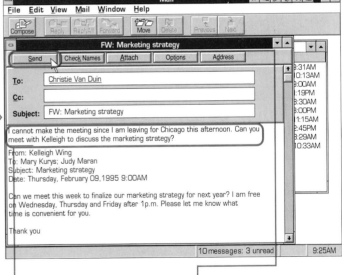

◆ This area displays the original message.

4 To specify the person you want to forward the message to, perform steps **2** to **5** starting on page 334.

5 To add your own comments to the message, move the mouse I over this area and then press the left button. Then type your comments.

6 To forward the message, move the mouse ⬉ over **Send** and then press the left button.

You can delete messages you no longer need.

DELETE A MESSAGE

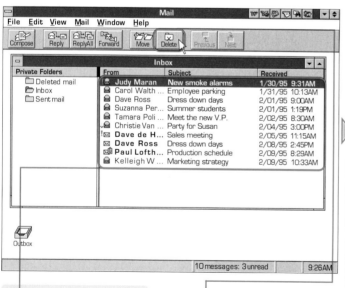

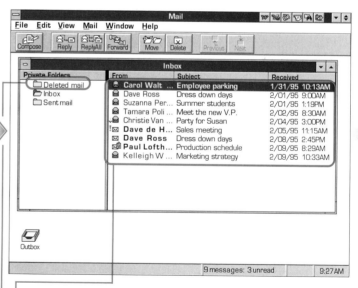

1 Move the mouse ⌖ over the message you want to delete and then press the left button.

2 Move the mouse ⌖ over **Delete** and then press the left button.

◆ The message disappears.

◆ Mail places deleted messages in the **Deleted mail** folder.

*Note: Your **Deleted mail** folder may be called **Wastebasket**.*

- Start Mail
- Send a Message
- Attach a File to a Message
- Read Messages
- Reply to a Message
- Forward a Message
- **Delete a Message**
- **Exit Mail**

At the end of each day, you should exit Mail before turning off your computer.

EXIT MAIL

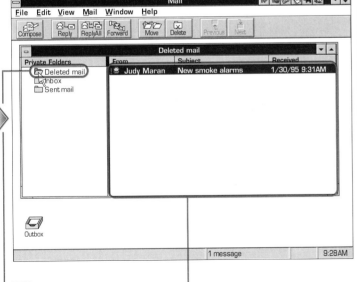

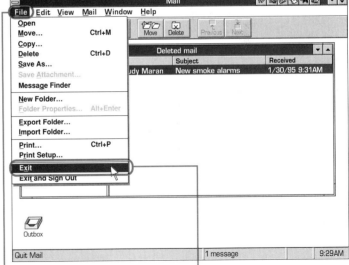

3 To view all the messages you have deleted, move the mouse over the **Deleted mail** folder and then quickly press the left button twice.

◆ This area displays all the messages you have deleted.

◆ These messages will be permanently deleted when you exit Mail.

1 Move the mouse over **File** and then press the left button.

2 Move the mouse over **Exit** and then press the left button.

EXCHANGE OBJECTS BETWEEN PROGRAMS

Linking and embedding allow you to create documents containing objects from other programs. For example, you can place a chart from Excel and a slide from PowerPoint into a Word document.

The source document supplies the object.

The destination document receives the object.

EMBED AN OBJECT

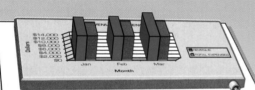

Source Document

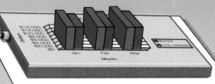

Destination Document

When you embed an object, it becomes part of the destination document.

When you make changes to the object in the destination document, only the destination document is affected.

The source document is no longer needed after you embed an object, since the destination document now contains the object.

OBJECT

The information you transfer between programs is called an object. An object can include items such as a picture, a chart, text, or a slide.

LINK AN OBJECT

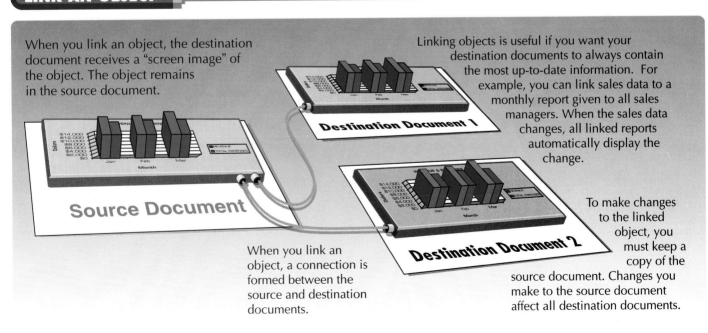

When you link an object, the destination document receives a "screen image" of the object. The object remains in the source document.

When you link an object, a connection is formed between the source and destination documents.

Linking objects is useful if you want your destination documents to always contain the most up-to-date information. For example, you can link sales data to a monthly report given to all sales managers. When the sales data changes, all linked reports automatically display the change.

To make changes to the linked object, you must keep a copy of the source document. Changes you make to the source document affect all destination documents.

Source Document

Destination Document 1

Destination Document 2

LINK OR EMBED AN OBJECT

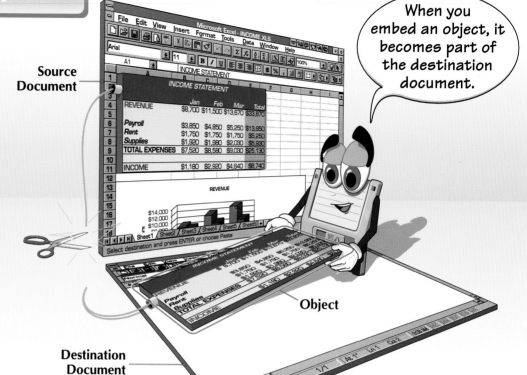

Source Document

> When you embed an object, it becomes part of the destination document.

Object

Destination Document

EMBED AN OBJECT

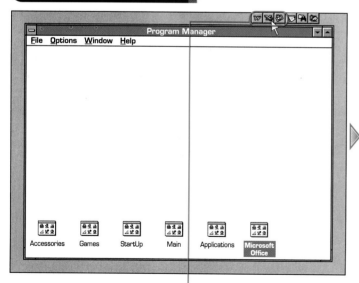

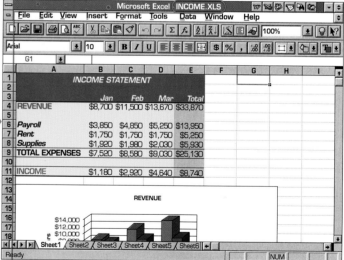

This example places an object from Excel in a Word document.

1 Start the program containing the object you want to place in another program (example: **Excel**).

Note: To start Excel, move the mouse over and then press the left button.

2 Open the document containing the object (example: **income.xls**).

Note: To open a document in Excel, refer to page 154.

352

- Introduction
- **Link or Embed an Object**
- Edit an Embedded Object
- Edit a Linked Object

LINK AN OBJECT

When you link an object, the destination document receives a "screen image" of the object. The object remains in the source document.

To link an object:

1 Perform steps **1** to **11** starting on page 352, selecting **Paste Link:** in step **9**.

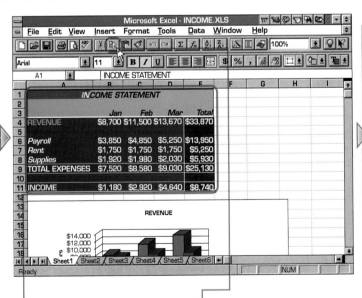

3 Select the object you want to place in another program.

Note: To select cells in Excel, refer to page 140.

4 To make a copy of the object, move the mouse ⬚ over ⬚ and then press the left button.

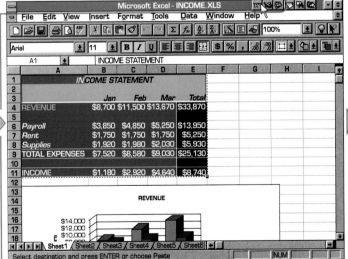

5 Start the program you want to display a copy of the object (example: **Word**).

Note: To start Word, move the mouse ⬚ over ⬚ and then press the left button.

CONTINUED

LINK OR EMBED AN OBJECT

Source Document

After you embed an object, the source document is no longer needed, since the destination document now contains the object.

Object

Destination Document

EMBED AN OBJECT (CONTINUED)

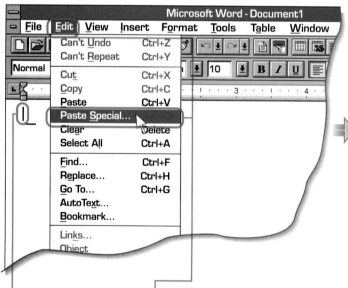

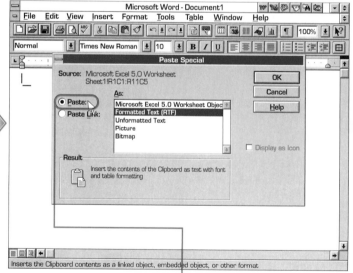

6 Position the insertion point where you want to place the object.

7 Move the mouse ⬡ over **Edit** and then press the left button.

8 Move the mouse ⬡ over **Paste Special** and then press the left button.

◆ The **Paste Special** dialog box appears.

9 To embed the object, move the mouse ⬡ over **Paste:** and then press the left button.

354

• Introduction
• **Link or Embed an Object**
• Edit an Embedded Object
• Edit a Linked Object

EXCHANGE OBJECTS
BETWEEN PROGRAMS

A document containing an embedded object takes up more space on your computer than a document containing a linked object.

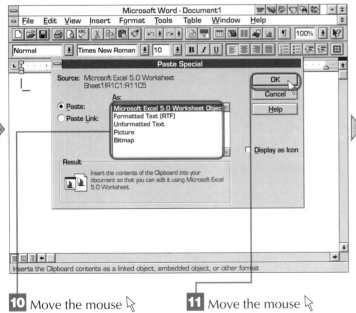

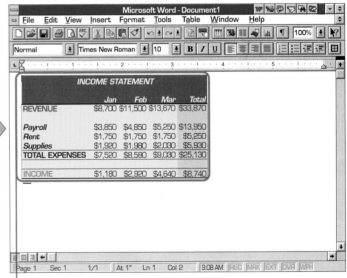

10 Move the mouse ⌖ over the option that ends with the word **Object** and then press the left button.

11 Move the mouse ⌖ over **OK** and then press the left button.

◆ The object from Excel appears in the Word document.

EDIT AN EMBEDDED OBJECT

You can easily make changes to an embedded object in your document.

Source Document

Destination Document

When you make changes to the object in the destination document, only the destination document is affected.

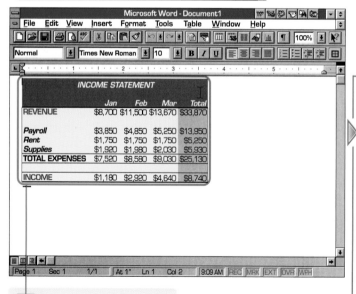

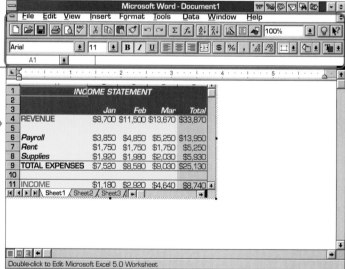

1 To edit an object, move the mouse I over the object and then quickly press the left button twice.

◆ In this example, the Excel menus and toolbars temporarily replace the Word menus and toolbars. This lets you access all of the Excel commands while working in the Word document.

• Introduction
• Link or Embed an Object
• **Edit an Embedded Object**
• Edit a Linked Object

EXCHANGE OBJECTS
BETWEEN PROGRAMS

A program that can link and embed objects supports OLE technology. OLE stands for Object Linking and Embedding.

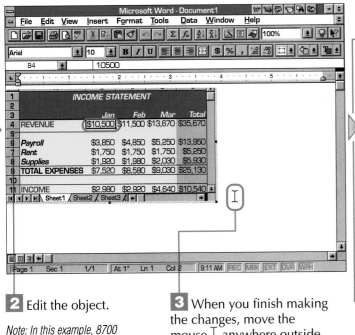

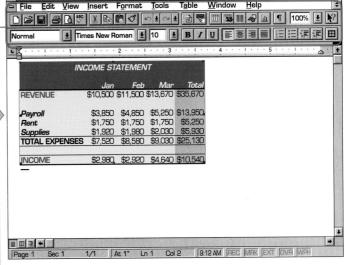

2 Edit the object.

Note: In this example, 8700 is changed to 10500.

3 When you finish making the changes, move the mouse I anywhere outside the object and then press the left button.

◆ The Word menus and toolbars reappear.

When you make changes to a linked object, all documents containing the linked object will also change.

Destination Documents

Source Document

EDIT A LINKED OBJECT

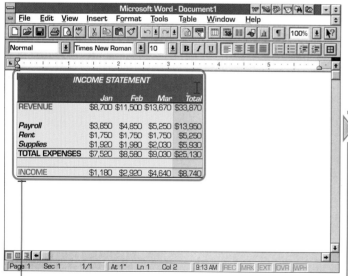

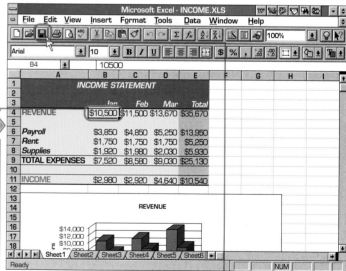

1 To edit an object, move the mouse I over the object and then quickly press the left button twice.

◆ In this example, the Excel program opens. This lets you access all of the Excel commands.

2 Edit the object.

Note: In this example, 8700 is changed to 10500.

3 To save the changes, move the mouse ⬚ over 🖫 and then press the left button.

358

- Introduction
- Link or Embed an Object
- Edit an Embedded Object
- **Edit a Linked Object**

CHANGE OBJECTS
BETWEEN PROGRAMS

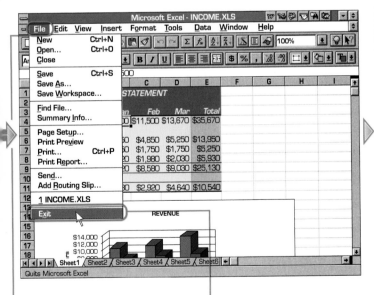

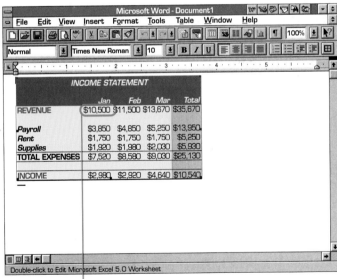

4 To exit Excel, move the mouse ⌖ over **File** and then press the left button.

5 Move the mouse ⌖ over **Exit** and then press the left button.

◆ The Word program reappears. The changes you made to the object in Excel appear in the Word document.

◆ All other documents containing the linked object will also change.

INDEX

Title	Author	ISBN #	Price
INTERNET/COMMUNICATIONS/NETWORKING			
CompuServe For Dummies™	by Wallace Wang	ISBN: 1-56884-181-7	$19.95 USA/$26.95 Canada
Modems For Dummies™, 2nd Edition	by Tina Rathbone	ISBN: 1-56884-223-6	$19.99 USA/$26.99 Canada
Modems For Dummies™	by Tina Rathbone	ISBN: 1-56884-001-2	$19.95 USA/$26.95 Canada
MORE Internet For Dummies™	by John Levine & Margaret Levine Young	ISBN: 1-56884-164-7	$19.95 USA/$26.95 Canada
NetWare For Dummies™	by Ed Tittel & Deni Connor	ISBN: 1-56884-003-9	$19.95 USA/$26.95 Canada
Networking For Dummies™	by Doug Lowe	ISBN: 1-56884-079-9	$19.95 USA/$26.95 Canada
ProComm Plus 2 For Windows For Dummies™	by Wallace Wang	ISBN: 1-56884-219-8	$19.99 USA/$26.99 Canada
The Internet Help Desk For Dummies™	by John Kaufeld	ISBN: 1-56884-238-4	$16.99 USA/$22.99 Canada
The3 Internet For Dummies™, 2nd Edition	by John Levine & Carol Baroudi	ISBN: 1-56884-222-8	$19.99 USA/$26.99 Canada
The Internet For Macs For Dummies™	by Charles Seiter	ISBN: 1-56884-184-1	$19.95 USA/$26.95 Canada
MACINTOSH			
Mac Programming For Dummies™	by Dan Parks Sydow	ISBN: 1-56884-173-6	$19.95 USA/$26.95 Canada
Macintosh System 7.5 For Dummies™	by Bob LeVitus	ISBN: 1-56884-197-3	$19.95 USA/$26.95 Canada
MORE Macs For Dummies™	by David Pogue	ISBN: 1-56884-087-X	$19.95 USA/$26.95 Canada
PageMaker 5 For Macs For Dummies™	by Galen Gruman & Deke McClelland	ISBN: 1-56884-178-7	$19.95 USA/$26.95 Canada
QuarkXPress 3.3 For Dummies™	by Galen Gruman & Barbara Assadi	ISBN: 1-56884-217-1	$19.99 USA/$26.99 Canada
Upgrading and Fixing Macs For Dummies™	by Kearney Rietmann & Frank Higgins	ISBN: 1-56884-189-2	$19.95 USA/$26.95 Canada
MULTIMEDIA			
Multimedia & CD-ROMs For Dummies™, Interactive Multimedia Value Pack	by Andy Rathbone	ISBN: 1-56884-225-2	$29.95 USA/$39.95 Canada
Multimedia & CD-ROMs For Dummies™	by Andy Rathbone	ISBN: 1-56884-089-6	$19.95 USA/$26.95 Canada
OPERATING SYSTEMS/DOS			
MORE DOS For Dummies™	by Dan Gookin	ISBN: 1-56884-046-2	$19.95 USA/$26.95 Canada
S.O.S. For DOS™	by Katherine Murray	ISBN: 1-56884-043-8	$12.95 USA/$16.95 Canada
OS/2 For Dummies™	by Andy Rathbone	ISBN: 1-878058-76-2	$19.95 USA/$26.95 Canada
UNIX			
UNIX For Dummies™	by John Levine & Margaret Levine Young	ISBN: 1-878058-58-4	$19.95 USA/$26.95 Canada
WINDOWS			
S.O.S. For Windows™	by Katherine Murray	ISBN: 1-56884-045-4	$12.95 USA/$16.95 Canada
Windows "X" For Dummies™, 3rd Edition	by Andy Rathbone	ISBN: 1-56884-240-6	$19.99 USA/$26.99 Canada
PCS/HARDWARE			
Illustrated Computer Dictionary For Dummies™	by Dan Gookin, Wally Wang, & Chris Van Buren	ISBN: 1-56884-004-7	$12.95 USA/$16.95 Canada
Upgrading and Fixing PCs For Dummies™	by Andy Rathbone	ISBN: 1-56884-002-0	$19.95 USA/$26.95 Canada
PRESENTATION/AUTOCAD			
AutoCAD For Dummies™	by Bud Smith	ISBN: 1-56884-191-4	$19.95 USA/$26.95 Canada
PowerPoint 4 For Windows For Dummies™	by Doug Lowe	ISBN: 1-56884-161-2	$16.95 USA/$22.95 Canada
PROGRAMMING			
Borland C++ For Dummies™	by Michael Hyman	ISBN: 1-56884-162-0	$19.95 USA/$26.95 Canada
"Borland's New Language Product" For Dummies™	by Neil Rubenking	ISBN: 1-56884-200-7	$19.95 USA/$26.95 Canada
C For Dummies™	by Dan Gookin	ISBN: 1-878058-78-9	$19.95 USA/$26.95 Canada
C++ For Dummies™	by S. Randy Davis	ISBN: 1-56884-163-9	$19.95 USA/$26.95 Canada
Mac Programming For Dummies™	by Dan Parks Sydow	ISBN: 1-56884-173-6	$19.95 USA/$26.95 Canada
QBasic Programming For Dummies™	by Douglas Hergert	ISBN: 1-56884-093-4	$19.95 USA/$26.95 Canada
Visual Basic "X" For Dummies™, 2nd Edition	by Wallace Wang	ISBN: 1-56884-230-9	$19.99 USA/$26.99 Canada
Visual Basic 3 For Dummies™	by Wallace Wang	ISBN: 1-56884-076-4	$19.95 USA/$26.95 Canada
SPREADSHEET			
1-2-3 For Dummies™	by Greg Harvey	ISBN: 1-878058-60-6	$16.95 USA/$22.95 Canada
1-2-3 For Windows 5 For Dummies™, 2nd Edition	by John Walkenbach	ISBN: 1-56884-216-3	$16.95 USA/$22.95 Canada
1-2-3 For Windows For Dummies™	by John Walkenbach	ISBN: 1-56884-052-7	$16.95 USA/$22.95 Canada
Excel 5 For Macs For Dummies™	by Greg Harvey	ISBN: 1-56884-186-8	$19.95 USA/$26.95 Canada
Excel For Dummies™, 2nd Edition	by Greg Harvey	ISBN: 1-56884-050-0	$16.95 USA/$22.95 Canada
MORE Excel 5 For Windows For Dummies™	by Greg Harvey	ISBN: 1-56884-207-4	$19.95 USA/$26.95 Canada
Quattro Pro 6 For Windows For Dummies™	by John Walkenbach	ISBN: 1-56884-174-4	$19.95 USA/$26.95 Canada
Quattro Pro For DOS For Dummies™	by John Walkenbach	ISBN: 1-56884-023-3	$16.95 USA/$22.95 Canada
UTILITIES			
Norton Utilities 8 For Dummies™	by Beth Slick	ISBN: 1-56884-166-3	$19.95 USA/$26.95 Canada
VCRS/CAMCORDERS			
VCRs & Camcorders For Dummies™	by Andy Rathbone & Gordon McComb	ISBN: 1-56884-229-5	$14.99 USA/$20.99 Canada
WORD PROCESSING			
Ami Pro For Dummies™	by Jim Meade	ISBN: 1-56884-049-7	$19.95 USA/$26.95 Canada
More Word For Windows 6 For Dummies™	by Doug Lowe	ISBN: 1-56884-165-5	$19.95 USA/$26.95 Canada
MORE WordPerfect 6 For Windows For Dummies™	by Margaret Levine Young & David C. Kay	ISBN: 1-56884-206-6	$19.95 USA/$26.95 Canada
MORE WordPerfect 6 For DOS For Dummies™	by Wallace Wang, edited by Dan Gookin	ISBN: 1-56884-047-0	$19.95 USA/$26.95 Canada
S.O.S. For WordPerfect™	by Katherine Murray	ISBN: 1-56884-053-5	$12.95 USA/$16.95 Canada
Word 6 For Macs For Dummies™	by Dan Gookin	ISBN: 1-56884-190-6	$19.95 USA/$26.95 Canada
Word For Windows 6 For Dummies™	by Dan Gookin	ISBN: 1-56884-075-6	$16.95 USA/$22.95 Canada
Word For Windows 2 For Dummies™	by Dan Gookin	ISBN: 1-878058-86-X	$16.95 USA/$22.95 Canada
WordPerfect 6 For Dummies™	by Dan Gookin	ISBN: 1-56884-032-2	$16.95 USA/$22.95 Canada
WordPerfect For Dummies™	by Dan Gookin	ISBN: 1-878058-52-5	$16.95 USA/$22.95 Canada
WordPerfect For Windows For Dummies™	by Margaret Levine Young & David C. Kay	ISBN: 1-56884-032-2	$16.95 USA/$22.95 Canada

IDG's 3-D Visual™ Series

from: **maranGraphics™**

**The Proven 3-D Visual Approach
to Learning Computers In
A Handy NEW Pocket Size**

**Excel 5 For Windows
Visual PocketGuide**

ISBN 1-56884-667-3
$14.99 USA/£13.99 UK

**Windows 3.1
Visual PocketGuide**

ISBN 1-56884-650-9
$14.99 USA/£13.99 UK

**Word 6 For Windows
Visual PocketGuide**

ISBN 1-56884-666-5
$14.99 USA/£13.99 UK

This is what reviewers are saying about our books…

Also Available

**Lotus 1-2-3 R5
For Windows
Visual PocketGuide**

ISBN 1-56884-671-1
$14.99 USA/£13.99 UK

**WordPerfect 6.1
For Windows
Visual PocketGuide**

ISBN 1-56884-668-1
$14.99 USA/£13.99 UK

Coming Soon!

**Windows 95
Visual PocketGuide**

ISBN 1-56884-661-4
$14.99 USA/£13.99 UK

Pending Software Release

FOR 3-D VISUAL CORPORATE ORDERS, PLEASE CALL : 800 . 469 . 6616 ext. 206

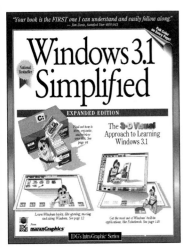

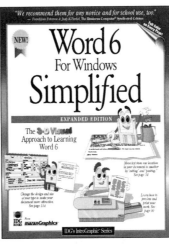
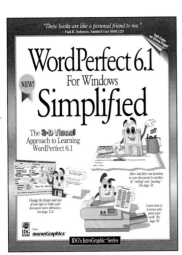

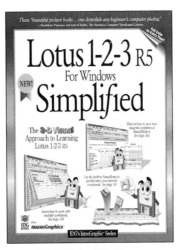

IDG BOOKS ®

TRADE & INDIVIDUAL ORDERS

Phone: **(800) 762-2974** *or* **(317) 895-5200**
(8 a.m.–6 p.m., CST, weekdays)
FAX : **(317) 895-5298**

CORPORATE ORDERS FOR 3-D VISUAL™ SERIES

Phone: **(800) 469-6616** *ext.* **206**
(8 a.m.–5 p.m., EST, weekdays)
FAX : **(905) 890-9434**

Qty	ISBN	Title	Price	Total

Shipping & Handling Charges

	Description	First book	Each add'l. book	Total
Domestic	Normal	$4.50	$1.50	$
	Two Day Air	$8.50	$2.50	$
	Overnight	$18.00	$3.00	$
International	Surface	$8.00	$8.00	$
	Airmail	$16.00	$16.00	$
	DHL Air	$17.00	$17.00	$

Subtotal _____

CA residents add
applicable sales tax _____

IN, MA and MD
residents add
5% sales tax _____

IL residents add
6.25% sales tax _____

RI residents add
7% sales tax _____

TX residents add
8.25% sales tax _____

Shipping _____

Total _____

Ship to:

Name _____

Address _____

Company _____

City/State/Zip _____

Daytime Phone _____

Payment: Check to IDG Books (US Funds Only)

Visa   Mastercard   American Express

Card # _____ Exp. _____ Signature _____

IDG Books Education Group
Jim Kelly, Director of Education Sales – 9 Village Circle, Ste. 450, Westlake, TX 76262
800-434-2086 Phone • 817-430-5852 Fax • 8:30-5:00 CST

IDG BOOKS WORLDWIDE REGISTRATION CARD

RETURN THIS
REGISTRATION CARD
FOR FREE CATALOG

Title of this book: Microsoft Office 4.2 For Windows Simplified

My overall rating of this book: ❏ Very good [1] ❏ Good [2] ❏ Satisfactory [3] ❏ Fair [4] ❏ Poor [5]

How I first heard about this book:

❏ Found in bookstore; name: [6]

❏ Advertisement: [8]

❏ Word of mouth; heard about book from friend, co-worker, etc.: [10]

❏ Book review: [7]

❏ Catalog: [9]

❏ Other: [11]

What I liked most about this book:

What I would change, add, delete, etc., in future editions of this book:

Other comments:

Number of computer books I purchase in a year: ❏ 1 [12] ❏ 2-5 [13] ❏ 6-10 [14] ❏ More than 10 [15]

I would characterize my computer skills as: ❏ Beginner [16] ❏ Intermediate [17] ❏ Advanced [18] ❏ Professional [19]

I use ❏ DOS [20] ❏ Windows [21] ❏ OS/2 [22] ❏ Unix [23] ❏ Macintosh [24] ❏ Other: [25]

(please specify)

I would be interested in new books on the following subjects:
(please check all that apply, and use the spaces provided to identify specific software)

❏ Word processing: [26]

❏ Data bases: [28]

❏ File Utilities: [30]

❏ Networking: [32]

❏ Other: [34]

❏ Spreadsheets: [27]

❏ Desktop publishing: [29]

❏ Money management: [31]

❏ Programming languages: [33]

I use a PC at (please check all that apply): ❏ home [35] ❏ work [36] ❏ school [37] ❏ other: [38]

The disks I prefer to use are ❏ 5.25 [39] ❏ 3.5 [40] ❏ other: [41]

I have a CD ROM: ❏ yes [42] ❏ no [43]

I plan to buy or upgrade computer hardware this year: ❏ yes [44] ❏ no [45]

I plan to buy or upgrade computer software this year: ❏ yes [46] ❏ no [47]

Name: _____ Business title: [48] _____ Type of Business: [49] _____

Address (❏ home [50] ❏ work [51]/Company name: _____)

Street/Suite#

City [52]/State [53]/Zipcode [54]: _____ Country [55] _____

❏ **I liked this book!** You may quote me by name in future
IDG Books Worldwide promotional materials.

My daytime phone number is _____

IDG BOOKS

THE WORLD OF
COMPUTER
KNOWLEDGE

❏ YES!

Please keep me informed about IDG's World of Computer Knowledge.
Send me the latest IDG Books catalog.